# International Politics and the Environment

D1550524

SAGE Series on the Foundations of International Relations

NEW IN 2009

Series Editors:
Walter Carlsnaes **Uppsala University, Sweden**
Jeffrey T. Checkel **Simon Fraser University, Canada**

**International Advisory Board:** Peter J. Katzenstein *Cornell University, USA*; Emanuel Adler *University of Toronto, Canada*; Martha Finnemore *George Washington University, USA*; Andrew Hurrell *Oxford University, UK*; G. John Ikenberry *Princeton University, USA*; Beth Simmons *Harvard University, USA*; Steve Smith *University of Exeter, UK*; Michael Zuern *Hertie School of Governance, Berlin, Germany*.

The SAGE Foundations series fills the gap between narrowly-focused research monographs and broad introductory texts, providing graduate students with state-of-the-art, critical overviews of the key sub-fields within International Relations: International Political Economy, International Security, Foreign Policy Analysis, International Organization, Normative IR Theory, International Environmental Politics, Globalization, and IR Theory.

Explicitly designed to further the transatlantic dialogue fostered by publications such as the *SAGE Handbook of International Relations*, the series is written by renowned scholars drawn from North America, continental Europe and the UK. The books are intended as core texts on advanced courses in IR, taking students beyond the basics and into the heart of the debates within each field, encouraging an independent, critical approach and signposting further avenues of research.

Forthcoming titles:
**International Security** – Christopher Daase
**International Relations Theory** – Colin Wight
**Globalization** – James Caporaso
**Foreign Policy Analysis** – Walter Carlsnaes

# International Politics and the Environment

Ronald B. Mitchell

Los Angeles | London | New Delhi
Singapore | Washington DC

First published 2010

SAGE Publications Ltd
1 Oliver's Yard
55 City Road
London EC1Y 1SP

SAGE Publications Inc.
2455 Teller Road
Thousand Oaks, California 91320

SAGE Publications India Pvt Ltd
B 1/I 1 Mohan Cooperative Industrial Area
Mathura Road
New Delhi 110 044

SAGE Publications Asia-Pacific Pte Ltd
33 Pekin Street #02-01
Far East Square
Singapore 048763

**Library of Congress Control Number: 2009929964**

**British Library Cataloguing in Publication data**

A catalogue record for this book is available from
the British Library

ISBN 978-1-4129-1974-6
ISBN 978-1-4129-1975-3 (pbk)

Typeset by C&M Digitals (P) Ltd, Chennai, India
Printed by MPG Books Group, Bodmin, Cornwall
Printed on paper from sustainable resources

To Kai Oliver Mitchell-Reiss and Jesse Cole Mitchell-Reiss

# CONTENTS

# ACKNOWLEDGEMENTS

For two decades, brilliant and generous colleagues have helped me learn everything I know about international environmental politics. This book introduces students to a range of arguments, concepts, theories, and cases at the core of international environmental politics, and particularly their intergovernmental aspects. Throughout, I provide citations to help the interested reader learn more and to 'give credit where credit is due' for the ideas on which I build. But, as I push back from my desk after completing the manuscript, I am well aware that the sources of this book run far deeper than ideas presented in particular articles or books.

My interest in international politics and the environment owes much to Howard Raiffa who encouraged me as a Master's student and, when I started my PhD in 1989, helped me shift my intellectual focus from national security to international environmental politics by allowing me to be the *rapporteur* for a Harvard faculty seminar on the policy, politics, economics, and science of climate change. The late Abram Chayes was, and William C. Clark and Robert O. Keohane remain, the best mentors a person could want, introducing me to the law, science, and politics of the global environment while consistently supporting me personally and challenging me professionally. Those with whom I started my PhD – Eileen Babbitt, Steve Block, James N. Miller, Manik Roy, and David Weil – as well as those with whom I completed it – Marc Levy, Edward Parson, and the late Vicki Norberg-Bohm – have been good friends and insightful colleagues throughout my career. In particular, many years ago, Marc Levy suggested a taxonomy of perspectives similar to that presented in Chapter 3.

My knowledge and conceptualization of international environmental politics have been expanded immensely through intense and sustained interactions through research collaborations with Thomas Bernauer, Edith Brown Weiss, David Cash, Antonia Handler Chayes, William C. Clark, Glenn Deane, Lisa Dilling, Peter Haas, the late Harold Jacobson, Robert O. Keohane, Barbara Koremenos, Charles Lipson, Karen Litfin, Ed Miles, Elinor Ostrom, Duncan Snidal, Detlef Sprinz, Arild Underdal, and Oran Young. Many scholars of international environmental politics have challenged me to think more clearly and critically, including Frank Alcock, Liliana Andonova, Steinar Andresen, J. Samuel Barkin, Michele

Betsill, Frank Biermann, Jennifer Clapp, Daniel Bodansky, Ken Conca, Geoffrey Dabelko, Beth DeSombre, Tamar Gutner, Jon Hovi, Ronnie Lipschutz, Urs Luterbacher, Anthony Patt, MJ Peterson, Tom Princen, Kal Raustiala, Miranda Schreurs, Olav Schram Stokke, Stacy VanDeveer, Paul Wapner, and Jørgen Wettestad. I also have benefited greatly from numerous invaluable exchanges on the GEPED listserv maintained by Michael Maniates of Allegheny College. More broadly, Virginia Page Fortna, Gary Goertz, Judith Goldstein, Lisa Martin, Helen Milner, Andrew Moravcsik, John Odell, Beth Simmons, and Mark Zacher have shared insights or critiqued my work in ways that have prompted me to construct arguments that generalize beyond the environment to security, economics, and human rights. Of course, I owe Jeff Checkel and Walter Carlsnaes a debt of gratitude for challenging me to put my views on international environmental politics, as well as causality, into a book that, I hope, contributes to the next generation of scholarship in this field.

A visiting research appointment at Stanford's Center for Environmental Science and Policy from 1999–2001, working with Pamela Matson and Walter Falcon, demonstrated to me how crucial interdisciplinarity is to understanding and explaining the causes of and solutions to international environmental problems. My appreciation of interdisciplinarity has been immeasurably extended by working with C. Susan Weiler and over 100 bright young scholars that have attended symposia hosted by the Dissertations Initiative for the Advancement of Climate Change Research (DISCCRS).

I have worked closely with superb graduate students like R. Charli Carpenter, Lada Kochtcheeva, Erin Graham, Patricia Keilbach, Jennifer Marlon, and Steve Rothman who have challenged and rewarded me throughout my teaching career. The many undergraduates who have taken my International Environmental Politics course over the years have helped me to present my views on international environmental politics more clearly and accessibly. As important, they regularly remind me of the multitude of reasons for optimism about our ability to resolve our international environmental predicament.

This book was written while I was supported by generous grants from several funders. These include funding from the National Science Foundation under Grant No. SES-0318374 entitled 'Analysis of the Effects of Environmental Treaties' (September 2003 through August 2008) and under grant No. EAR-0435719, entitled 'Fostering Cross-Disciplinary Relationships and Early-Career Development to Advance Interdisciplinary Research on Climate Change and Impacts' (January 2005 through February 2009). I also have been supported by the University of Oregon's Summer Research Award and Richard A. Bray Faculty Fellow programs, Stanford University's Center for Environmental Science and Policy, an International Studies Association Workshop Grant, and an American Philosophical Society Sabbatical Fellowship. The opinions, findings, conclusions, and recommendations expressed are those of the author and do not necessarily reflect the views of any of these funders. I also wish to thank the Hillsdale Branch of the Multnomah County Library in Portland, Oregon, for providing a comfortable and beautiful place to work on so many days.

Finally, my friends and family provide the love and concern so central to all of human life and so necessary to bringing joy and fulfillment to this mortal coil. Malka Kopell and Karen Seto seamlessly combine the skills and virtues of friend and colleague in ways too numerous to mention. My parents, Lee Mitchell and Edith Bertsche Mitchell, gave me the ocean that provides the constant background music to my life. Curtis Mitchell, Linda Mitchell, and Janet Letalien listen and understand, which often is enough. And, my life would not exist without the constant and deep love and support of Amy Susan Reiss. And Kai Oliver and Jesse Cole help me laugh and love, every day – what could be better than that!

# EXPLAINING INTERNATIONAL ENVIRONMENTAL POLITICS

International environmental politics is the study of the human impacts on the environment that garner international attention and the efforts that states take to address them. If international relations is the study of both the conflicts that arise among states and the cooperative efforts states make to address such conflicts as well as shared problems, international environmental politics is the study of the cooperation and conflict among governments that surround environmental degradation, natural resource use, and other human-generated impacts on the Earth and the efforts to address them.

Humans have been transforming the natural environment for thousands of years (Turner et al., 1990). So long as humans lived in relatively small groups of hunter-gatherers, their impacts did not differ much in kind or magnitude from those of other species. But, as humans developed tools, they began to use natural resources and the natural environment in ways that differed in kind from other species and that allowed human populations to grow at faster rates and with fewer constraints than other species. The agricultural revolution and, then, the industrial revolution produced explosions in the range and types of human environmental impacts, allowing the human population to grow even faster while also increasing the amount of natural resources each human used, the environmental degradation each caused, and their life span. The fossilized footprints left by early humans in Tanzania have been replaced by the larger and longer-lasting carbon footprints of modern humans. Human impacts increasingly exceed the bounds of natural variation and the environment's ability to absorb and rebound from them. Although many environmental impacts are local, an increasing number of these cross borders or evoke concern among people in other countries. And much environmental damage has become global in nature, with impacts and implications for people in most, if not always all, countries in the world. In the last several decades, growing concerns about these problems have made international environmental problems an increasingly common and important part of international relations and foreign policy.

If international environmental *problems* are those impacts that humans have on the natural environment that raise concern in other countries, international environmental *politics* consists of the self-conscious efforts by some people to reduce these impacts and the response (or lack of response) to those efforts, whether by supporters, opponents, or indifferent bystanders. If we consider international conflict to involve situations in which one or more countries consider the existing state of the world as suboptimal relative to alternative states of the world, then international environmental politics is the study of why and when such conflicts arise over environmental issues and why and when efforts to resolve them succeed or fail.

## Goals of the Book

This book seeks to help the reader understand international environmental politics and explain why it unfolds as it does. It focuses on the 'why' rather than the 'what' of international environmental politics. It engages many, though not all, of the major issues studied by scholars of international environmental politics. It introduces readers to the substance of international environmental politics through an explanatory rather than a descriptive framework. The book defines what international environmental agreements are and then reviews explanations of why humans harm the natural environment, why some of these harms emerge on the international scene, why negotiations sometimes succeed and sometimes fail, and why some international environmental treaties alter behavior and others do not. The book summarizes those explanations while helping the reader to think rigorously about how to identify the most compelling and convincing of several competing explanations of particular outcomes in international environmental politics. Chapters focus on particular outcomes as dependent variables, identify the 'independent' variables claimed to cause those outcomes, and delineate the logics by which, and the conditions under which, those causes operate. The book also includes causes proposed by scholars representing a range of schools of thought with the view of providing readers with the theoretical foundations for adjudicating between competing explanations of particular outcomes in international environmental politics of interest to them.

I provide tools designed to facilitate the reader's own analysis of the major political aspects of any international environmental problem. Careful analyses of each stage of numerous international environmental problems have been, and will continue to be, undertaken in articles, books, and edited volumes by an increasingly large group of international relations scholars. Those analyses provide far more careful and rigorous explanations of particular cases than would be possible here. My goal, instead, is to offer a framework for thinking carefully about how we identify the causes of different outcomes in international environmental politics and to provide a list of 'likely suspects' that one must consider in explaining those outcomes. Thus, the book seeks to encourage readers to undertake more in-depth analyses of particular cases, or groups of cases, to expand our knowledge of why and when international society succeeds in addressing international environmental problems.

This book does not attempt to inform the reader in any depth about the many international environmental problems currently facing humanity nor the wide variety of efforts that have been and are being made to address them. Some important international environmental problems receive little or no attention in the pages that follow. Yet, as the number of international environmental problems has grown, generating a comprehensive list of those problems – let alone describing and explaining each – has become an encyclopedic task. The book also does not summarize several major debates that have engaged scholars and policy-makers, including those on sustainable development, nongovernmental organizations (NGOs), world civic politics, and multi-national corporations. All of those issues have received extensive and well-informed treatment in other venues. It also focuses on international environmental *politics*, in the process giving less depth to the many important contributions from the fields of international law and international economics (Birnie and Boyle, 1992; Sands, 1994; Cameron et al., 1996; Swanson and Johnston, 1999; Barrett, 2003).

The book engages the issues of international environmental politics by focusing primarily on *intergovernmental* politics, the politics of interactions among governments. To be sure, there are limits to 'green diplomacy' among governments (Broadhead, 2002). And NGOs, scientists and epistemic communities, and large domestic and multinational corporations play increasingly important roles in how humans respond to international environmental problems (see, for example, Haas, 1992c; Garcia-Johnson, 2000; Betsill et al., 2006; Betsill and Corell, 2008). Such actors often contribute to intergovernmental efforts but also generate and implement innovative new ideas of their own, sometimes with and sometimes without any involvement by governments. Individuals as well as municipal and provincial governments often adopt 'unilateral' actions to address international environmental problems, actions that may not be coordinated with efforts in other countries but, nonetheless, help mitigate such problems. My focus here should not be taken as suggesting that non-intergovernmental attempts to address international environmental problems are unimportant or ineffective but instead as simply a choice to concentrate on the dynamics and processes of intergovernmental efforts.

I have structured my discussion of international environmental politics as a series of four policy stages. Those stages include the creation of international environmental impacts, their emergence as international problems, the negotiation of intergovernmental solutions, and the effectiveness of those solutions. Within the international environmental politics literature, differing theoretical, normative, and methodological perspectives generally coexist in complementary ways that enrich our understanding of global environmental politics. Analyzing international environmental politics in terms of the causes of major outcomes at each of these stages facilitates the desire here to have an inclusive list of potentially explanatory variables for such outcomes. The book's approach also highlights that structural constraints on choices, on the one hand, and the participation, choices, and influence of state and non-state actors, on the other, may differ from one policy stage to the next.

Finally, this book reflects that both explanations based on structure and those based on agency are central to international relations and international environmental politics (Wendt, 1987; Dessler, 1989). Almost all international environmental outcomes in which we are interested reflect the influence of both deep-seated structural variables that are relatively unsusceptible to immediate and direct human manipulation and of people – human 'agents' – making decisions that provide more proximate explanations of outcomes, decisions that could have been made differently. Indeed, careful study of international environmental politics can prompt an uneasy tension between pessimism and optimism. Pessimism arises in response to evidence that environmental degradation is globally, historically, and culturally ubiquitous and results from deep-seated, difficult-to-change, structural forces that appear to make the creation of international environmental problems common but their resolution rare. Optimism arises from the (perhaps unwarranted) belief that humans can make better choices and evidence that sometimes such problems emerge on the international agenda, that sometimes states negotiate agreements to address them, and that sometimes those agreements effectively resolve problems. Fully) understanding outcomes at different stages requires recognizing that structural factors do constrain the choices agents can make but leave room for political skill and energy in determining which of a more or less narrow range of potential outcomes actually occurs (Keohane, 1996: 24; Underdal, 2002: 37). Equally important, human choices, over time, can transform the 'normally invariant' structural forces that 'shape how publics and officials ... experience and cope with the diverse challenges posed by environmental issues' (Dessler, 1989: 461; Rosenau, 1993: 262).

# A History of the Field

The study of international environmental politics is inherently interdisciplinary, since understanding 'what is going on' in a particular environmental realm often requires understanding political science and economics, biology and chemistry, law and philosophy, and atmospheric and oceanographic modeling. Outcomes that seem obvious when only factors of interest to one discipline are considered become puzzles when factors of interest to other disciplines are brought in and, conversely, outcomes that are puzzling from a particular discipline's perspective make eminent sense when other disciplines' perspectives are taken into account. Thus, understanding the adoption of protocols under the Convention on Long-Range Transboundary Air Pollution in which countries accepted 'differentiated obligations' that entailed significantly different costs for different countries requires an understanding of the political forces that were operating within a context in which atmospheric modelers, ecologists, and economists had demonstrated the environmental ineffectiveness and the economic costs of simply continuing the 'common obligations' approach of prior protocols. The application of cost-sharing formulas from a treaty addressing chloride pollution of the Rhine to one addressing chemical pollution of the Rhine becomes surprising only after recognizing the scientific and economic realities that France was the primary source of the former problem but was only one of many sources of the latter (Bernauer and Moser, 1996). The inclusion of a progressively diverse range of disciplines in the Intergovernmental Panel on Climate Change since its first assessment reflects the increasing recognition that climate change cannot be properly understood and effectively addressed without interdisciplinary collaboration and understanding.

As detailed in Chapter 2, environmental problems were already on the international scene by the end of the nineteenth century. Countries had begun protecting various fish species, whales, and seals before the Second World War and had made efforts to address habitat degradation, endangered species, and river and marine pollution by the 1950s. Yet, international environmental politics only emerged as a subfield of international relations in the 1970s, in the wake of growing environmental concern, particularly in the United States. Almost four decades ago George Kennan called for the prevention of a 'world wasteland' (Kennan, 1970). Harold and Margaret Sprout, Richard Falk, Lynton Caldwell, and others authored books in the early 1970s that analyzed the issues raised at the United Nations' 1972 Conference on the Human Environment (UNCHE), including in a special issue of *International Organization* (Falk, 1971; Sprout and Sprout, 1971; Caldwell, 1972; Kay and Skolnikoff, 1972; Utton and Henning, 1973). Through the 1970s and into the 1980s, several scholars dedicated significant attention to international environmental politics but they were joined by relatively few others (LeMarquand, 1977; Ophuls, 1977; Orr and Soroos, 1979; M'Gonigle and Zacher, 1979; Caldwell, 1980; Young, 1981; Carroll, 1983, 1988; Kay and Jacobson, 1983; Young, 1989b). Articles analyzing international environmental politics appeared infrequently in major international relations and political science journals. However, the field began to expand in the late 1990s, as additional scholars and practitioners took an interest in international environmental politics (Peterson, 1988; Benedick, 1989; Haas, 1989, 1990; Mathews, 1991).

The end of the Cold War, and the 1992 UN Conference on Environment and Development (UNCED) held in Rio de Janeiro, made international environmental issues both politically and intellectually more salient. Two journals dedicated to the issues were launched – *International Environmental Affairs* and the *Journal of Environment and Development* – and articles on international environmental politics became more common in mainstream international relations journals. Several university presses (including MIT Press, Columbia University Press, and SUNY Press) developed series on international environmental politics that provided outlets for this growing scholarship. Sole authored and edited books dedicated to international environmental issues became more common (Choucri, 1993; Haas et al., 1993; Lipschutz and Conca, 1993; Sjostedt, 1993; Young and Osherenko, 1993b;

Young, 1994a; Keohane and Levy, 1996; Underdal, 1998b; Underdal and Hanf, 2000). A new group of scholars began publishing doctoral and subsequent research (Litfin, 1994; Mitchell, 1994a; Princen and Finger, 1994; Sprinz and Vaahtoranta, 1994; Bernauer, 1995a; Miller, 1995; Wapner, 1996; Dauvergne, 1997; O'Neill, 2000). Major debates were engaged related to environmental security and the trade–environment relationship (Deudney, 1990; Homer-Dixon, 1990; Bhagwati, 1993; Daly, 1993; Zaelke et al., 1993; Esty, 1994b; Levy, 1995). Since 2000, this trend has continued as researchers have examined an increasingly broad spectrum of issues including the environmental influence of the World Bank and other international financial institutions (Gutner, 2002), the role of the European Union (Andonova, 2004), the influence of unilateral state policies (DeSombre, 2000), and the influence of science on international environmental policy (Social Learning Group, 2001a, 2001b; Walsh, 2004; Mitchell et al., 2006b). The field has now grown to the point that articles on international environmental politics appear regularly in mainstream journals and as near-essential elements in edited volumes covering the major issues in international relations. Indeed, recent growth in the amount and diversity of the literature has made it increasingly difficult to track.

This research has generated numerous theoretical propositions and a corresponding number of careful empirical studies. Initially, deductive theories generated little follow-up in terms of operation-alization and testing while inductive case studies generated useful insights that often were not framed in ways which could facilitate their application and evaluation in other environmental realms. As a result, different terminologies and taxonomies of causal factors often overlapped with, but seemed unaware of, competing or complementary ones. Over the last decade, however, the field has begun to mature in several ways. Concentrated scholarly attention has generated considerable progress in the areas of international environmental regime effectiveness and the role of NGOs in international environmental governance (Underdal, 1992; Haas et al., 1993; Princen et al., 1995; Werksman et al., 1996; Brown Weiss and Jacobson, 1998; List and Rittberger, 1998; Simmons, 1998; Victor et al., 1998a; Wettestad, 1999; Young, 1999a; Betsill and Corell, 2001, 2008; Miles et al., 2002). Scholars increasingly engage critically with the work of other scholars (Sprinz and Helm, 1999; Hovi et al., 2003a, 2003b; Young, 2003) and pay increasing attention to methodological issues (Mitchell and Bernauer, 1998; Mitchell, 2002; Sprinz and Wolinsky-Nahmias, 2004; Underdal and Young, 2004). Databases that allow large-N studies have begun to be developed to complement the extensive set of case studies of global environmental governance (Miles et al., 2002; Mitchell, 2003, 2008; Breitmeier et al., 2006). This book builds on the theoretical and empirical insights developed by this extensive literature, organizing and summarizing it in ways that facilitate its application by the next generation of scholars.

# Causation

This book presents a causal account of international environmental politics. It provides a foundation for understanding and explaining the dynamics and outcomes involved in the creation and resolution of the wide range of past, current, and likely future international environmental problems. It also focuses on the 'whys' of international environmental politics rather than the 'whos', 'whats', 'whens', and 'wheres'. As background, this section delineates the perspectives on causation adopted in this book.

The following chapters investigate four analytic questions that correspond to the major stages of international environmental politics. First, why does the world face such a wide variety of international environmental problems? Second, why do some of these environmental problems emerge as issues on the international agenda while others do not? Third, why do countries devise intergovernmental solutions for some of these problems more quickly than for others? Fourth, why do some intergovernmental policies succeed at mitigating – and sometimes eliminating – the problems they address while others fail? These questions are preceded, in Chapter 2, by a discussion of what defines international environmental problems, what distinguishes them from other environmental and international problems, and of the various ways in which such problems can differ in politically important aspects of their 'problem structure'.

I have also sought to develop the reader's ability to think carefully about causes, about why certain outcomes *and not others* emerge during particular policy stages. To do so, it develops a theoretical framework designed to foster empirical explanation. Theory, whether arrived at inductively or deductively, provides insights that allow for generalization across a range of cases and supply the causal logic and predictions that are crucial to convincing explanations. Empirical explanation provides us with nuanced and accurate understandings of existing cases and allows us to provide nuanced and accurate policy advice about future cases. This book adopts an inclusive approach to theoretical claims in the belief that we can best understand and explain outcomes in international environmental politics by exploring all the potential explanations, rejecting them as unsatisfactory *after* consideration rather than precluding them *from* consideration.

## Causal claims: theory and its empirical application

This book seeks a balance between an excessively theoretical treatment and an excessively empirical one. The usual theoretical distinctions made in international relations between rationalism and constructivism; realism, institutionalism, and liberalism; or power-based, interest-based, and knowledge-based certainly apply to international environmental politics (Hasenclever et al., 1997; Ruggie, 1998; Fearon and Wendt, 2002; Zürn and Checkel, 2005). Collectively, these schools of thought have identified various independent or explanatory variables alleged to drive outcomes in international relations in general, and, by extension, in international environmental politics. They have developed theoretically compelling logics for why, how, and under what conditions we should expect certain independent variables to cause certain effects. They delineate how a 'cause' under certain conditions makes an 'effect' more likely to occur or, phrased more carefully, how an independent variable having a specified value when other independent variables also have specified values makes it more likely that a dependent variable will have a specified value.

Yet, theoretical claims about causation pose two challenges to those interested in empirical explanation, namely the opera-tionalization and isolation of variables. First, consider the challenges of operationalization. Scholars usually design theoretical claims to explain a broad class of phenomena. Even when scholars explicitly reject the value of generalization, other scholars may pick up explanations of particular cases and evaluate how well they apply to other cases. Because theoretical claims are generally made in abstract terms, applying them to explain a particular case requires the interpretation and judgment of operationalization, of mapping theoretical concepts to empirical realities. Theory can tell us how outcomes in Tragedies of the Commons are likely to differ from those in upstream/downstream problems, but knowing which outcomes are likely in any particular case requires that we classify the case as a Tragedy of the Commons or an upstream/downstream problem. Using theory to understand empirical cases, whether in international environmental politics or other realms of international relations, requires operationalizing abstract terms and concepts in ways that accurately reflect both the theoretical claims and the empirical realities of the cases being analyzed.

Second, consider the challenge posed by the tendency of theory to treat variables in isolation. Understanding how a particular independent variable operates, how it influences some dependent variable, is often clarified by considering the variable's average influence over a range of conditions or under specified conditions. We often best understand one variable's influence by considering it in isolation from all other variables. Yet, the clarification that comes from a *ceteris paribus* – 'holding other variables constant' – approach can shift our focus away from the fact that most outcomes (and satisfactory explanations of most outcomes) reflect the influence of a large number of independent variables. Put differently, an independent or explanatory variable having a particular value rarely constitutes a sufficient condition that produces a particular outcome under all conditions; that variable's influence almost always depends on other explanatory variables (the 'control variables') having particular values. Most causes generate certain outcomes only in particular contexts. We may focus on the proximate causes of certain anthropogenic environmental impacts, of the emergence of an international environmental problem on the international agenda, or of the success of negotiations. However, the causal power of these 'triggers' almost always depends on a 'causal field' of deep or enabling causes which, had the values of the variables constituting that causal field been different, would have led to different outcomes (Brady and Seawright, 2004). Thus, even the most environmentally-damaging behaviors would pose little environmental risk if the global population were six million rather than six billion. Superb intellectual leadership on an environmental issue will not lead to a successful conclusion of negotiations if powerful states fail to see an agreement as in their interests. The most carefully drafted environmental treaty will produce sought-after behavioral changes only if background levels of concern remain reasonably high.

The incentives and dynamics of theory development in international relations pose a deeper obstacle to clear thinking about the causes of international environmental problems and the sources of their resolution. International relations has often been dominated by 'great debates' between competing schools of thought. Carr and Morgenthau juxtaposed their versions of realism to the idealism of Wilson and others (Carr, 1964; Morgenthau, 1993). Waltz (1979) posited his structural neo-realism as an alternate but distinct means of explaining international politics which neoliberal institutionalists led by Keohane and Nye (1989) directly and explicitly sought to refute. The ensuing debate often involved scholars taking diametrically opposed positions that ceded little intellectual territory to the other side and often altogether discounted variables that the other side considered central (see Krasner, 1983; and in particular, Strange, 1983). More recently, the realist/institutionalist debate has been replaced by a rationalist/constructivist debate in which both sides often posit their preferred explanatory variables as central and the other side's as, at best, peripheral (Ruggie, 1998; Wendt, 1999; Fearon and Wendt, 2002). These debates have been productive in identifying, developing, and rigorously evaluating a range of variables as potential explanations of outcomes in international relations. Yet the development of international relations theory through debates can produce a climate in which explanatory variables are precluded from consideration on theoretical grounds rather than excluded as explanations on empirical grounds. The major debates can, nonetheless, help those interested in explaining international environmental outcomes if they lead to accepting the variables and arguments put forth by all sides as potentially explanatory while rejecting the claims that alternative variables are not, and cannot possibly be, explanatory. In short, theory provides a rich, and well-developed, list of variables that may help explain any particular empirical case or set of cases. However, the adjudication of which variables best explain a case should be based on confirmatory empirical evidence rather than on logically compelling theory alone.

This book remains agnostic regarding any particular independent variable's ability to explain any specific empirical case. For each outcome or 'dependent variable' focused on in succeeding chapters, I use prior theoretical and empirical work, often from competing paradigmatic perspectives, to identify a list of potential explanatory variables. By delineating the conditions under which, and the logic by which, each independent variable having a given value is alleged to lead to the dependent variable having a particular value, the chapters provide the tools for evaluating whether evidence from a particular case supports or refutes a claim of that independent variable's influence in that case. It leaves to the empirical analyst, rather than the theorist, the task of investigating which of various proposed variables best explain a particular case and which do not. The book also assumes that most explanations will involve only a subset of proposed explanatory variables, with careful analysis allowing the development of strong empirical and logical arguments for the influence of some variables and, equally important, against the influence of others.

## Deterministic *vs* probabilistic causality

It is worthwhile at this point to clarify the view of causation adopted here. I have assumed that the causal processes involved in international environmental politics are best treated as probabilistic rather than deterministic. In a deterministic causal model, to say X causes Y is to make one of two claims. Such a claim can mean that X is a sufficient cause of Y and corresponds to the claim that – under some specified set of conditions, whether broad or narrow – when X occurs, Y will occur. That is, given that specified conditions have been met and that X *did* occur, there is a 100 per cent probability that Y will occur. Alternatively, such a claim can mean that X is a necessary cause of Y and corresponds to the claim that, given that X *did not* occur, there is a 0 per cent probability that Y will occur, regardless of any other conditions (on necessary and sufficient conditions, see Goertz et al., 2008).

In a probabilistic causal model, however, the claim that X causes Y corresponds to the claim that when X occurs, it makes Y (as opposed to 'not Y') more likely to occur than had X not occurred. That is, neither X's presence nor its absence generates an unambiguous prediction of the value of Y, but instead simply makes it more likely that Y will take on a particular value. Explanatory variables make things likely – rather than cause things – to happen. Discussions of causation in international relations often invoke natural science analogies with corresponding images of deterministic causality in which the outcome being explained is influenced by a relatively small number of identifiable variables whose values can be observed. Thus, water can be counted on to freeze at 0 degrees C and boil at 100 degrees C so long as the water is at sea level and contains no impurities. But complex natural systems – and certainly international relations and international environmental politics – involve causal processes that are either ontologically or episte- mologically probabilistic (Clark et al., 2006). When the occurrence of a particular outcome (for example, the emergence of an international environmental problem or the negotiation of an intergovernmental agreement to address it) depends on a large number of factors, then claims that any one of those factors 'causes' that outcome, almost necessarily, depend on other variables having particular values. Given that the likelihood of that constellation of variables having their specified values will almost always be less – and often significantly less – than one, the claim that a particular variable is a cause is necessarily probabilistic. Even if the constellation of other conditioning or enabling variables frequently does coalesce in ways that allow the variable of interest to have its alleged influence, we might still perceive that influence as probabilistic simply because we cannot know what all the enabling and conditioning variables are, let alone observe their values.

Although I reject the notion that explaining particular cases is fostered by thinking in terms of necessary or sufficient conditions, thinking in those terms can shed light on the tension between pessimism and optimism in the study of international environmental politics. The pessimism that often pervades the study of international environmental politics reflects the sense that international environmental problems are common and their resolution is rare. We can explain that pattern of outcomes in broad strokes as due to the fact that international environmental problems have few necessary conditions but several sufficient conditions, and that both types of conditions are common. Such problems can be generated by numerous causes under numerous conditions. Their resolution is rare, however, because they have few sufficient conditions and many necessary conditions, and the simultaneous occurrence of both is rare.

## Building convincing causal claims: correlations, counterfactuals, and process tracing

An important element of this causal analytic approach is an identification of the 'observable implications' of each explanatory variable and the mechanisms by which they work, which together clarify what we should expect to see in the real world if a particular explanatory variable were the cause of a particular outcome. Causal theories can generate two types of observable implications: predictions about correlations and predictions about causal processes. We strengthen a claim about a particular variable's causal influence by validating those predictions against correlational evidence and process tracing the causal mechanisms.

Correlations between dependent and independent variables are crucial to causal analysis because they provide a fundamental and necessary piece of evidence underlying any causal claim. The importance of correlational evidence is not to contradict the adage that 'correlation does not imply causation' (Tufte, 2006: 159). Numerous important features of the world correlate with each other for various non-causal reasons. Correlations can arise when underlying conceptual definitions are vague or are tautological. The failure to define key concepts unambiguously can lead to collecting evidence that, perhaps unintentionally, necessarily confirms a hypothesis rather than evaluates it. Tautological definitions result from theory that fails to provide the means of identifying the value of the independent variable with evidence distinct from that used to identify the value of the dependent variable. Thus, claims that negotiations succeed when political conditions are ripe (that is, that 'ripeness' causes negotiation success) will be true necessarily unless we delineate ways of determining whether political conditions are 'ripe' that are independent of whether negotiations have succeeded (Zartman, 1985). Correlations can also reflect changes in a dependent variable and an alleged independent variable because both are effects of another, unidentified or discounted, independent variable. Indeed, a central realist claim that international institutions, including international environmental agreements, are epiphenomenal involves just such a claim: that the correlation of state behavior with treaty rules designed to regulate those behaviors result from the fact that both are effects of the constellation of state power and interests, with compliance being an artifact of states designing international law to codify their existing interests and expected future behavior (Strange, 1983; Mearsheimer, 1995). Many important social variables also tend to increase over time, creating correlations that are simple coincidences. By almost any metric, we have seen increases in the number of international environmental problems over the past century at the same time as we have seen increases in the global population, the number of countries in the world, the number of democracies in the world, the amount of international trade, the percentage of people speaking English in the world, and the number of books written about international environmental problems. While all of the latter variables have increased, only some are even potentially causes of the increase in international environmental problems. Indeed, the last example highlights that correlations – at least simple ones – cannot identify the direction of causation. The number of books written about international environmental problems has increased over the past century, but that is more likely the effect of the increase in international environmental problems rather than its cause.

Evidence of correlation supports causal claims not so much by its presence but by its absence. Correlation is a necessary condition for causation (Tufte, 2006: 159). The correlation or covariation of two variables need not imply that one causes the other. The absence of such covariation, however, does imply that the two are not causally connected, at least given the existing background conditions. As important, evidence that a dependent variable and an independent variable covary provides the foundation for a compelling argument that the latter caused the former once other potential causes have been excluded as explanations because they do not covary with the dependent variable or because no convincing logical arguments can be made of their causal power.

Counterfactuals are an important element in the causal approach adopted here. Counterfactuals are thought experiments designed to be cases that are identical to the actual state of the world with the exception of the value of the explanatory variable being evaluated. By comparing the outcome in that counterfactual case with the actual outcome, counterfactuals can help assess whether an independent variable was or was not the cause of that outcome. Counterfactuals are, necessarily, hypothetical cases because of the fundamental problem of causal inference (King et al., 1994). Consider an observation that both A and B occurred and the corresponding causal claim that A caused B. The latter claim implies that – in a context identical to the one observed – if A had been absent, B would also have been absent. The fundamental problem of causal inference arises because it is impossible to identify a situation that perfectly meets the conditional clause of 'in a context identical to the one observed'. In medicine, researchers often place identical twins in identical contexts and adopt double-blind protocols with placebos to approximate, as closely as possible, a world in which the medical treatment being evaluated is the only difference that could even potentially explain any differences in outcome. The movie *It's a Wonderful Life* nicely illustrates a perfect counterfactual – the angelic intervention that takes place allows us to observe in the movie's second half how the world of the movie's first half would have been different had everything been the same *except* that the protagonist had never lived. In short, counterfactuals are attempts to identify 'what would have happened otherwise', with 'otherwise' defined as 'had the alleged causal variable taken on some other value'.

The ability of counterfactuals to support a causal claim depends on the plausibility of the assertions that the counterfactual world could have existed and that the claimed outcome would have occurred as posited in that world (Fearon, 1991; Tetlock and Belkin, 1996). Counterfactuals are less plausible when it is difficult to imagine the independent variable in question having a different value than it had given the values of the other variables that the counterfactual seeks to hold constant. Thus, many claims about the influence on state behavior of those regimes established by particular international environmental agreements (IEAs) rely on descriptions of 'no regime' counterfactual worlds and further claims about how states would have behaved in those worlds (Biersteker, 1993; Hovi et al., 2003a). The plausibility of those counterfactuals, and the causal claims they are designed to support, depends on how convincing the claim is that within the extant international political context the IEA and the surrounding regime might not have formed. No-regime counterfactuals are less plausible for IEAs whose formation was overdetermined and all but inevitable and more plausible for IEAs whose formation appears to have been highly contingent on various factors, where the absence of any one might have led it not to form.

Counterfactuals become particularly plausible when the independent variables in question can be shown to have had different values in similar circumstances. Comparative case studies are convincing to the extent that they approximate a counterfactual, thereby providing empirical support that the claimed counterfactual world could exist and that outcomes actually turned out as had been claimed in that world. Cases selected so that the independent variable of interest varies between them – but so that other independent variables known to influence the dependent variable do not – are compelling precisely because they provide us with empirical evidence that the independent variable not only *could have had*, but in a real case *did have*, a different value under otherwise-similar circumstances.

Quantitative research evaluates covariation and can be understood in similar terms. Regression equations generate coefficients for each of the included independent variables that are estimates of how much the dependent variable changes in response to a one-unit change in each independent variable, after having held all other independent variables constant at their average values. Thus, the coefficient for an independent variable that can be operationalized as either present or absent (that is, a dummy variable) is an estimate of the difference between the value of the dependent variable with that independent variable present and its value with it absent, holding the other variables constant. Notably, regression can only estimate the influence of such variables if the researcher has collected data from counterfactual-like cases, that is, cases in which the dummy variable was absent.

Process tracing is often as central to convincing causal claims as correlation and counterfactuals. Process tracing involves looking for the 'footprints and fingerprints' that can satisfy us that observed correlations are causal rather than spurious. It involves creating convincing causal narratives that 'assess causality by recording each element of the causal chain' (Zürn, 1998: 640). Theories about causal relationships are never merely correlational in nature. Such theories involve claims that two variables will covary that derive from descriptions of *how* the independent variable causes variation in the dependent variable. They delineate causal mechanisms, causal chains, and compelling logics of why and under what conditions we should expect the independent variable to wield influence. Theories generate observable implications about correlation but also about the processes of causal influence. Thus, NGOs are theorized as influencing the outcomes of international negotiations by introducing novel ideas rather than through more material sources of power (Betsill and Corell, 2001). That claim, in turn, suggests looking for their influence by examining ideas proposed to negotiators by NGOs and the degree of 'congruence' between those ideas and 'the ideas embedded in an international agreement' (Betsill and Corell, 2001: 75). Agreements that contain specific text, principles, or ideas that originated with NGOs rather than other actors provide compelling evidence of their influence because it conforms so closely to the logic and processes proposed by theory (Betsill and Corell, 2001: 75).

Compelling explanations of the international environmental outcomes in which we are interested are built by combining elements of both correlation and process tracing. Correlational studies – whether involving large-N quantitative studies, comparisons of more limited numbers of carefully selected cases or of variation over time within a single case, or through carefully constructed counterfactuals – convince us that an independent variable was a cause by providing evidence *that* the dependent variable had a different value when – or would not have had that value if – that independent variable had a different value and that the dependent variable changed its value only after the independent variable changed its value. Process tracing and causal narratives can also convince us that an independent variable was a cause by providing evidence of *how* the independent variable caused the change in the dependent variable. The most compelling causal claims are those that bring all these elements together, combining strong theoretical logic, considerable empirical evidence that matches theoretical predictions and that demonstrates empirical correlation, plausible counterfactuals, and careful process tracing. Done well, such claims help both researchers and their audience understand and explain the world of international environmental politics.

## Outline of the Book

This chapter has provided a brief history of the field of international environmental politics and has introduced the reader to major elements of the causal framework that informs the rest of the book. Chapter 2 defines what international environmental problems are and provides a brief overview of the history of international environmental problems, from early attempts to regulate shared fisheries to current efforts to address more and more varied environmental problems. It then delineates politically important ways in which international environmental problems vary as the basis for explaining why some problems are more difficult to address than others and why the type of solutions and their effectiveness varies significantly across problems.

Chapters 3 through 6 address the 'why' questions that are specific to the four key stages in the international environmental policy process. Chapter 3 asks why international environmental problems arise as frequently as they do. It also summarizes the various explanations of why so many human behaviors result in international environmental harm and why some behaviors do not produce such results. The chapter starts by describing the IPAT (Impacts = Population*Affluence*Technology) identity as an initial model of the sources of human environmental impacts. The chapter then reviews six perspectives on the sources of environmental harms and the appropriate strategies for addressing them, looking at the roles of values, knowledge, law, incentives, incapacity, and power. The chapter ends with a discussion of why environmental degradation is so common and ubiquitous; why environmental degradation is more common – and its resolution less common – in the international arena than the domestic one; and how these six perspectives can be used in conjunction to identify the causes of particular international environmental problems.

Chapter 4 explores why some international environmental problems receive international attention as soon as they are recognized, why others take decades to receive such attention, and why still others that scientists have known about for years continue to receive scant international attention. The chapter develops the argument that issue emergence results from the development of sufficient knowledge, concern, and urgency around an environmental impact. Recognizing an environmental impact as a problem, getting it on the international agenda for discussion, prioritizing the issue for action, and framing the issue are distinct functions of the agenda setting or 'issue emergence' stage of international environmental politics. These functions are fostered by different actors and any variation in both the nature of the problem and in the contextual conditions can help or hinder the efforts of those actors.

Chapter 5 examines explanations of the success of states at forming intergovernmental institutions to address international environmental problems. The chapter starts by delineating the background conditions that can foster action on particular types of international environmental problems. It then looks at the processes of international negotiation by which knowledge and concern are transformed into specific provisions that enough states find mutually acceptable to gain acceptance of an international environmental agreement. The chapter also explores the factors that can influence agreement content, looking at the fundamental form that international institutions take, the degree to which they incorporate scientific advice, the flexibility that states are granted, and the types of primary rules, information systems, and response mechanisms they adopt.

Chapter 6 engages questions of institutional effectiveness. It looks at the methodological issues involved in assessing institutional effectiveness, particularly those related to the choice of compliance, goal achievement, or behavior change as the indicator of influence. The chapter delineates two models of actor behavior – a logic of consequences and a logic of appropriateness – that provide overarching frameworks for understanding why states respond as they do (or fail to respond) to the commitments they undertake in international treaties. The chapter lays out the different pathways and sources of institutional influence within these logics and then details the features and strategies that intergovernmental institutions use to influence behavior. The chapter also examines the exogenous contextual conditions that, despite being beyond institutional control, play an important role in determining whether an institution succeeds in its efforts to induce behavioral change.

Chapter 7 concludes by identifying patterns in the influence of variables, actors, and processes that emerge by looking across policy stages and how those patterns vary depending on what outcomes we seek to explain. It revisits issues related to thinking causally about international environmental politics and then briefly describes debates in international environmental politics that are related to trade and the environment, the environment and security, the erosion of sovereignty, and the value of a World Environment Organization. The chapter concludes by identifying several important questions related to international environmental politics that remain unanswered and highlights the importance of conducting policy-relevant research.

# DEFINING AND DISTINGUISHING INTERNATIONAL ENVIRONMENTAL PROBLEMS

Before analyzing the processes of international environmental politics, it is useful to define what international environmental problems are, to review the history of their development, and to develop conceptual categories of such problems. This chapter starts by defining international environmental problems and by asking how we can distinguish environmental problems from other problems, domestic problems from international problems, and problems from non-problems. It then describes the appearance of international environmental problems on the international agenda and how the mix of problems addressed on that agenda has changed over time. The rest of the chapter outlines categories that allow the identification of similar political patterns and dynamics across problems that are quite diverse, in an ecological and environmental sense. It also asks, how do the politically-important characteristics of international environmental problems vary? What aspects of such problems deserve our attention if we want to understand international environmental politics? These categories provide the foundation for analyzing, in future chapters, the sources of international environmental problems, the forces that can lead to their emergence on the international agenda, the dynamics that can influence the success of negotiations, and the factors that can explain when states are likely to reduce their environmentally-damaging behaviors.

## Defining International Environmental Problems

If we define international environmental *politics* as the array of political efforts to address international environmental *problems*, then understanding the former requires a meaningful and useful definition of the latter. Such a definition should meet certain criteria. It should correspond as much as possible to standard usage. It should not be so broad as to identify all human impacts on the environment as problems and all environmental problems as international. But it should allow us to identify 'latent' international environmental problems; if we define international environmental problems as those addressed by international environmental politics, then it precludes engaging crucial questions of why some are addressed rapidly, others slowly, and some not at all. Finally, the definition should acknowledge that international environmental problems are socially constructed. It should allow us to distinguish between the environmental *impacts* humans have on nature – which are objective facts – and environmental *problems* – which involve subjective assessments, perceptions, and valuations that are often contested. Given these criteria, we can define international environmental problems as 'those impacts on the natural environment of human activities that some significant set of people view as negative and that have either a transboundary or international commons aspect'. This definition has three parts: an 'environmental' part, a 'problem' part, and an 'international' part.

Let us start with the 'environmental' part: 'those impacts on the natural environment of human activities'. Many, and perhaps most, international issues are situations in which some human activity influences other humans. And, in many cases, war, trade, globalization, and human rights violations involve processes that also harm the environment. But those environmental impacts are not central to what those concerned consider to be 'the problem'. Environmental impacts are, however, central to many problems that have been, and still remain, on the international agenda. The definition here seeks to distinguish issues in which the state of the natural environment plays a central role from those in which it does not. This includes issues such as the exploitation or destruction of living natural resources like trees, fish, other plant and animal species, biodiversity, and habitats. It encompasses issues in which environmental well-being also plays some role, even if it is a secondary one. Thus, nuclear weapons testing should be treated as an environmental problem if concerns about it extend beyond the security realm and involve the damage such testing causes to the environment. The definition excludes the exploitation of non-living natural resources (such as oil and mineral deposits) except to the extent that the processes by which we extract and use such resources generate concern about environmental well-being. The definition also excludes the impacts of naturally-generated hurricanes, drought, earthquakes, tsunamis, and disease; although these forces drastically alter the environment and have major impacts on people, it seems useful to treat them as environmental only if they are caused, exacerbated, or altered by human activities.

The definition's 'problem' aspect is 'that some significant set of people view as negative'. 'Environmental problems' are not objectively identified or discovered but are defined by human judgments regarding our influences on nature. The objective affects of clear-cutting a square kilometer of forest have changed very little over time but doing so was considered 'progress' in the 1700s and is considered a 'problem' today. The killing of whales and fur seals has changed from being viewed as an appropriate economic activity to being viewed as a problem of unrestrained exploitation reducing any future harvest to being viewed as a problem of overexploitation threatening a species to being viewed as a problem entailing environmental 'immorality' (D'Amato and Chopra, 1991). Wetland drainage was the intended goal of much development policy for many years before wetland loss came to be considered a major problem. Although this part of the definition introduces an admittedly unsatisfying imprecision by defining an environmental impact as a 'problem' only if a 'significant set' of people consider it as negative, it seems superior to the alternatives. If nobody considers an impact as negative, then surely it is not a problem; if everybody considers that impact as negative, then surely it is. Like 'folk theorems' in game theory (Fudenberg and Tirole, 1991), the goal is to capture the intuition that, somewhere between these extremes, lies a point at which when 'enough' people consider certain impacts to be negative then they become, subjectively, problems. We cannot specify that point in advance, since what constitutes a 'problem' depends on both how many people are concerned and how concerned they collectively are. But we can say that when a large number of people or a small number of politically important people become sufficiently concerned, most people would agree that 'a problem exists'. 'Some significant set' of people need not be most people on the planet but may consist of a few activists, scientists, or others who observe an impact, consider it a problem, and self-consciously attempt to convince others likewise.

The definition contends that problems exist when people consider human impacts on nature as negative, whether or not the human benefits of the responsible activities generate more-than-offsetting benefits and whether or not solutions are available and sufficiently cheap that people support their adoption. A problem must exist before efforts to assess taking action and to devise solutions can begin. Indeed, recognizing an activity's environmental harm is usually what prompts the creative social processes that generate potential solutions. The definition proves analytically useful because it allows us to engage the question of why some impacts become 'problems' quickly, some slowly, and some not at all. It also excludes those human impacts that few, if any, people consider as negative. Thus, the industrial pollution of rivers has been of international concern for decades but the active chlorination and fluoridation of water that many countries undertake to promote human health also contributes to environmental impacts that have yet to become significant environmental concerns.

The 'international' part of the definition is that they 'have either a transboundary or international commons aspect'. Environmental problems are international if the responsible activity, the impacts of that activity, or the concern about (and solutions to) those impacts do not all exist within one country's borders. Certain problems are more likely to receive international attention. At one extreme, norms of sovereignty hinder efforts to internationalize environmental problems that exist solely within one country. Those norms legitimize the rights of national governments to balance, and to differ in how they balance, the interests of the former and those of the latter. Thus, land use change – the conversion of forests into cropland, wetlands into residential areas, and coastal zones into aquaculture farms – dramatically alters the environment but has received little international attention because the responsible activities, their immediate impacts, and the concerns they raise tend to be contained within one country's borders. Likewise, the pollution of rivers or lakes that exist within one country's borders has rarely received international attention: pollution of the Mississippi River, the Amazon or Lake Baikal, or the desiccation of Mono Lake or the Aral Sea (before the breakup of the Soviet Union) have generally not been treated as *international* environmental problems.

As the spatial span of activities, impacts, or concern grow, however, problems are more likely to be considered international. Activities that occur wholly within one state's borders but have impacts on the atmosphere, transboundary rivers and lakes, or ocean zones are more likely to prompt concern in other states and, hence, to become international. Regional problems such as acid rain, river pollution, and marine pollution tend to arise on the international agenda only when their impacts cross borders. Acid rain has generated more international attention in Europe than in North America because closer borders mean that economic activities that generate few transborder impacts in the United States generate many such impacts in Europe. Although such transborder impacts are often the unintended consequences of economic activities, they can result from conscious efforts to displace environmental problems, as in the export of hazardous waste, transforming otherwise local environmental problems into international ones (Wapner, 1997: 228).

Activities that take place on or influence shared resources, like transboundary rivers and lakes, will become international issues relatively rapidly if the victims of those activities find domestic routes for redress ineffective. Activities within a country's borders that have impacts on a global commons will become international only after those impacts are identified and concern about them grows. Thus, stratospheric ozone depletion and climate change are caused primarily by activities occurring within countries' borders whose impacts affect the global atmospheric commons, so they became international issues only after scientists identified those impacts and concern grew in various countries. By contrast, activities that occur on a global commons often 'begin life' as international problems precisely because neither the activities nor their impacts exist within any single government's realm of sovereignty. High seas fisheries, Antarctica, and outer space are considered global commons with the assumption that whether, what, how, and how much of given activities take place on them is an appropriate subject for international dialogue. Marine pollution is international in at least three respects: land-based pollution from most states degrades the world's oceans; pollution from international shipping on the commons also degrades the commons; and pollution that occurs on the commons also degrades the environment of ocean-bordering states.

Two other factors make it likely that environmental problems will become international. First, the activities and impacts of some environmental problems can occur within a single country but become international when citizens in other countries become concerned about those impacts. Just as human rights violations become internationalized because citizens in other countries express concern even when they are not directly affected, environmental impacts that appear to be domestic can become international because of concern in other states. Thus, the local extinction of a species due to local activities – such as the endangerment of various species in the United States – may remain a domestic environmental problem because the citizens of other countries express little concern about them. By contrast, species endangerment generally is an international problem because, in the aggregate, people from many countries are concerned about preserving species and biodiversity both in the global commons and in other countries. Second, some environmental problems are local but ubiquitous, involving truly local environmental problems that happen to occur in many countries. Such problems can become internationalized if international cooperation appears to offer advantages in understanding or addressing the problem. Globalization fosters such perspectives since international trade means that consumers' choices in one country have environmental impacts in others and international media means that people are better informed about environmental degradation abroad. As tropical deforestation demonstrates, local companies still do considerable local environmental damage but they do it increasingly on behalf and under the scrutiny of foreign customers (Dauvergne, 1997).

This book's focus on *international* environmental problems should not obscure the many important *domestic* environmental problems. Pollution of rivers that do not cross national borders occurs in many countries but receives less international attention than that of transboundary rivers. The local extinction of local populations of plants or animals may go unnoticed beyond the affected country's borders if populations are thriving elsewhere. Toxic, hazardous, and nuclear waste disposal within a waste-generating state's borders poses a major, but usually domestic, environmental problem. Efforts to internationalize temperate and boreal deforestation have been less successful than those targeting tropical deforestation. Urban air pollution, despite its ubiquity, remains almost exclusively a domestic, and even a municipal, concern.

The definition here is intended to define international environmental problems in ways that highlight – and allow us to better engage – important political questions as to why certain environmental impacts become 'problems', why certain environmental problems get addressed on the international agenda, and why international environmental problems differ, and are treated differently, from non-environmental problems.

## A Brief History of International Environmental Problems

Given this definition, what is the list of all current international environmental problems and how has that list changed over time? This section notes the obstacles to generating such a list but then seeks to provide a plausible sense of the history of international environmental problems.

How can we generate a comprehensive list of international environmental problems? One might start with those problems that states have addressed through bilateral or multilateral treaties. One might then add government efforts to foster environmental improvements in other countries through financial aid, investment, technology transfer, training programs, and policy diffusion. One might further add the many international environmental projects undertaken by nongovernmental organizations and international organizations. But such a list includes those international environmental problems *that have been addressed* but not *all* international environmental problems. Indeed, it would be surprising (pleasantly, to be sure) if we currently have addressed – even if inadequately – all international environmental problems. But many human behaviors that harm the environment are not yet treated as international environmental problems. Indeed, knowing which problems have *not* been addressed is crucial for identifying where environmental progress is slow, why some problems are addressed and some are not, and why those that are addressed are addressed when they are. How can we identify these unaddressed problems, these 'dogs that didn't bark' to use Sir Arthur Conan Doyle's metaphor? Conceptually, given the definition above, the list of international environmental problems should start with all human influences on the environment, should take from that the subset that a significant set of people consider a problem, and should then take from that the subset that are international in character.

No ready-to-hand source exists for such a task. But the list of existing international environmental agreements does provide some insight even though it fails to capture those problems that have been recognized but still remain unaddressed at a particular point in time (the following history draws from Mitchell, 2008). The precursors to what would now be considered 'environmental' problems emerged on the international agenda as early as 1351, when England and Castile (the predecessor of Spain) negotiated an agreement to address fisheries (Giordano, 2002a: 608). By 1875, various countries had signed more than 40 bilateral agreements addressing the problems of fisheries' access or allocation (Giordano, 2002b). These initial fisheries' agreements were not environmental, at least in the present-day sense. They were created to avert conflicts that might otherwise have arisen over the terms under which each country's nationals had rights to the fish in a shared river or in international waters. Catch levels were rarely so high as to threaten the health of the underlying stock but international conflicts could still break out on the high seas or in rivers if one country's catch impinged on another's or conflicts among fishers of different nationalities threatened to generate larger problems. Although most current international fisheries are plagued by collective overappropriation, the distribution problems central to these early treaties continue to trouble international fisheries management (see Krasner, 1991). Although over-appropriation had not become a problem for most fisheries, it had for fur seals. By the late 1800s, seal populations were so decimated that states agreed to limit the season for sealing near Jan Mayen in the Arctic and to ban pelagic sealing in the north Pacific. Present-day problems of invasive species were also already visible by the late 1800s in the transnational propagation of contagious animal diseases and of wine parasites (*phylloxera vastatrix*). River management had also become part of international affairs, with conflicts arising over the diversion and distribution of water and over efforts to channel river flow. States had recognized and begun to address all these problems by the late 1800s.

From 1900 through 1950, a wider range of human environmental impacts emerged on the international agenda. Threats to, and the value of preserving, certain species were recognized in a 1900 treaty in which six European countries and the Congo banned all hunting of giraffes, gorillas, chimpanzees, mountain zebras, and several other species 'on account of their rarity and threatened extermination' (Convention for the Preservation of Wild Animals, Birds, and Fish in Africa). By 1933, various colonial states had recognized that many African plants and animals could only be preserved by creating large natural parks and reserves (Convention Relative to the Preservation of Fauna and Flora in their Natural State). The hunting of birds had taken such a toll that it was regulated under multilateral treaties in 1902 and 1950, as well as in bilateral agreements between the USA and Canada, Denmark and Sweden, and the USA and Mexico. Contagious diseases of livestock and plants transmitted through trade continued to show up on the international agenda, as did locust plagues that harmed international agriculture. Transboundary pollution was recognized in the regulation of the transport of flammable substances on the Rhine, in international regulations regarding the use of lead in paint, and in the damage caused in Washington State in the United States from air pollution from Canada's Trail Smelter. The League of Nations unsuccessfully tried to address marine oil pollution in the 1920s. Whaling was regulated by a 1931 convention and other fisheries continued to receive much international attention, with countries negotiating over 100 fisheries agreements, including many that addressed overappropriation as well as allocation. The increasing ability to dam rivers for flood control and energy production also prompted efforts to manage the international implications of such engineering.

Since 1950, the number and range of international environmental problems have continued to increase. Fisheries, river management, and the protection of endangered species remain central to the international landscape. Endangered species have been treated as both global and regional problems and as individual species and within frameworks that address large ranges of species. Environmental problems began to be viewed in more interconnected terms, with an increasing focus on habitats and not just species. Marine oil pollution began being addressed in the 1950s, and was soon followed by marine pollution from the dumping of waste, chemicals, sewage, and other substances, as well as river and lake pollution. These problems have been addressed within global frameworks and as problems requiring region-specific solutions, often within the context of protecting a particular sea or a particular part of the ocean. International efforts were made to manage nuclear energy and to eliminate the radioactive pollution from atmospheric nuclear testing in the early 1960s. Acid rain became an international issue in the 1970s among European and North American states but has received little international attention in other regions. Stratospheric ozone depletion emerged on the international agenda in the late 1970s and early 1980s, while climate change, biodiversity loss, and desertification emerged in the late 1980s and early 1990s.

If we use negotiation of treaties as an available, if inadequate, proxy, we observe that states have paid increasing international attention to environmental problems over time. Discussions of international environmental problems were rare until the last half of the twentieth century. Until the 1920s, such issues were the topic of international negotiations only two to three times per year. From 1925 to 1949, that rate increased to four to five times per year and, in the 1950s, to 15 per year. International agreements were signed approximately 25 times per year in the 1960s, 50 times per year in the 1970s, 35 times per year in the 1980s, and almost 80 times per year in the 1990s (these statistics include bilateral and multilateral discussions that generated new agreements, protocols, or amendments: see Mitchell, 2008).

Successful agreements also document changes in what environmental problems states think about and how they think about them. Fisheries and species protection were the focus of 80 to 90 per cent of all environmental negotiations until the 1950s but now constitute only 40 to 50 per cent. Pollution of rivers, the marine environment, and the atmosphere constitutes 25 to 30 per cent of recent multilateral environmental negotiations. States treat an increasing proportion of the environmental problems on the international agenda as multilateral rather than bilateral problems. Multilateral agreements were rare early on in the history of international environmental affairs but now constitute 30 to 40 per cent of all agreements, despite dramatic increases in the number of bilateral agreements. And states increasingly frame environmental problems in eco-systemic terms, increasingly seeing the preservation of habitats and eco-systems as valuable in its own right as well as essential for preserving particular species.

## Distinguishing Environmental Problems

To begin to understand international environmental politics requires us to distinguish among the range of international environmental problems in ways that shed light on why the politics surrounding one problem can differ so markedly from those surrounding another. This demands categories that reflect politically important differences rather than ecologically important ones, categories that account for the interests, power, and knowledge of states that are so central to explanations in other realms of international relations (Hasenclever et al., 1997). Scholars have often looked at the characteristics of an activity, issue area, or problem for explanations of why states cooperate in resolving some international problems but not others (Rittberger, 1993: 13). There is a compelling logic to the idea that 'certain inherent characteristics of issues or conflicts predetermine the way in which ... issues or conflicts will be dealt with' (Rittberger, 1993: 14). Problem structure becomes important because certain problems seem more difficult for states to resolve than others, that is, some problems are likely to be more malign than others (Miles et al., 2002). Problem structure is also assumed to influence what solutions states will adopt to resolve their conflicts (Young, 1999b: Chapter 3; Mitchell, 2006). Game theory has provided invaluable insights into how the relationship among two or more states' incentives can make international environmental cooperation difficult, even under the most simplified conditions (Martin, 1992b; Zürn, 1998). The discussion that follows builds on game theory's insights that incentives are important causes of environmental problems but notes that incapacity, power, knowledge, and values also play important roles in why international environmental problems occur or don't, why they make it onto the international agenda or don't, why states adopt cooperative solutions or don't, and why states succeed in implementing those solutions or don't.

Before detailing the factors that cause or exacerbate international environmental problems, it is helpful to delineate two important overarching distinctions among environmental problems. The first is the distinction overappropriation, degradation, and accidental harms. The second is the distinction among Tragedies of the Commons, upstream/downstream situations, and incapacity problems.

## Overappropriation, degradation, and accidental harms

People derive value from environmental resources in one of three ways: through consumptive use; through non-consumptive use; or through simple knowledge of their existence. Consumptive use involves people extracting units that flow from an environmental resource and using them in ways that preclude their use by others and also preclude their being returned to the environment in the form in which they were extracted. Examples here include fishing and hunting. Non-consumptive use involves actions that do not prevent others from taking the same action but do decrease the quality of the environmental resource in question. Examples include air, river, and marine pollution, as well as habitat degradation. Existence value involves actions that, when taken, do not preclude others from taking the same action and do not reduce either the flow from, or the quality of, the environmental resource. Examples include the pleasure that people derive from enjoying nature or from simply knowing that certain species are protected from extinction.

The behaviors by which people derive existence value do not impinge on other people or harm the environment and, so, do not create environmental problems. But both consumptive and non-consumptive uses can have environmental impacts and reduce the value, including the existence value, that other people derive from the environment, and hence these can become environmental problems. Environmental impacts occur whenever the level of human use exceeds the environmental amenity's 'carrying capacity', defined as the environment's ability to restore itself promptly to its pre-use condition. If environmental impacts become large enough that a significant set of people consider them negative, they will generate two types of environmental problems. Excessive consumptive use will produce overappropriation problems while excessive non-consumptive use will produce degradation problems.

Overappropriation problems can be defined as problems in which people derive value from some environmental resource by appropriating a flow of units from it, in which they value the amenity based on how many units they can appropriate, and in which one person's use of a unit precludes its use by another. Overappropriation involves *consumptive* use that exceeds the resource's ability to *replenish* itself and decreases the *quantity* of that resource available to others. Imagine a large lake used for fishing. Individual fish reproduce and die at rates that generate an annual 'recruitment rate' for the fish stock as a whole. Given a certain stock size, that recruitment rate (percentage of stock per year) produces a certain number of fish that can be caught each year without reducing the stock size. Overappropriation occurs if more than that number of fish is caught, leading to a declining stock. Such overappropriation makes it increasingly difficult for those who rely on fishing to catch the same number of fish and, eventually, the stock decline may make it so costly to catch a species that it becomes 'commercially extinct', if not ecologically extinct. The threats to and decimation of various species, including whales and other marine mammals as well as terrestrial animals including elephants, tigers, rhinoceroses, and others have resulted, at least in part, from overappropriation. Likewise, agricultural water use – in which water drawn from a river returns to aquifers rather than the river – also involves an overappropriation problem.

Degradation problems, by contrast, can be defined as problems in which people derive value from some environmental amenity by having access to the stock of that amenity, in which they value the amenity based on the quality of that stock, and in which the use of the stock by one human has little impact on the *ability* of others to use that stock but does influence the quality of the stock. Degradation involves *non-consumptive* use that exceeds the resource's ability to *restore* itself and decreases the *quality* of that resource available to others. Imagine a long river that provides municipal, industrial and agricultural water and serves as a repository or 'sink' for intentional discharges of chemical pollutants and sewage and unintentional runoff of agriculture pesticides and fertilizers. Downstream water users can still take water from the river, but upstream polluters have decreased the quality of that water, making it more costly to provide the quality of water needed for downstream drinking, agricultural use, or industrial purposes. Sewage, garbage, and oil and chemical pollution disposed of by tankers, container ships, and other large ocean-going vessels decrease the quality (not the quantity) of ocean water, making bathing, beach-combing, and other ocean-related activities less enjoyable.

Overappropriation and degradation problems can, therefore, be distinguished by asking whether people derive value from the environmental resource by consuming units of the resource (for example, harvesting animals from a stock) or by non-consumptive uses that degrade the resource by discharging something into it or by extracting it temporarily from the environment and then returning it at a lower level of quality than before. Some environmental resources exhibit both types of features, of course, and then it becomes important to recognize both the distinct aspects of each problem type and the interplay between them.

Because overappropriation often produces immediate and visible resource shortages, it can generate more political conflict than degradation problems (Koremenos et al., 2001). Overappropriation often involves an inherent competition among appropriators unrelated to its environmental impacts, a problem that does not exist in degradation settings. Overappropriation conflicts are never merely – and often not centrally – about how current use levels impact future use levels, but are over allocating the current appropriation: over who gets more water, fish, whales, or polar bears today. Indeed, in arid regions like the Middle East, the conflict over freshwater is quite intense even though current use has little influence on future availability (which is driven by precipitation and recharge rates). Shortages caused by one state's overuse of a resource can create economic conflicts that are exacerbated by national loyalties in which the overappropriation of water, fish, and other environmental resources by foreigners is considered far less politically acceptable than overappropriation by fellow citizens. Indeed, the heatedness with which both international water and international fisheries conflicts are fought (in contrast to the rarity of such conflicts with respect to international pollution problems) provides strong, if anecdotal, evidence of this dynamic (Hart, 1976; Gleick, 1993; Lowi, 1995; Postel, 1999; Barkin and DeSombre, 2002).

The overappropriation/degradation distinction also maps onto how alternatives are perceived. Pollution and other degradation problems are usually the unintended by-products of activities undertaken for other reasons. Because their impacts are unintended, resistance to addressing them tends to depend on the availability, cost, and logistical obstacles to transitioning to environmentally-friendly alternatives. The environmental impacts of most over-appropriation problems, however, are inherent to the responsible activity. Fish cannot be simultaneously harvested and left in the ocean to reproduce; trees cannot be simultaneously harvested for timber and left standing. Resolving these problems requires changing the level of the activity and not the process by which it is conducted. Demand for the resource in question must be reduced or redirected into other activities.

Both overappropriation and degradation problems become problems only at the point at which aggregate human demands on the resource approach the resource's ability to meet those demands, that is, its carrying capacity. For centuries, people could catch fish, kill polar bears and rhinos, cut down trees, and draw irrigation water without impinging on the ability of others to do the same. Likewise, levels of land, air, and water degradation from various human activities remained well within the regenerative capacities of the environment for centuries. International environmental problems have become – and are likely to become more – common because population growth and economic growth together have increased aggregate human demands on the environment dramatically, leading to a growing number of environmental resources being overappropriated or degraded.

Finally, some environmental impacts result from accident-prone activities. Some behaviors have unintended environmental effects that the responsible parties themselves would prefer to (and may well already be making efforts to) avoid. Consider oil or chemical spills in the ocean or in rivers, nuclear reactor accidents, and toxic releases. Such problems attract international attention whenever their impacts have been or may be international. For these activities, any resistance to engaging the environmental problem will depend on the degree to which the immediate economic interests of the responsible parties are harmed by the accident, independent of any additional environmental harm.

## Tragedies of the Commons, upstream/downstream problems, and incapacity problems

Another important distinction among environmental problems is that among Tragedies of the Commons, upstream/downstream problems, and incapacity problems. The first two problem types are distinct in terms of the types of incentives that lead to environmental damage and both, in turn, are distinct from problems in which incapacity rather than incentives are the cause of environmental damage.

We can distinguish between Tragedy of the Commons and upstream/downstream situations by considering the degree to which those concerned about some form of environmental degradation (the 'victims') are also the 'perpetrators' of that damage. Environmental impacts exist on a spectrum in this regard. At one end are Tragedies of the Commons, in which – at least in the stylized case – all relevant actors are both perpetrators *and* victims. Thus, in Hardin's original example, the problem arises only among those placing cattle on the commons; the impacts they have on villagers who might prefer to enjoy the commons for hiking or picnicking are not considered (Hardin, 1968). Because the perpetrators are also victims, they would prefer that the environmental problem be resolved even while they would prefer not to contribute to its resolution.

In 'upstream/downstream' problems, at the other end of the spectrum, none of the victims concerned about the problem have caused it and none of those perpetrating it consider their interests harmed by it. In such situations, the perpetrators remain indifferent as to whether the environmental problem is resolved or not. It is only the victims who seek its resolution. Put differently, actors in Tragedy of the Commons situations are situated symmetrically and have 'mixed motives', wanting to continue to engage in the environmentally-harmful behavior themselves because of the benefits they receive by doing so but also wanting others to stop engaging in that behavior because of the environmental harm it causes. Actors in upstream/downstream problems are situated asymmetrically and have one of two 'pure motives' with respect to resolving a problem, since the perpetrators receive all the benefits but bear none of the costs of their environmentally-harmful behavior while the victims bear all of the costs but receive none of the benefits. River pollution often involves such situations, but air pollution may do the same. More to the point, any asymmetric situation in which those concerned about an environmental problem are distinct from those causing it can be referred to as an upstream/downstream problem. Thus, international efforts to protect endangered species, including whales, tigers, and rhinos, are more upstream/downstream problems than Tragedies of the Commons, since many of the 'downstream' states concerned about those species are not involved in their endangerment while many of the 'upstream' states harvesting or failing to protect them are not concerned about their endangerment.

Despite important differences, in both problem types environmental damage emerges because those responsible for the problem lack sufficient incentives to take action to address it effectively. Yet environmental damage, especially in the developing world, often results from incapacity rather than incentive problems. When environmental problems arise from governments *failing* to take certain actions, that is from acts of omission rather than commission, incapacity may lead governments to leave unaddressed problems they would indeed prefer to see addressed. The discharge of untreated sewage into rivers in many countries occurs because of financial limitations and not because of a lack of concern about health and environmental impacts. Indeed, sewage treatment one of the first environmental problems governments address as they develop. Incapacities can be administrative as well as financial. Governmental institutions in states that lack financial and administrative capabilities may be unable effectively to control fishing companies operating from their ports, industries that pollute the air or water from within their borders, or individuals that clear forests to create farmland for their families (Brown Weiss and Jacobson, 1998). Indeed, many developing country governments committed to species and habitat protection, pollution reduction, and other environmental goals can dedicate only the most limited resources to the education and regulation campaigns central to such efforts. Technical incapacities also can generate environmental problems. Thus, although most governments have strong incentives to dispose of nuclear waste safely, nuclear waste disposal is an environmental problem largely because no technology that achieves environmental objectives within economic, political, and social constraints exists. It might seem that incapacity issues would generally remain domestic issues. However, issues of incapacity become international when states other than the one involved become concerned about it. Whether motivated by an altruistic concern about the human toll of certain environmental problems, or more instrumental concerns about how those problems have impacts abroad, other 'victim' states may find it worthwhile to help alleviate financial, administrative, or technological incapacities so the 'perpetrator' state can address the environmental problem to the benefit of both the perpetrator and the victim.

Why does this three-part distinction matter? Mixed motive, Tragedies of the Commons, situations are more likely to end up on the international agenda because those perpetrating the problem – at least collectively – have incentives to address the problem, have knowledge about the types and levels of environmentally suspect behaviors, and have the capacity to reduce or eliminate those behaviors. By contrast, pure motive, upstream/downstream, problems come to light only if and when those concerned about some environmental amenity become aware that it is being harmed; only if and when those harms are sufficiently evident and sufficiently large to outweigh the obstacles to mobilizing for action; and only if and when those concerned bring sufficient pressure to bear on the perpetrators to take action. Incapacity problems tend to enter the international arena when the countries causing the problem bring them up, realizing that other states may have incentives to contribute to ameliorating their own domestic environmental problem. Differences can also influence the design of solutions, since the reciprocal tit-for-tat strategies appropriate to Tragedies of the Commons are either unavailable or ineffective in upstream/ downstream problems (Axelrod, 1984; Mitchell and Keilbach, 2001). In the international fisheries that are so often examples of Tragedies of the Commons, each country's threats to restrain their catch only if others do so can contribute, under the right conditions, to keeping catch levels lower than they would be otherwise. By contrast, in pollution cases, the actions of downstream or downwind states do not influence upstream and upwind states and, therefore, threats by the former to increase their pollution levels make no strategic sense. Incapacity issues also dictate certain types of solutions: threats are obviously non-starters; more capable states must supply the resources the less capable state lacks; but they also must ensure that the recipient state applies the resources for their intended purpose rather than diverting them for other uses.

## The strength of incentives

If the distinction among Tragedies of the Commons, upstream/ downstream problems, and incapacity problems sheds light on whether and which states have the incentives to take action on an environmental problem, how strong those incentives are depends on the costs of taking – and of failing to take – action to protect the environment, who bears those costs, and when those costs occur.

The cost magnitude of both action and inaction clearly matters. Environmental problems that impose large costs if unaddressed tend to get addressed before those that impose smaller costs. Likewise, those that are cheaper to address tend to get addressed before those that are more expensive. For people and states who are indifferent to some environmental degradation, this cost magnitude is irrelevant. But those who consider their interests to be harmed by such degradation are more likely to investigate, mobilize against, incur costs to address, and follow through on commitments to avert those problems that entail large costs if left unaddressed.

Environmental problems and their solutions also differ in terms of cost incidence, that is, in terms of who pays the costs of action and inaction. Who the victims of environmental degradation are, at both the domestic and international levels, influences both how capable and how motivated they are to address the problem. An environmental problem that affects only the United States, Japan, and France will tend to be addressed sooner and more effectively than one with larger impacts on India, Indonesia, and Brazil which, in turn, will tend to be addressed sooner and more effectively than one that devastates small island, developing states like Fiji, Kiribati, and Samoa. 'Who' feels the environmental pain also matters at the domestic level. Environmental degradation that harms major corporations will tend to receive more rapid and complete attention than that which harms the interests of individuals, particularly disenfranchised individuals such as indigenous and tribal peoples. Likewise, the costs of action often fall differentially on different actors. Environmental diplomats spend considerable amounts of their time trying to craft solutions that will distribute costs in ways that all parties will find bearable. Once states recognize the costs to them of environmental inaction, they must then choose among policy alternatives based on the costs to them of action. Costs of action and inaction can also differ in terms of how concentrated they are. The more states that must cooperate to address an environmental problem, the more difficult it is to achieve such cooperation (Olson, 1965; Koremenos et al., 2001). As the number of actors who must cooperate increases, so does the likelihood (and each actor's awareness of the likelihood) of free-riding and shirking by other actors who want the problem resolved but prefer to avoid contributing to its resolution.

Finally, environmental problems exhibit different time sequencing. The resolution of some requires incurring both direct economic costs today and foregone economic growth to reap future environmental rewards. Resolution of others may provide near-term economic co-benefits, for example, in the form of competitive advantages for those who develop environmentally-benign alternatives. The resolution of yet others may entail large up-front costs but may also provide substantial long-term non-environmental returns, as is evident in climate change policies that limit fossil fuel use by restricting oil imports and thereby improve national security or that reduce speed limits and thereby also reduce traffic accidents.

## Power and influence

Power can both cause and exacerbate international environmental problems (Victor et al., 1998b: 9ff). International relations scholars often speak of state power as stemming from the control over military or economic resources (Waltz, 1979). A state with more 'systemic' power often can influence the behavior of weaker states in various arenas. States that control significant economic resources can use these to push less powerful states into cleaning up environmental problems without having to make corresponding efforts. The United States, for example, has threatened and used economic sanctions to push various states to reduce their commercial whaling even though, as a state not then engaged in such whaling, it could not exercise a corresponding restraint (Stoett, 1997; DeSombre, 2000). Hegemonic states, when they are concerned about an environmental problem, can foster its speedy resolution (Kindleberger, 1981; Martin, 1992a). Powerful states can also play an important role by taking the lead in support of, or opposition to, international environmental protection. Domestic political pressures have led the United States government to take unilateral action on many international environmental problems, thereby prompting international action (DeSombre, 2000). Groups of states, like the European Union, may have a 'go it alone' power stemming from a coincidence of domestic politics favoring particular policies and the view that those actions, even if they address only part of a problem, make it worthwhile to take action before others do (Gruber, 2000).

States may also have issue-specific power, being able to use their control over environmental resources and the concerns of other states about protecting those resources to give them more influence than a systemic-based assessment of power would predict (Keohane and Nye, 1989). Thus, oil-exporting states are weaker than the United States and European countries in systemic power, but can still exercise considerable issue-specific influence with respect to energy production and consumption. Issue-specific power is evident environmentally in how the relative flows of pollutants between countries alter the incentives of countries to address a problem. Imagine two countries, each with industries that generate $1000 in revenue (benefits) and $1200 of environmental damage, half of which ($600) is transported to the other country, for example, because the upstream state discharges pollutants into a river but is downwind – and hence receives air pollution – from that downstream neighbor. This state of affairs will lead to both states receiving $1000 in economic benefits but $1200 in environmental costs – $600 from its own industry and $600 from its neighbor's. This situation gives both sides incentives to cooperate to address the problem because, if they do not, they will both be worse off. However, those incentives change if one country's industry is only half the size of its neighbor's (generating $500 in revenue and imposing only $300 in environmental damage on its neighbor). The larger country then has far weaker incentives to address the problem since it receives $1000 in economic benefits and only $900 in environmental costs – $600 from its own industry and $300 from its neighbor's.

Interdependence among states also provides an important source of influence in international relations. The political, economic, informational, cultural, and social linkages that constitute international interdependence provide opportunities for those states concerned about an environmental problem to press other states to understand and address that problem. Scientific and informational linkages can increase the speed with which an international environmental problem is identified. And economic and political ties can provide mechanisms by which concerns in one country can be promoted in other countries. Thus, we might expect faster responses to identical environmental problems among the highly interdependent states of Europe than among the less interdependent states of Asia.

## Number of actors

As already noted, the number of actors causing, or potentially contributing to resolving, an environmental problem will influence how readily it can be resolved. Because a larger group of actors finds it more difficult to organize but can be more readily regulated, it matters whether there are a large number of victims, a large number of perpetrators, or both (Olson, 1965; Koremenos et al., 2001). Collective action problems make it more difficult for a large number of victims to mobilize in a coordinated way, reducing the pressure for action (Olson, 1965). These same dynamics imply that if there are relatively few perpetrators, they will find it relatively easy to mobilize to resist international regulation. Notably, however, if regulations are adopted, the smaller the number of perpetrators, the more readily their behaviors can be monitored and sanctioned (Jacobson and Brown Weiss, 1998: 521). The power and visibility of actors also come into play. Multinational corporations have formidable resources with which to resist efforts at environmental protection. But they can also present highly visible, readily identified targets that are often more susceptible to environmental pressures and consumer boycotts because they 'have bureaucratic structures that enforce control, and they prefer to conduct their activities in stable and uniform regulatory environments' (Jacobson and Brown Weiss, 1998: 521).

Whether actors are considered 'potentially relevant' to an environmental problem depends on objective characteristics of that problem – how many countries cause the problem and how many are harmed by it – but also on social perceptions about who the necessary 'players' are and institutional norms regarding which actors to involve. Some problems such as climate change, ozone depletion, and marine pollution tend to be treated as global problems because almost all countries are either the causes of the problem, or are affected by it, or both. Others (like most transboundary river and lake pollution) have a limited number of potentially relevant actors consisting only of the two, three, or four countries that share the river or lake in question. Efforts to regulate international whaling, however, illustrate that which actors are 'potentially relevant' reflects political dynamics and subjective judgments: the initial treatment of international whaling as a Tragedy of the Commons among a few whaling states progressively shifted to its treatment as a moral question about preserving the global resource of whales, a question that made all countries 'potentially relevant' actors whether or not they had ever hunted whales (Mitchell, 1998a).

## Domestic political alignments

The power of domestic political actors harmed by or benefiting from efforts to avert environmental degradation also matters. If corporate or nongovernmental actors concerned about environmental degradation are powerful in a state, that state's government is more likely to be pro-environmental as well and, if that government is powerful internationally, then those voices are more likely to be heard than if they were raised by citizens of a less powerful country (Keck and Sikkink, 1998). As debates about environmental racism and environmental justice clarify, however, many forms of environmental degradation impact sub-national actors who are disenfranchised in their own countries and also those countries that lack international power, and such problems are therefore less likely to be recognized or addressed internationally.

Environmental problems also vary as to whether they generate conflict or cooperation between environmental activists and industry groups. When regulatory strategies pit environmental interests against economic interests at the domestic and international level, they inhibit efforts to address environmental problems (Oye and Maxwell, 1994). But in some situations, regulated firms will benefit from the subsidies, constraints on substitutes, price fixing, or barriers to new rivals that are adopted (Oye and Maxwell, 1994). Regulations that serve the interests of regulated actors can lead firms to join environmentalists in forming powerful 'Baptist-bootlegger coalitions' in support of environmental protection (DeSombre, 1995). When these dynamics emerge in internationally powerful states, they can then create strong pressures for their governments to internationalize domestic regulations to avoid placing domestic industries at a competitive disadvantage (DeSombre, 2000; Young, 1999a).

## Knowledge and uncertainty problems

Environmental problems can be caused or exacerbated by knowledge inadequacies related to the existence and magnitude of a problem, the actions and actors causing a problem, and potential solutions to a problem; inadequacies that can influence agenda setting, negotiations, and the implementation of international environmental agreements.

Many environmental problems initially arise because as humans we are unaware of the environmental impacts of our behaviors. The environmental impacts of most behaviors prior to the twentieth century were unknown, but even today the environmental impacts of new technologies and new behaviors are initially unknown. Often, there is little reason to suspect environmental harm. Chlorofluorocarbons (CFCs, developed in the 1920s) promised large benefits in refrigeration and insulation and, because they are inert and non-toxic, appeared to pose few health or environmental risks (Nordhaus and Kokkelenberg, 1999: 209). Until Molina and Rowland (1974) proposed a theory linking CFCs to stratospheric ozone loss, continuing human degradation of the ozone layer could be explained as due to an ignorance that CFCs had such impacts. Although such ignorance of environmental impacts is rarely a sole cause of an environmental problem, it is certainly a sufficient condition for such problems – if we don't know our behaviors are harmful, we will make no effort to reduce those harms.

Ignorance and uncertainty are sometimes reduced by scientists investigating theoretically-expected impacts, as with the linkage of CFCs to stratospheric ozone loss and acid rain to forest die-off (Haas, 1992a; Jäger et al., 2001). In other cases, scientists or laypeople may look for the causes of puzzling environmental changes, as in efforts to explain high rates of frog mutations, bee colony collapse, and bat die-offs in the 1990s and 2000s (United States Geological Survey, 2001; Gill, 2007; Minkel, 2007; New York State Department of Environmental Conservation, 2008). Nor does knowledge that certain behaviors damage the environment always go hand in hand with knowledge of the magnitude or extent of that damage. Whether discovered by scientific studies or lay observation, the identification of environmental impacts often begins in delimited locales and it may take decades to assess how widespread a problem is. Indeed, knowledge of the impacts even of suspicious activities may remain limited for long periods. Thus, the potential impacts of the agricultural application of massive quantities of fertilizer remain understudied and poorly understood (Vitousek et al., 1997).

In turn, how quickly knowledge of a problem spreads may depend on how visible, immediate, and attention-grabbing it is. Environmental problems that result from dramatic accidents receive more recognition more quickly than more serious problems that have resulted from ongoing and incremental processes. For these and other reasons, some problems will prompt political mobilization and action more effectively than others.

Environmental problems also vary with respect to knowledge about their causes. The greater the uncertainty about a problem's causes, the more challenging it becomes to get that problem addressed. Some problems have known, clear, and un-complex causes. Some behaviors have direct impacts that require little scientific mediation to understand. Most people readily recognize that oil spills cause the deaths of birds, otters, and seals and that excessive harvest of a species will threaten the continuation of historical rates of harvest. But other problems have uncertain, ambiguous, and quite complex causes. The links between a behavior and its impacts can be numerous and complicated. Environmental problems may result from multiple causes, from interactions among those causes, or from factors whose causal influence is poorly understood or contested by scientists. The complexity of environmental systems, as well as scientific uncertainty and ignorance of those systems, often makes it impossible to make unambiguous claims about what behaviors have caused a problem or who has engaged in them.

Finally, environmental problems vary as to knowledge about potential solutions. Unless offered alternatives, those engaged in an environmentally-harmful behavior are likely to choose continuing that behavior over abandoning the goals that motivated that behavior in the first place. Available alternatives, by contrast, allow actors to pursue pre-existing goals through less environmentally-harmful means. If alternatives do not exist, conflicts over goals can emerge, which are typically harder to resolve than conflicts over means (Rittberger and Zürn, 1991). Although the search for solutions will generally start only after a problem and its causes have been identified, certain problems will present far greater challenges to finding such solutions.

## Transparency regarding behaviors

Environmental problems vary in the ease with which the behaviors that cause them can be identified. The impacts of some behaviors are immediate, visible, and clearly linked to those behaviors. The impacts of others occur decades later, are difficult to observe, and are hard to link to the responsible behaviors. Satellite technology makes it easy to identify deforestation but is not particularly useful at identifying those responsible for it. Marine oil spills are more likely to be detected than marine chemical spills because oil floats. Shipwrecks that spill oil and chemicals become public quickly because ship owners cannot hide the loss of such valuable assets, but intentional operational discharges of oil and chemicals are difficult to detect both, in aggregate and individually (Mitchell, 1994a). Wetlands can be destroyed by actions that can be immediately and unambiguously linked to a responsible party, as in hotel construction, or by actions that are gradual, hard to detect, and impossible to link to any responsible party, as in dehydration or pollution from numerous upstream water users.

Environmental problems also vary in how attenuated the links are between impacts, responsible behaviors, and responsible parties. Some impacts can be easily linked to both the behaviors causing them and the responsible actors. Others can be linked to the responsible behaviors but not the responsible actors. And still others can result from interactions among many causal factors that cannot be isolated. Thus, nuclear irradiation in Spain in 1966 and Greenland in 1968 clearly were caused by the accidental release of nuclear weapons, with the United States being the only potentially culpable actor (Center for Defense Information, 1981). River or lake pollution due to detergents and sewage or to fertilizers and pesticides can be unambiguously attributed to municipal and agricultural activities, respectively. But recent fish stock declines reflect current and past overfishing, pollution, and climate change, as well as interactions among these factors, making identifying their causes, let alone the responsible parties, all but impossible.

## Values and social inertia

How willing people and societies are to shift to less environmentally harmful behaviors also influences international environmental politics. The environmental impacts of behaviors that are, and have been, central to everyday life will be more resistant to change than new behaviors in which relatively few people engage. Thus, the relatively rapid response to stratospheric ozone depletion and the much slower response to climate change reflect, in part, how much more central fossil fuels are to existing economic behavior than are

CFCs. As alternatives become available and economically competitive, they can reduce the resistance to efforts to address an environmental problem.

Environmental problems vary in the types of value conflicts they entrain. Some involve differences in the priority different actors give to environmental protection relative to economic or other concerns. In value prioritization conflicts, all sides believe in environmental protection but disagree about what economic costs should be incurred to ensure it. Such conflicts can be challenging to resolve. Other conflicts can arise among those committed to environmental protection due to disagreements about the 'necessary evils' of harmful activities that fulfill 'legitimate' human needs and equally harmful activities that are considered illegitimate. Developing states have sought to frame climate change as caused by necessary and legitimate 'subsistence' emissions and illegitimate luxury emissions (Biermann, 2006b). Indeed, for long periods of time, relevant actors often accept some environmental damage as legitimate if the offsetting benefits to humans are large enough. Conflicts then arise over what constitutes 'large enough'. Thus, efforts to eradicate mosquitoes or viruses that plague humans (but contribute to biological diversity) are relatively uncontroversial. Likewise, wetland drainage, pesticide use, and the killing of animals that prey on livestock have often been treated as non-controversial, with their human benefits considered to outweigh their environmental costs.

However, some environmental conflicts reveal deeper differences in values, differences over whether environmental protection should reflect a logic of consequences or a logic of appropriateness. In a logic of consequences, people choose actions based on the relative costs and benefits of their alternatives; in a logic of appropriateness, people choose actions based on the moral and social appropriateness, the rightness and wrongness, of their alternatives (March and Olsen, 1998). Environmental conflicts can emerge when relevant actors disagree about whether decisions should be based in the former or latter logic. Thus, the international regulation of whaling since the 1970s has involved a conflict between those who support commercial whaling so long as it does not threaten whale species and others who contend that all killing of whales is wrong, regardless of its environmental impacts (Mitchell, 1998a). Such fundamental value conflicts 'usually defy cooperative conflict management' because they 'leave very little room for compromise' (Rittberger, 1993: 14). In some – though not all – environmental problems, states adopt a logic of appropriateness in which a behavior, once abandoned, becomes inappropriate to re-adopt, even as a strategic bargaining chip. Therefore, most states consider it legitimate to intentionally and strategically increase their fish catch to 'punish' other countries for exceeding their established international quotas, but would not consider it appropriate to increase their levels of pollution to 'punish' other countries for violating international emission standards.

## Distinguishing the Problem Structure of 'Real World' Problems

Two caveats about these distinctions regarding the problem structure of environmental problems are in order. The first is that most international environmental problems reflect combinations of these characteristics. To be sure, some environmental problems can be appropriately characterized as having certain problem structure features. Thus, characterizing international fisheries as Tragedies of the Commons, the pollution of river basins as upstream/downstream problems, and threats to endangered species in developing states as incapacity problems often captures their most important political characteristics. But trying to pigeon-hole other environmental problems into only one of these categories can seriously mislead with respect to the political dynamics involved. The stratospheric ozone depletion problem and the climate change problem have both Tragedy of the Commons and upstream/downstream characteristics depending on which set of countries is considered. A Tragedy of the Commons exists among concerned states that also perpetrate the problem, but an upstream/downstream problem exists between those concerned states that contribute relatively little to these problems and the unconcerned ones that contribute much to them. Likewise, current efforts to regulate international whaling involve a Tragedy of the Commons among the whaling states and an upstream/downstream problem between whaling and anti-whaling states. Many current global environmental problems reflect incapacity problems for developing states but incentive problems for developed states. The categories outlined above can help our analysis to the extent that they clarify why environmental politics unfold as they do and, at times, that requires recognizing that a single problem has multiple facets that make it best understood as a 'hybrid' with features of multiple different categories.

The second caveat is that many environmental resources provide multiple eco-system services (Daily, 1997). When different actors value a single environmental resource differently, their interactions can exacerbate environmental problems and create political conflict. One type of resource use can influence significantly the value that others derive from that resource. The value many Northern countries and their citizens place on preserving elephants, rhinos, and tigers conflicts with the value that many Southern countries and their citizens place on killing individuals of those species for food or to protect themselves and their livelihood from destruction. The health of marine fish stocks is increasingly influenced not merely by catch but by marine and land-based pollution as well as by escapement and pollution from fish farming. Most international rivers provide freshwater for drinking and agriculture; habitat for fish and other freshwater species; electric power; wildlife habitat and wilderness – and also serve as sinks for municipal, agricultural, and industrial pollution. We may be able to intellectually and conceptually compartmentalize such multiple uses and classify one aspect as a Tragedy of the Commons and another as an upstream/downstream problem, but in doing so we will miss important dynamics and interactions among these facets that complicate such problems but may also offer opportunities for their resolution.

## Conclusion

International environmental problems are 'those impacts on the natural environment of human activities that some significant set of people view as negative and that have either a transboundary or international commons aspect'. This definition is designed to correspond to standard usage, to distinguish domestic from international problems, to allow the identification of 'latent' problems before attempts are made to resolve them, and to recognize that what constitutes a 'problem' is socially constructed. Both human impacts on the environment and the recognition of those impacts as problems had emerged in international affairs at least by the late 1800s. Before the 1950s, international efforts had already begun on the problems of overfishing and whaling, the threats to birds and various land species, contagious diseases and invasive plant species, and marine and river pollution. Since then, the number of environmental problems considered as international has increased dramatically, with hundreds of multilateral and bilateral environmental agreements being signed to address them.

Understanding why these problems emerge on the international agenda, why states do (or do not) address them, what affects the responses states adopt to each, and a variety of other crucial questions requires distinguishing politically-important characteristics that can clarify political similarities across ecologically different problems. Two broad sets of distinctions include those among overappropriation, degradation, and accidental forms of environmental damage, and among Tragedies of the Commons, upstream/downstream problems, and incapacity problems. In addition, environmental problems vary in terms of the strength of states' incentives, their relative power, the number of states involved, the political alignments of domestic actors, the levels of knowledge and uncertainty, the transparency regarding behaviors, and the values that states hold. Each of these categories captures concepts that can help explain differences in the political dynamics surrounding the identification and recognition of international environmental problems, the efforts states make to address them, and the extent to which those efforts lead to successful negotiation and implementation of international environmental policy.

The range of characteristics identified here highlights that understanding the politics surrounding a given international environmental problem requires evaluating many different facets of its structure. Knowing that a problem involves overappropriation and not degradation, and that it more closely approximates a Tragedy of the Commons than an upstream/downstream problem, provides a place to start in analyzing when problems will be identified and addressed and their solutions successfully implemented and not a place to stop. Incentives play an important role in defining a problem's structure but so do power, knowledge, transparency, and values. For any given problem, some of these facets may make resolution easier while others may make it harder. Fully understanding and answering the questions raised by subsequent chapters requires that we recognize how the various facets of a problem's structure contribute to or inhibit the political processes surrounding that problem's recognition and resolution.

# SOURCES OF INTERNATIONAL ENVIRONMENTAL PROBLEMS

Why does the world face so many and such diverse international environmental problems? Why do people engage in so many activities that harm the environment? Under what conditions do people engage in environmentally-harmful activities? Under what conditions do people stop, or refrain from, such activities? This chapter starts by delineating the 'IPAT' identity that explains human environmental impacts as resulting from population, affluence, and technology. The chapter then offers six categories into which we can place various scholars' more elaborated and diverse perspectives on the causes of our environmental predicament: ecophilosophical, scientific, legal, economic, capacities, and political. The chapter concludes by delineating why environmental problems are more common internationally than domestically.

## The IPAT Identity: Impacts, Population, Affluence, and Technology

The IPAT identity provides a simple but useful starting point for understanding the factors that determine human impacts on the environment. The IPAT identity posits the level of those impacts (I) as a function of population (P), affluence (A), and technology (T) (Commoner, 1971; Ehrlich and Holdren, 1971, 1972a, 1972b; see also, Fischer-Kowalski and Amann, 2001; Chertow, 2002; Waggoner and Ausubel, 2002). Mathematically, this can be expressed as:

$$I = P * A * T$$

This is a mathematical 'identity' because – if we express population as '# of people', affluence as per capita income ('GDP/population'), and technology as 'impact per dollar of GDP' – it is mathematically true by definition. Multiplying '# of people' times '$ per person' times 'impact per $' produces impact.

This identity has considerable analytic value. It is generic rather than specific, promising to explain any environmental problem as well as variation across problems. It highlights the equifinality of many environmental problems, that is, that a given level of environmental degradation can result from quite different combinations of social forces. River pollution, for example, can be generated by many poor people using relatively primitive technology for waste disposal or by far fewer rich people using various modern technologies intensively. Many countries emit similar levels of greenhouse gases despite significant differences in their levels of population, affluence, and technology. Indeed, even individuals can generate similar annual greenhouse gas emissions despite differences in their affluence and access to technologies, with poor farmers contributing to climate change by clearing forests by hand to plant crops while middle-class suburbanites contribute to it by driving their cars and heating and air conditioning their homes. The IPAT identity also highlights the multifinality of environmental causes, since 'impact' (and its incorporation in the technology term) can be measured in any environmental units. Multifinality involves the notion that a population with a given level of affluence and technology access will generate numerous environmental impacts, ranging from air, land, and water pollution to habitat degradation and species loss.

The IPAT identity clarifies the often-overlooked influence of population on levels of environmental degradation. A fundamental cause of the increase in environmental problems over the past two hundred years is the dramatic growth in the human population. The total impact of any activity that degrades the environment depends on the number of people in the world, each of whom may engage in it. Indigenous societies had far less environmental impact than modern ones, at least in part, because their population levels placed them much farther from the carrying capacities of the different environmental resources on which they depended. The IPAT identity highlights (a) that a world of billions of people necessarily implies a large environmental impact and (b) that maintaining or reducing current impacts requires that any population growth we accept be offset by corresponding decreases in affluence or improvements in technology.

The IPAT identity also highlights the role of affluence in limiting or facilitating our environmental impact. Given particular value structures about how resources should be expended, the more income and wealth people have, the more environmental damage they will do. Put differently, the environmental impacts humans have are limited by the economic resources they have available.

Finally, the IPAT identity recognizes that technology – put simply, how humans pursue their goals – is central to how much they degrade the environment. In this identity, the 'impact intensity' of available technologies is defined and measured as the 'environmental impact per dollar' (or other currency). A society relying exclusively on solar or wind power would emit far less greenhouse gases than would one relying on fossil fuels. Changes in technology usually have two effects, comparable to the economic distinction between the income and substitution effects of price changes. Consider, for example, the difference between eighteenth century and twenty-first century transportation options. The 'environmental substitution' effect of replacing horses with cars is that cars generate far more atmospheric pollution than horses to get a person from point A to point B. The 'environmental income' effect of replacing horses with cars is that far more people go from point A to some other point now that cars are available. Some technological changes, like that from horses to cars, increase our environmental impact because they increase the 'impact per unit' of an activity *and* lead people to engage in that activity more. But even those that appear environmentally beneficial because they decrease the 'per unit' damage of an activity may increase the total environmental impact because those decreases are more than offset by the increases in how much people engage in that activity.

The IPAT definition of technology as 'impact per dollar of GDP' can be usefully split into an environmental efficiency component ('impact per unit') and a cost component ('units per dollar', the inverse of price). Thus, the technology term for evaluating the carbon dioxide emissions of computers ($CO_2/\$$) combines carbon emissions per computer ($CO_2/computer$) and the inverse of a computer's price (computers/$). Separating these components clarifies that the rate at which humans transform resources into environmental damage depends on both the technologies available and their prices. While prices influence our choices among available technologies, technological availability also constrains our choices since, at any given time, certain technologies may not be available at any price, such as zero-pollution cars.

Although valuable, the original IPAT identity overlooks two important forces. First, it ignores consumption rates or the 'intensity of use' (Waggoner and Ausubel, 2002). It implicitly assumes that each dollar of affluence is expended on consumptive or environmentally-degrading technologies. It ignores the possibility that some affluence is either saved or expended in environmentally-beneficial activities. Yet, some societies exhibit a process of 'dematerialization' in which they have reduced their resource use even as they have become more affluent (Waggoner and Ausubel, 2002). Consumption rates reflect what humans value, not merely in the tradeoff between saving for the future and consuming in the present but also in choices among different types of consumption. Values determine what goals people pursue and hence their choices about how, and even whether, to expend those resources. The extensive environmental Kuznets curve literature, for example, demonstrates that environmental impacts do not correlate linearly with affluence (Grossman and Krueger, 1995; Chertow, 2002: 23ff; Harbaugh et al., 2002). Countries vary in their environmental impacts, even after accounting for population, affluence, and technology. The environmental footprints of otherwise comparable European and American people and cities differ because people make choices that (intentionally or unintentionally) lead them to have greater, lesser, or different environmental impacts within the constraints of affluence and technology (see Inglehart, 1990, 1995).

Second, and relatedly, the IPAT identity obscures how social organization, customs, and institutions influence how people organize themselves to conduct certain activities and, therefore, the types and levels of damage they impose on the environment. Although we can define 'technology' to capture this, it seems more useful to separate it analytically. Social organization affects what happens, how it happens, and where it happens. Free trade, urbanization, the preference for coastal living, the social choice not to price environmental services, and explicit efforts to manage environmental impacts are all forms of social organization which, when organized differently, produce societies that have quite different environmental impacts.

Whether as originally proposed or taking these other concerns into account, the IPAT identity clarifies those forces that contribute to environmental degradation and explain the variation in environmental impacts across countries and over time. It helps us predict national environmental trajectories, the magnitude of potential problems, and targets for policy intervention. Thus, many developing countries are on environmental trajectories involving growing populations, increasing affluence, and the adoption of more environmentally-harmful technologies. The trajectories of most developed countries with slower or flat population growth more likely will be driven by the latter two factors. And the IPAT identity reminds us that policies to address global environmental impacts may include those that reduce population growth, slow economic growth, shape human values, develop lower-impact technologies, or alter price structures.

# Six Perspectives on the Sources of Environmental Problems

An alternative way of identifying the sources of international environmental problems emerges by categorizing the various claims about why we face these problems. The literature on environmental problems reflects six perspectives: ecophilosophical, scientific, legal, economic, capacities, and political. Each contains certain beliefs about why humans degrade the environment, with corresponding implications for what would be necessary to transform existing behavior patterns into more environmentally-friendly alternatives. Some articles, authors, and arguments can fit neatly into one of these categories. But many – and perhaps most – people understand environmental degradation as a result of a combination of factors, with some types of environmental degradation best explained by one perspective, other types best explained by another perspective, and yet other types best explained by a combination and/or interaction among variables from several perspectives. Therefore, this categorization seeks to avoid pigeon-holing arguments, articles, or authors, while providing a rubric that recognizes commonalities among nominally competing arguments and differences among nominally similar arguments.

## The role of values – an 'ecophilosophical' perspective

In what can be called ecophilosophical perspectives, our environmental problems arise because people individually and societies collectively place insufficient value on environmental protection. Given this, resolving our environmental problems requires altering the value people place on the environment and environmental protection through such tactics as education, persuasion, and direct action. Ecologists, ecological activists, ecofeminists, and environmental philosophers have developed theories of deep ecology, the Gaia principle, ecofeminism, and religious environmentalism which, while differing in many respects, share a commitment to the notion that our environmental problems are rooted in an individual and collective failure to value the natural world sufficiently.

Deep ecologists contend that all life forms have intrinsic value, independent of their use to humans; that we have an ethical obligation to other species and other natural things; and that humans are part of – rather than separate from – the environment (Naess, 1973; Devall and Sessions, 1985). Proponents of Gaia theory contend that the Earth is properly understood in a holistic sense as a 'complex, bounded, self-organizing, adaptive organism' and a 'living entity ... regulat[ing] the planet's geochemistry to the benefit of the whole' (Litfin, 2005: 502; see also Lovelock, 1979, 1990; Miller, 1991). Gaia theory has come to blend scientific claims that the Earth is a living organism in an empirically verifiable sense with spiritual claims regarding the Earth as an interdependent and dynamically complex being that 'evokes a sense of awe and reverence' (Litfin, 2005: 516). The needs to maintain the Gaian system for its own sake and to sustain human life obligate humans 'to harmonize our social, economic and political systems with Gaia' (Litfin, 2005: 506).

Other scholars argue that environmental degradation reflects certain fundamentally anthropocentric tenets of western philosophical traditions (Sessions, 1991), particularly the secular liberal notion that human freedom should be constrained only when it conflicts with another human's freedom and the historically religious notion that man is separate from and placed over – rather than being part of – the natural world. Taken together, these tenets imply a separation between humans and nature in which humans need be concerned only with their own well-being and not that of nature. That perspective, in turn, generates a wide variety of environmental insensitivities (Westing, 1988: 7).

Ecofeminists, in turn, see environmental problems as different manifestations of a fundamental alienation of humans from nature (see, for example, Diamond and Orenstein, 1990; Gaard, 1993; Warren and Wells-Howe, 1994; Merchant, 1996; Warren, 2000). The same factors that have produced the historical degradation and domination of women by men globally have also produced the degradation and domination of nature globally. Masculine fear and resentment generate the male urge to dominate both women and nature and this, in turn, produces hierarchical, militaristic, mechanistic, and industrialized social structures that, in turn, generate a plethora of extant environmental problems. Resolving our global environmental predicament, and its many local manifestations, requires mending 'the alienation of women and men from each other and both from nature' (Merchant, 1990: 103). This requires a radical transformation in human values, a 'new philosophical underpinning of civilization' in which 'technocratic alienation and nihilism' are replaced with an empathetic cultivation and honoring of 'our direct connections with nature' (Spretnak, 1990: 11–13). Modern, Judaeo-Christian, anthropocentric philosophies need to be replaced with ecocentric, nature- or Goddess-worshipping philosophies that resurrect, re-establish, and reinforce the earth-nature connection (Diamond and Orenstein, 1990). Women are 'uniquely placed' to challenge the dominant national and international norms that both create environmental problems and obstruct the efforts to address them (Bretherton, 2003: 116).

To be sure, these views (and other ecophilosophies not discussed here) have large and important differences that should not be overlooked. Yet they share a core assumption that environmental problems arise because the moral and ethical underpinnings of almost all human behavior place insufficient value on protecting the natural world. And they share the view that effectively addressing our numerous environmental problems requires engaging the long-term project of modifying these deep-seated foundations of modern societies.

## The role of knowledge – a 'scientific' perspective

A second approach entails a 'scientific' or knowledge-based perspective, which could just as aptly be called an 'epistemic' or 'technological' perspective. If ecophilosophical perspectives see environmental problems as resulting from 'a lack of the right values', scientific perspectives see them as the result of 'a lack of the right knowledge'. At its simplest, this view attributes environmental degradation to ignorance. We may not know that environmental degradation is occurring. We may know it is occurring but not whether it reflects natural cycles or human influences and, if the latter, what behaviors are responsible. And we may know that it is occurring and know its human causes but not know any means for resolving it.

Given ignorance and uncertainty as the problem, information and technology are the solutions. We can reduce or eliminate environmental problems by ensuring people know how their behaviors influence the environment and also know of and have access to more environmentally-benign options. This suggests investing in research on what environmental degradation is occurring and what human behaviors cause it, the research and development of potential solutions, and the dissemination of the results of both as widely as possible. Combining a better knowledge of human impacts with the technologies that can mitigate those impacts offers a prescription for our environmental problems. Improved knowledge and technology allow us to respond to environmental changes by changing the technology component of the IPAT identity. Within this perspective, there is increasing recognition that whether scientific knowledge influences international policy or, more directly, the behaviors that cause environmental damage depends on whether that knowledge is scientifically credible while also being relevant to current policy and economic decisions and reflecting inclusive and legitimate knowledge-generating processes (Mitchell et al., 2006b).

Thus, a stylized scientific interpretation of the resolution of the stratospheric ozone depletion problem would go something as follows. After being created in the 1920s, the production and use of CFCs and related chemicals developed as they did only because humans were unaware that these harmed the stratospheric ozone layer. In the early 1970s, scientists hypothesized that CFCs were depleting that layer (Molina and Rowland, 1974). Other scientists subsequently collected evidence supporting that hypothesis (Haas, 1992a; Benedick, 1998; Parson, 2003). Policy-makers began negotiations to address the problem in response to this evidence (Parson, 2003). Knowledge of these chemicals' environmental effects, and particularly the compilation of that knowledge into 'authoritative scientific assessments' within a context in which chemical alternatives to CFCs were available and became increasingly economically viable, fostered initial agreement on and then progressive tightening of international targets and timetables to phase out CFC use. Although few would accept this as a full and accurate accounting, it captures, in broad strokes, the explanatory value of knowledge that is central to a scientific perspective.

## The role of law –
## a 'legal' perspective

A third, 'legal', perspective sees the range of environmental problems as resulting from the failure of existing legal structures to define rights and obligations appropriately. Legal rights should ensure that those actors seeking to protect the environment have appropriate legal standing. Legal obligations should link better definitions of environmentally inappropriate behaviors with more effective legal mechanisms for reducing them.

One line of research argues that a fundamental cause of environmental problems is that modern legal systems do not grant an
appropriate legal status to those who have incentives to protect the
environment. Thus, precisely because future generations cannot
represent and defend their own interests, present generations have
an obligation to take those interests into account and, thereby, to
promote intergenerational equity (Brown Weiss, 1989). Current legal
systems intended to adjudicate between individuals with
competing rights fail to protect the environment because they
allow little, if any, representation of the views and concerns of
future generations. Existing legal systems fail to provide even for
intragenerational equity because they provide little if any
representation for poor, indigenous, and disenfranchised people
and communities in society. The environmental justice and
environmental racism literature argues that racial and socio-
economic discrimination correlates with environmental degradation: disenfranchised communities – which are often more aware
of and more concerned about environmental protection – are
systematically denied a legal voice, allowing the mainstreams
within societies to displace their environmental problems onto
these communities without fear of a legal response (Buttel, 1995;
Anand, 2003).

This line of argument has been extended by those who contend
that the problem lies in limiting legal rights to humans. In a legal
parallel to the arguments of deep ecologists, other species and the
environment itself should have legal rights that, when violated,
provide for recourse and remedies within domestic and international
courts. Thus, scholars have argued that trees should have legal
standing and that whales should have a 'right to life' (Stone, 1974;
D'Amato and Chopra, 1991).

The dominant strain of international legal scholarship does
not view the international legal system as systematically flawed
in its ability to protect the environment. Rather, it considers
international law as an as-yet-imperfect set of definitions of good
and bad, appropriate and inappropriate, and right and wrong
behavior. It fosters the overexploitation of fish stocks by
treating the high seas as a global commons to which all
countries have legal access and by failing to regulate catch on
that commons. Most fisheries agreements have been agreed to
after the problem is well-advanced, set quotas that rarely reflect
scientific recommendations, and have only weak mechanisms to
discourage non-compliance (Peterson, 1993). And, even when
bad international law is not causing environmental problems, it
can help resolve them. An additional flaw in the international

legal system involves the inability effectively to enforce international laws that are 'on the books' in the form of conventions, treaties, protocols, or amendments. There are all-but-ubiquitous calls for 'treaties with teeth' at the same time as there is all-but-ubiquitous recognition that states rarely agree to the incorporation of rigorous monitoring and sanctioning in treaties and that, when they do, those provisions are rarely used (Chayes and Chayes, 1993). Just as an economic perspective (see below) implies that almost any behavior can be induced with appropriate, and sufficiently large, incentives, so a legal perspective implies that almost any behavior can be reduced or eliminated with appropriate, and effectively enforced, laws.

The common thread within a legal perspective is the sense that appropriately designed legal institutions can play an important role in averting environmental degradation. Where international law is non-existent or poorly formulated, better law can be identified and states can be convinced to adopt it. And there is an extensive literature identifying what this 'better' international law might look like, including discussions of the virtues of hard *vs* soft law (Brown Weiss, 1997; Abbott and Snidal, 2000); of sanctions *vs* incentives *vs* capacity-building (Chayes and Chayes, 1995; Downs et al., 1996); of norms *vs* more instrumental influences on behavior (Parker, 1997; Pettenger, 2007); and of international *vs* nongovernmental organizations as implementors of international law (Smith, 1972; Werksman et al., 1996; Simmons, 1998; DeSombre, 2007).

## The role of incentives –
## an 'economic' perspective

A fourth perspective sees the sources and solutions to environmental problems as economic, or incentive-based. From this perspective, environmental degradation occurs because the use of natural resources is not appropriately priced. If the proximate influences on our choices among available behaviors are the relative costs and benefits of each, then the best explanation of why humans harm the environment is that environmentally-harmful behaviors are insufficiently expensive. Low or non-existent prices for polluting and extracting natural resources lead people to engage in undesirably high levels of those activities. The history of economic development treated many natural resources as 'free for the taking', effectively priced at zero. The extraction of other resources often has been subsidized by governments that subsidize extraction costs directly, provide the infrastructure to facilitate extraction, or ensure the price of the resultant raw materials or products. Governments rarely monitor pollution discharges or charge those who use the atmosphere, rivers, and oceans as pollution sinks. Environmental harms arise because the costs of engaging in environmentally-degrading activities, if there are any such costs, are too low. In short, natural resources and environmental services are not 'priced right', either being free or having a price that fails to reflect the benefits to society that would come from more behavioral restraint.

Central to an economic perspective is the concept of 'negative externalities' (Baumol and Oates, 1975; Cornes and Sandler, 1986; Tietenberg, 1988). An externality arises whenever an economic transaction affects people who are not involved in – that is, are 'external' to – that transaction. Usually in an economic transaction, the buyer gives up money for a product they value more highly and the seller gives up that product for a sum of money they value more highly. We accept that both the buyer and seller are 'better off', at least in their own estimation, so long as they engage in this transaction voluntarily. And we assume that the transaction does not help or harm others. Externalities arise, however, when the 'private' costs people must pay to engage in an activity are lower than the full 'social' costs that arise as a result of their engaging in such activity. More broadly, these externalities involve behaviors, whether involving economic transactions or not, that will affect the well-being of other actors who have no influence over whether or not that behavior is engaged in.

Externalities can be either asymmetric or symmetric. In asymmetric externalities, costs are imposed on others who do not engage in the environmentally-harmful activity. Asymmetric externalities can involve actors from one country creating environmental harms that are quite costly to actors in other countries, as illustrated by pollution from smelters in Canada and Russia polluting the United States and Finland, respectively (Darst, 2001; Bratspies and Miller, 2006); in oil tankers discharging oil from tank-cleaning operations to save costs while that oil fouls beaches and kills marine life (Mitchell, 1994a); in French discharges of chlorides into the Rhine to reduce potassium mining costs while increasing Dutch costs of desalination for municipal and agriculture uses (Bernauer, 1996); and in British powerplants being built tall enough to avoid local environmental damage but causing significant acidification of Scandinavian lakes and forests (Levy, 1993). In these and similar cases, those engaged in certain economic activities reduce their costs of production – and, presumably, the prices charged to consumers – but impose environmental costs on others who are not engaged in that activity.

In symmetric externalities, or Tragedies of the Commons, the externalized costs are imposed on others engaged in the same activity.

That is, asymmetric externalities involve actors who are *either* the perpetrators or victims of an environmental harm while symmetric externalities involve actors who are *both* the perpetrators and victims of an environmental harm. The defining characteristic here is that each resource user is imposing costs *on other resource users*. Although Hardin explains the tragedy as resulting from the social institution of the commons, what defines the commons, in economic terms, is the choice to grant costless access (Hardin, 1968). International fishing fleets regularly replicate the dynamics described by Hardin even decades after they become aware that they are collectively overfishing fish stocks. This overfishing occurs because the boat that catches a certain tonnage of fish receives all the economic benefits of doing so but the economic costs of that catch are borne by other boats that, as a consequence, have a lower chance of catching fish in the future.

An economic perspective sees the common source of these environmental problems as social institutions sending 'price signals' that lead to the overuse of natural resource and environmental service, that is, a level of use above that which is considered socially optimal. Resolving Tragedy of the Commons problems requires internalizing social costs, that is, ensuring that those choosing to engage in certain activities or economic transactions experience all the social costs of that activity. This can be accomplished through legal strategies such as privatization (providing a single country or actor with exclusive legal access) or economic strategies such as imposing taxes or user fees for engaging in those activities. Subsidies can be removed when unsubsidized prices better reflect social costs. And there can be cooperative efforts such as treaties involving 'mutual coercion, mutually agreed upon' (Hardin, 1968: 1347). Incentives can also address asymmetric externalities, either by granting perpetrators the right to generate externalities and victims the right to demand compensation or by precluding perpetrators from generating externalities unless they compensate victims (Coase, 1960). All such strategies work on the basis of creating social institutions that expose those actors choosing to engage in certain activities to the full social costs of those actions, costs that, in the absence of those institutions, would be borne by others.

## The role of incapacity – a 'capacities' perspective

Incapacity can also explain why certain international environmental problems emerge. From this perspective, environmental problems arise when actors with incentives to protect the environment lack the technological, administrative, or financial capacities that would allow them to do so. Constrained by the technologies available at a given time, the choice to engage in certain activities necessarily implies certain environmental impacts. Technology currently limits efforts to reduce carbon emissions from coal-burning powerplants, the efficiency with which photovoltaics transform solar energy into electricity, and the capacity of batteries for use in electric cars. Technologies do not as yet exist to generate electricity efficiently from a river without dams, and to thereby avoid numerous environmental impacts. Efforts to develop more environmentally benign technologies usually only begin after human environmental impacts are identified and acknowledged as problems. After those efforts begin, slow technological progress can leave those impacts unaddressed for years or decades simply because of a lack of alternatives.

Financial incapacities may also explain environmental degradation. Economists note that people's willingness to pay often exceeds their ability to pay. An individual's 'willingness to pay' for some action that would protect the environment depends on whether their values and knowledge leading them to believe that action's benefits will exceed its costs. Yet, their 'ability to pay' may preclude them from taking that action. Valuing certain benefits does not imply having the resources to pay the corresponding costs. Although some argue that environmental protection is a 'luxury good' that is valued more highly by the rich than the poor, some research has demonstrated that developing and developed countries do not differ significantly in their levels of environmental concern (Kolstad, 2000; Dasgupta, 2001). Thus, most developing countries continue to dump raw sewage into their rivers, generating major human and environmental costs, because they lack the financial wherewithal to provide sewage treatment rather than the incentives to provide it (UNEP GEMS/Water Programme, 2007).

Government administrative incapacities may also allow environmental problems to continue unabated. Weak or failed states often cannot provide their populations with the most basic services, let alone protect the environment. But a much longer list of governments lack the infrastructures needed to implement environmental laws effectively or have administrative capacities that are hampered by corruption and inefficiency. And, governments will protect their environmental resources less well when their administrative capacities or stability are undermined, whether this is because of political, economic, or other changes.

Incapacity can sometimes be more environmentally fortuitous, however. Environmental problems are sometimes avoided or delayed because those who might engage in environmentally-harmful activities lack the technological, administrative, or financial capacities to do so. Environmental problems may not occur or may emerge later in some countries simply because of slow technological development. Nuclear waste disposal emerged as a problem only after nuclear weapon and nuclear power technologies were developed by certain states and it is not yet a problem in many countries that cannot afford to purchase the technology from those countries that have developed it. The different levels and trajectories of greenhouse gas emissions across countries – both how quick they are rising and that they are not rising faster – reflect variation in economic and technological incapacity as much as other factors. And improvements in countries' administrative, financial, and technological capacities and infrastructures can resolve environmental problems even when no other significant changes have occurred.

## The role of power – a 'political' perspective

Politics, or power-based theories, offer a sixth perspective on the causes of international environmental problems. In this view, environmental problems arise because those with power lack incentives to protect the environment and those with incentives to protect the environment lack the power to do so. Thucydides' oft-quoted line that 'the strong do what they can while the weak suffer what they must' (Thucydides, 1982: V–89) implies that the powerful will displace environmental degradation on the disenfranchised, both within and across a country's borders. Environmental protection will be provided if it coincides with the interests of the powerful but not otherwise.

This perspective finds it unsurprising that the developed world, having overexploited its own resources, now extracts the resources it needs from developing countries. Likewise, developed countries commonly address their nuclear and hazardous waste problems by exporting those wastes to less powerful developing countries rather than by reducing waste generation or by designing technologies for its safe domestic disposal (Princen et al., 2002).

At the international level, a political perspective sees environmental problems as reflecting that political boundaries do not match environmental ones. Norms regarding sovereignty and the sanctity of national borders admonish states not to intervene in the internal affairs of other states, including with respect to environmental destruction (Krasner, 1999; Conca, 1994). Efforts to provide international protection to biodiversity, wetlands, rivers, and forests that exist within a country's borders have taken decades to develop and change only slowly. Indeed, many environmental treaties explicitly protect the 'sovereign rights' of countries to exploit natural resources within their borders.

The lack, weakness, and poor design of international environment laws also reflect that the anarchic nature of the international system discourages states from creating effective international institutions. That system creates incentives for states to prioritize security over all other concerns (Waltz, 1979). Despite the many arguments put forward that environmental protection is and/or should be central to states' conceptions of national security, most governments' behavior reflects the fact that the physical security and economic security of their citizens always trump environmental protection (Ullman, 1983; Mathews, 1989; Homer-Dixon, 1999). Most government institutions, and particularly militaries, are centralized and hierarchical, making them poorly suited to address environmental problems. The traditional focus on defense against other states leads them to view threats as caused by others and hierarchical and centralized military responses as effective responses. Yet, environmental problems frequently result as much from our own actions as from the actions of others and effective solutions often require distributed, non-hierarchical, and inclusive forms of cooperation that engage all sectors within a country as well as multiple countries working together (Deudney, 1990, 1991).

The traditional focus of states on their security and defense also predisposes states toward zero-sum, relative-gains calculations in which one country's loss is assumed to be another's gain and, therefore, collective efforts to address problems become the exception rather than the rule (Snidal, 1985; Krasner, 1991; Powell, 1991). The lack of trust among countries and the fear that gains in one realm will be used for coercion in others make states both reluctant to cooperate with other states and less experienced with, and cognizant of, the benefits of doing so.

Political power structures within states also tend to preclude the recognition of, and responses to, environmental concerns. Government structures, even in democracies, are often responsive to the most powerful sectors of their societies. When those sectors lack incentives to protect the environment, then governments will be reluctant to address environmental problems, either domestically or internationally. Resolving international environmental problems, therefore, requires devolving political power to different institutions, whether up to intergovernmental organizations or down to nongovernmental organizations and transnational activist networks (Keck and Sikkink, 1998). If the powerful – either domestically or internationally – do not consider it in their interests to protect the environment, then protecting it requires creating social processes and institutions that empower those who *do* consider it in their interests to protect the environment.

## Six perspectives in overview

I have delineated these perspectives as logically distinct and competing perspectives. Indeed, some authors present their perspectives as mutually exclusive and antithetical to others. Yet, much can be learned about the sources of international environmental problems by recognizing how the factors identified by these perspectives align and reinforce each other in some areas but undercut or contradict each other in others.

Thus, proponents of deep ecology share views with both scientific and political perspectives. After delineating that values were the root of much environmental degradation, Arne Naess argued that 'the implementation of ecologically responsible policies requires in this century an exponential growth of technical skill and invention' – a view that is much more in line with a scientific perspective (Naess, 1973: 98). Other elements of deep ecology correspond with the central components of a political perspective, such as the notion that resolving most environmental problems requires decentralization, local autonomy, and respecting the knowledge and sensitivity of local people to local conditions and the fact that environmental damage often arises because decision makers are distant from, unaware of, and unconcerned about the environmental impacts of the policies they approve.

Likewise, the incentives that are central to an economic perspective derive from and are driven by underlying legal structures. Tragedies of the Commons arise because users of the commons do not pay for their use, but land becomes a commons (rather than multiple private farms) only because of the way property rights are established legally. Fisheries on the high seas have been plagued by Tragedy of the Commons dynamics because states do not pay for the fish they harvest. But this situation exists because states have not chosen to divide the high seas into nationally controlled jurisdictions, although the redefinition of exclusive economic zones stretching 200 miles out constituted movement in this direction. And a political perspective provides considerable insight into why such legal structures are as they are. Both domestic and international laws are created by and reflect a political process of powerful actors domestically and powerful states internationally striving to promote their interests. Similarly, the knowledge derived from the research and development that a scientific perspective prescribes is more likely to influence behavior if economic incentives and legal structures also are adapted to promote the behaviors that such scientific understandings suggest are the sources of our problems.

A synthetic view of our environmental dilemma can be developed by seeing how these different perspectives collectively contribute to our understanding of why we face so many environmental problems and what would be necessary to change, in any fundamental way, our impacts on the Earth. A synthetic view recognizes that human value structures (stressed by ecophilosophical perspectives), and the place of environmental protection in those structures, are fundamental determinants of the goals people have, the behaviors they adopt (or reject) in pursuit of those goals, and, therefore, the impacts they have on the environment. Choices among behaviors – and the many behaviors people engage in without conscious choice – are, in turn, heavily influenced by our knowledge of the impacts of those behaviors and the technological alternatives available to us (stressed by the scientific and capacities perspectives). Given available alternatives for pursuing their goals and knowledge about the environmental consequences of their choices, people are also influenced by legal proscriptions and prescriptions regarding their options and the larger legal and institutional structures that channel much human activity (stressed by a legal perspective). Those legal structures, in turn, shape economic markets in ways that determine the costs and benefits of alternative behaviors (stressed by an economic perspective), which, in turn, influence which behaviors people choose and which they reject. And the legal and economic structures that shape the choices people and countries have, in turn, reflect the political structure of the world and the interests, incentives, and values of those actors who have power in the system (stressed by a political perspective).

Effective solutions also tend to require a recognition, if not an incorporation, of the elements of these different perspectives. Deciding what environmentally-harmful behaviors to tax and what environmentally-benign behaviors to subsidize requires significant scientific knowledge about existing and new alternatives. Although social norms and values can be altered by long-term normative processes, domestic and international legal changes can help establish and strengthen environmental norms. How much effort is put into scientific endeavors depends, at least in part, on support from governments and private donors, which in turn depends on both political structures and the value placed on environmental protection generally. In short, these differing perspectives each provide insight into why environmental problems are so ubiquitous and help us categorize the wide range of solutions to them.

# The Causes of International Environmental Problems

How can the IPAT identity and the six perspectives just outlined help us to understand why we face so many international environmental problems, why certain types of problems are so common, and why particular problems emerge when and where they do? A central question of international environmental politics is why there are so many international environmental problems. What can explain why we degrade the international environment in so many ways? Equally important questions revolve around why certain types of environmental problems are so common internationally, why certain activities and economic sectors appear particularly prone to them, and why some countries generate certain types of environmental problems while others generate different types. A third set of questions arises when we try to identify why a particular international environmental problem exists or emerged when it did? This section illustrates how the perspectives on international environmental problems identified above can help answer these questions.

## Understanding the causes of our general international environmental predicament

These six perspectives offer various explanations as to why international environmental problems emerge. The ubiquity and diversity of such problems alone suggest a discouraging multifinality: environmental degradation arises under a wide set of conditions and as the result of a wide range of variables. It arises in such varied economic sectors and political contexts that it seems unlikely that it is always caused by the same variable or even the same constellation of variables. Scientific ignorance of an activity's impacts can lead even environmentally-enlightened states to collectively abuse an environmental resource. Even when environmental impacts are clearly known and understood, the failure of economic markets to fully reflect those impacts can produce the same result. And groups of environmentally-sensitive states that carefully husband environmental resources within their own borders can fall prey to Tragedy of the Commons dynamics on an international commons.

Because environmental problems tend to illustrate multifinality – in the sense that most causes proposed by the six perspectives are individually sufficient to cause environmental degradation – individual environmental problems often are over-determined. That is, most environmental problems arise from several of these forces working together, with each deserving a significant, and overlapping, share of the blame for the observed degradation. Early on, ignorance about the existence and magnitude of a problem and its human causes often coincides with a lack of concern about the environmental harm itself and government subsidies that reduce the costs of engaging in the responsible activities. Indeed, the coincidence of factors that often cause environmental degradation is not always accidental; the nature of some variables means that synergies, interactions, and interdependencies among them are particularly likely. Thus, value systems that deprioritize environmental protection tend to produce political structures that give leaders few incentives to protect the environment, economic structures that are unlikely to reflect environmental costs in prices, and legal structures that grant rights and obligations that do not inhibit, and may promote, environmental degradation. Likewise, ignorance of an activity's environmental consequences creates a context in which maintaining the resource as open access, failing to regulate such access, and even subsidizing appropriation may appear as reasonable policies even among environmentally-sensitive governments.

Put differently, environmental protection is rare because it depends on so many, and sometimes all, causal forces being properly aligned. A wide range of necessary conditions must be met. It requires not only knowledge of the effects of our actions but also concern about those effects and the existence of both domestic and international institutions that allow for a quick and effective expression of those concerns in policies that establish appropriate legal rights and obligations and ensure that the costs of environmental damages are reflected in market prices. Failing to meet even one of these conditions can easily lead to environmental degradation in a context that might otherwise seem conducive to environmental protection. Given that so many human activities – at least when conducted at high aggregate levels – pose a risk of environmental harm, that environmental degradation can emerge as a result of so many forces, and that environmental protection requires so many variables to be properly aligned, it becomes less surprising that we face an international landscape in which environmental problems are so distressingly common.

## Understanding why environmental problems are more common internationally

To argue that, collectively, the factors delineated above make international environmental problems likely does not preclude assessments of which factors play greater, or lesser, roles in the emergence of certain, or certain types, of problems. Several factors stand out as particularly powerful explanations of why environmental problems are more common internationally than domestically. First, any environmental amenity is more susceptible to overuse or pollution and degradation if it is international simply because an international setting places greater and more diverse demands on an amenity, making it more likely that the carrying capacity will be exceeded. Consider an environmental amenity access to which has traditionally been limited to a particular country's nationals. Allowing international access to this amenity – either by allowing foreigners direct access or by fostering international trade in the resources extracted from, or generated by use of, that amenity – increases both the diversity of demands placed on the amenity and the quantity of demand.

International common access places more diverse demands on an environmental amenity than does national access. Because countries vary in their social, cultural, and economic preferences, even if the citizens of one country value an environmental amenity only for its existence benefits (or do not value it at all), citizens of other countries may value it for its consumptive or nonconsumptive benefits. Thus, allowing international access to an amenity makes it more likely that some actors will make consumptive and/or nonconsumptive use of the amenity. Consider the sea urchin population in the state of Maine in the United States. Maine sea urchin landings were less than 0.2 million pounds from the early 1960s through 1986, but development of a Japanese market for sea urchin roe increased landings to over 40 million pounds in 1994 with a subsequent crash back to less than five million pounds after 2004 (Maine Department of Marine Resources, 2004, 2008). Allowing global access (even if via American divers serving the Japanese sushi market) placed consumptive demands on a resource that had previously provided only existence value, thereby creating the possibility of  overappropriation. The more nations and cultures that place demands on an amenity, the greater the likelihood that some of that demand will involve consumptive or nonconsumptive benefits, introducing the possibility for overappropriation or degradation.

Even when granting international access (directly or through trade) does not alter the *types* of demands placed on an amenity, it can increase the *total* demand placed on it. One nation's demand on an amenity may not, by itself, create an overappropriation or degradation problem, but transforming that resource from a national to a global amenity can generate aggregate international demand that exceeds that amenity's carrying capacity. Thus, international trade makes regional fish species (such as Chilean sea bass or various tuna species) susceptible to global demand for food and makes local elephant, tiger, polar bear, and other endangered species stocks susceptible to global demand for luxury goods, medicines, or sport trophies. Today's globalized economy generates more rapid tropical deforestation because forests supply both local firewood demand and foreign lumber demand (Dauvergne, 1997). Bhutan's opening up to international tourism will produce more rapid congestion of its wilderness and the degradation of environmentally-sensitive habitats than if access continued to be restricted to Bhutanese. Even when transnational preferences are homogeneous, that is, the amenity provides only consumptive benefits, aggregate demand will increase as more humans have access to it.

The challenges to precluding access to – or regulating the use of – an international commons make environmental problems particularly likely. Many governments reasonably treat amenities for which domestic demand is far below carrying capacity as public goods, choosing not to limit access or preclude appropriation by their citizens. National parks often need few limits on use until they become international tourist destinations. Many fisheries within countries' exclusive economic zones (EEZs) go largely unregulated by domestic governments. National boundaries serve as important, if often unrecognized, barriers to excessive demand that helps protect environmental amenities. By contrast, the high seas and many shared lakes and rivers are treated as open access commons, lacking even the basic mechanism of national citizenship as a means of limiting access.

International anarchy, relative gains concerns, interstate rivalry, nationalism, and a weaker sense of community at the international level also tend to reduce the incentives for self-restraint that might protect an environmental amenity. States that would benefit from protecting some international environmental amenity face two potential futures: if other states do not help protect it, that amenity will not be protected and therefore their restraint entails a present cost with no future benefit; if other states' restraint does protect the amenity, the state can receive future benefits from the amenity without having to incur the present costs that restraint would entail. In the international context, even if the state might realize an absolute gain by contributing (that is, future benefits would exceed present costs), the fears of relative losses may increase the perceived value of shirking. Indeed, rivalries over international environmental amenities can be intensified by nationalism and pride that do not enter into conflicts over domestic environmental amenities. The Anglo-Icelandic Cod War and the Spanish-Canadian Turbot War both illustrate how fish stocks and other environmental amenities can generate volatile forms of rivalry when they involve two or more nations (Hart, 1976; Barkin and DeSombre, 2002).

Upstream/downstream problems illustrate particularly clear distinctions between the domestic and international spheres. River pollution, in the form of a firm's chemical waste or a farmer's pesticide residue, imposes externalities on downstream users. To be sure, norms do not fully inhibit firms or individuals from engaging in such activities when doing so harms citizens of their own country. Yet, whatever inhibitory power such norms exert is even weaker when those harmed are foreign nationals. And even when such norms are absent, interdependencies among nationals of a country can generate restraint among polluters due to instrumental mechanisms involving economic, social, or political retaliation and reputational effects, mechanisms that are likely to be less available in the case of transnational externalities because such inter-dependencies are less prevalent across than within borders.

Likewise, people's stronger sense of allegiance and obligation to fellow nationals than to an international or global community makes them more likely to contribute voluntarily to the maintenance and enhancement of national goods than to international goods. National identity remains an important element in people's decision making, and restraint to preserve a fish stock shared by other nationals, however unlikely, is more likely than such restraint to preserve a fish stock shared by foreigners. Thus, pressures for overfishing are strong *within* national EEZs but are even stronger *outside* them. A 'common purpose' or 'common goal' may not always persuade people to contribute to national efforts at environmental protection but their absence tends to make people even less likely to contribute to corresponding international efforts.

## Identifying the causes of particular international environmental problems

The IPAT equation and the six perspectives delineated here shed light on the reasons that particular international environmental problems appear in particular sectors, among particular countries, and at particular times. To argue that a range of causes, collectively, makes international environmental problems likely and makes them more likely than in domestic settings is unlikely to prove compelling when we are interested in understanding or identifying the causes that produce a particular environmental problem.

In identifying the causes of a particular international environmental problem or a particular set of problems, many international environmental problems are either overdetermined by the convergence of multiple sufficient causes or reflect the interdependencies and convergence among multiple necessary forces, none of which is a sufficient cause in itself. Closely related to the problem of causal interdependencies is the distinction between permissive causes and triggering (or 'catalytic') causes. Permissive causes are necessary, or at least contingently necessary, background conditions that explain why a certain problem was likely (Goertz et al., 2008: 10). Triggering causes, by contrast, are temporally and/or spatially proximate variables that explain why a certain problem emerged at a particular time and place.

These considerations challenge those seeking to identify 'the' cause of an international environmental problem. In this regard, it helps to consider the distinction between a cause and the 'causal field' within which that cause operates (Brady and Seawright, 2004). Efforts at causal explanation of one case almost always entail an explicit or implicit comparison to some other case or cases. The nature of those other cases, whether chosen consciously or not, dictates which variables or factors fade into a background causal field and which variables or factors emerge as potential causes of the case being evaluated. Regardless of whether a causal explanation relies on case material, counterfactual thought experiments, or careful process tracing, any such effort involves choices that background some variables in the causal field (where convincingly demonstrating their causal force becomes challenging) and foreground other variables whose causal influence can be more readily and carefully evaluated. By necessity, selecting cases for comparison leads to certain variables being constant across the cases and others that vary across them. Whether intended or not, the shared features become the background conditions or causal field within which the international environmental problem emerges and therefore can, and indeed must be, set aside as causes (Brady and Seawright, 2004: 9). The features that differ across the cases then constitute the set of variables that are potential causes of that problem. In short, the cases selected for comparison limit the set of potential, and potentially convincing, explanations of any given international environmental problem.

More generally, how satisfactory we find a given explanation, and whether we consider one cause more important than another, depends on our analytic goals, on the correlational evidence and/or the counterfactual plausibility we can bring to bear, and how convincingly causal mechanisms can be delineated and supported. First, whether we find a causal explanation satisfying or not depends on whether we want to understand by specifying the causes of a particular case or by generalizing the causes of many cases. A satisfyingly detailed explanation of a specific case requires attention to both the deep, structural, enabling, or permissive causes that make up the causal field and the proximate, triggering, or catalytic causes. Enabling causes – the generally stable background conditions that make an environmental problem's emergence possible – are shared across the many situations in which particular environmental problems emerge but are missing from those in which those problems do not emerge. Such causes may not meet the strict definition of necessary conditions but, nonetheless, make environmental problems more likely. For example, ecophilosophical claims focus our attention on structural causes, arguing that worldviews dominated by shallow ecological, masculine, or technocratic norms are more likely to produce environmental degradation than those imbued with deep ecological, feminist, or spiritual norms. Catalytic causes are those more proximate factors that convert a latent environmental problem into a realized one. Those who are interested in full and rich explanations of particular cases develop causal explanations that invoke both types of causes. They may explain a fire by drawing our attention to the convergence of catalytic causes (a lit cigarette, the spark from a passing car, or a lightning strike) and deeper enabling causes (wood and underbrush, seasonal variation, and drought) (Nye, 2000). By contrast, those interested in generalizing across cases tend to focus their attention on the deeper enabling causes, documenting how certain international environmental problems emerge across various contexts that differ in many ways but have one or relatively few features in common.

Thus, consider an effort to explain the overexploitation of North Pacific fur seals at the end of the nineteenth century (Dorsey, 1998). Someone with an ecophilosophical bent could readily argue that fur seal overexploitation was driven by a culture that placed more value on fashionable hats than on the lives of animals whose skins were used for those hats. A scientific perspective might highlight the poor understanding of fur seal stock sizes and population dynamics. A legal perspective might highlight that international law treated the high seas as a commons and did not restrict access to resources such as seal stocks, thereby creating a Tragedy of the Commons among Russia, the United States, Japan, and Canada. An economic perspective would highlight how treatment of the ocean as a commons and government subsidies made the private costs of sealing (the costs to those conducting it) lower than their social costs, thereby leading to overharvesting (Wilen, 1976). A capacity-based perspective might point out that then-current technologies allowed the killing of seals on land and at sea but that the latter was technologically inefficient with many seals sinking before their carcasses could be brought on board. And a political perspective might identify the competition among the countries as a source of pressure to exploit fur seal stocks and to gain economic and geopolitical advantage, and of obstacles that delayed mutual resolution of the problem until 1911. Arbitrating among these competing causal claims requires reliance on correlational evidence and counterfactuals as well as the convincingness of the logic and evidence for causal mechanisms.

Second, the fit of correlational evidence with a causal claim and the plausibility of counterfactuals have a major influence on how convincing a causal claim appears. Although frequently dismissed for not providing correlational evidence, many single case studies shed powerful light on the causes of international environmental problems by highlighting that a problem emerged only at a particular point in time. By carefully evaluating when a problem emerges, alleged causes that did not occur until after the problem emerged and those that occurred long before the problem emerged can be dismissed, strengthening claims about those causes that occurred immediately before the emergence of that problem. Indeed, case studies can often prove particularly compelling because, unlike much quantitative analysis, they provide a temporal resolution that documents an alleged cause as having occurred before rather than after an environmental problem, thereby eliminating the possibility of it having been an effect rather than a cause. Of course, many international environmental problems are caused by – in the sense of 'would not have occurred in the absence of' – a large range of enabling or permissive factors. So, such temporal evaluations tend to discount the favorable background conditions that constitute the causal field and highlight as 'causes' the catalytic or triggering factors or events that prompt an international environmental problem to emerge from that favorable context. Thus, the catalytic cause of overexploitation is often one of demand reaching the point of exceeding a resource's carrying capacity. When technological constraints limit resource extraction, a technological innovation may become the catalytic cause of overexploitation. However, global trade liberalization also can be identified as a catalytic cause of some international environmental problems simply because growth in international trade has dramatically increased the aggregate demand for most environmental resources. Studies of specific cases tend to prove less compelling (though arguments regarding causal mechanisms can significantly mitigate this problem, see below) when they argue for the causal influence of variables that did not vary during the period studied and, therefore, for which the case provides no empirical evidence that whether the environmental problem would not have emerged in their absence. Thus, claims blaming international environmental problems on the capitalist economic system, male-dominated or masculinity-dominated hierarchies, or modernity, however logically compelling in their own right, become more so when they are derived from comparisons that present empirical evidence that such problems emerged less frequently in non-capitalist economic systems, female-dominated or femininity-dominated hierarchies, or traditional cultures.

Efforts to evaluate the power of particular alleged causes of international environmental problems can be designed in two different ways that parallel Mill's distinction between the method of agreement and the method of difference (Mill, 1950). Researchers can select cases that differ widely in most respects but, in all of which, particular international environmental problems emerged and then can look for the one or two factors common to these otherwise-divergent cases. Such strategies prove particularly useful in identifying deep, structural causes that enable or permit environmental problems to emerge, making them more likely than under other circumstances. Alternatively, studies can compare cases that are similar in most respects but that differ with respect to one variable of interest to assess whether international environmental problems tend to be present when that alleged cause is present and tend to be absent when it is absent. Particularly when such strategies only compare a small number of cases, or multiple observations within a single case, they tend to obscure or ignore deeper, enabling causes that made the emergence of the problem likely and focus our attention on more proximate or triggering causes. And as Mill noted, although these latter 'method of difference' strategies can distinguish causal from irrelevant factors more readily than can single case studies, they do less well at distinguishing whether a causal factor is acting alone or is simply 'an indispensable part of the cause, of the phenomenon' (Mill, 1988: 280).

Counterfactuals are central to compelling causal arguments of any type (Fearon, 1991; Biersteker, 1993; Tetlock and Belkin, 1996;

Goertz et al., 2008). Counterfactuals differ from Mill's method of difference largely in whether the case that differed with respect to the one variable of interest was a real-world case or a 'thought experiment' in which the 'evidence' consists largely of making a conjecture about how the world would have differed *if* only that one variable of interest had been different. Because thought experiment counterfactuals generate strictly hypothetical, 'what would have happened if', evidence, they contribute to a convincing causal claim in proportion to their plausibility. Thus, the claim that stratospheric ozone depletion was caused by the invention of chlorofluorocarbons in the 1920s (and the subsequent development of related chemicals) is convincing both because (a) had such inventions not occurred, it is difficult to identify other reasons that the ozone layer would have become depleted and (b) it seems quite plausible that such inventions could have failed to occur and, had that happened, modern economic development would not have proceeded in any fundamentally different ways than it did anyway. By contrast, a claim that present climate change has been caused by any *particular* technological development seems far less convincing because (a) climate change is caused by greenhouse gas emissions from such a range of human activities that delays in the technological development of any one of those would have had only a marginal effect on overall rates of climate change and (b) the greater economic pressures to develop coal, oil, gas, and wood as energy sources and the lower technological obstacles to doing so were much more likely than in the chlorofluorocarbon case to have been overcome in any event. Similarly, in the fur seal example, we might be more convinced by an ecophilosophical than a scientific argument if we believe that, given then-current scientific knowledge, a change in values would have reduced the annual seal kill significantly whereas, given then-current values, a change in scientific knowledge would have reduced that kill only minimally. Both correlational evidence and counterfactuals generally strengthen causal claims not so much by 'ruling in' certain causes but by 'ruling out' alternative explanations until only a relatively few alleged causes are left standing. Apparently logical and convincing claims often lose their validity in the face of evidence or counterfactuals that, when examined, easily and convincingly undermine the causal claim. Causal claims gain validity, in contrast, when the careful and rigorous development of correlational evidence and plausible counterfactuals *fails* to undermine a causal claim.

Third, causal claims are strengthened by narratives involving logical mechanisms that convincingly link causes and effects and leave observable traces (Young, 1999a; Brady and Seawright, 2004: see particularly Table 1(3) and 31; George and Bennett, 2005). Since correlation can exist in the absence of causation and since counterfactuals involve hypotheticals that lack empirical evidence, our faith in a putative cause lies in being able to observe correlation and develop plausible counterfactuals and, then, in being able to observe empirical evidence of theoretically-predicted links in the cause-effect chain. Consider how we identify the timing of the international emergence of environmental problems. Why did the overexploitation of North Pacific fur seals become a problem in the late 1800s but not earlier? Why did global stratospheric ozone loss and European acid rain problems appear in the late 1960s and 1970s but not earlier? Explaining why these impacts on environmental resources became problems focuses our attention on those potentially causal factors that vary (over time or across cases) in ways that correspond with the emergence or existence of that environmental problem. Thus, with respect to fur seals, ozone loss, and acid rain, we would tend to focus on whether aggregate demand finally approached the carrying capacity sufficiently that it became both noticeable and of concern. We would also tend to dismiss explanations that highlight that these situations involve Tragedies of the Commons or negative externalities or that the behaviors involved arose from anti-environmental worldviews since those causes, while potentially useful in understanding why people engaged in certain behaviours, seem less useful in understanding why a certain problem emerged at a particular point in time.

A full explanation of why most international environmental problems emerge would require attention to most, if not all, of the variables identified above. Thus, the growing problem of acid precipitation in Europe until the 1970s and in much of the rest of the world even today could appropriately reference, inter alia, the drive for economic progress unconstrained by environmental concern; increasing populations and affluence; heightened levels of economic development; technologies that could convert fossil fuels (particularly coal) into electricity but did so by producing atmospheric pollution; ignorance of environmental impacts; the lack of institutional mechanisms to address those impacts; and the happenstance that geopolitically weaker states tended to be downwind from stronger states. Whether one or more of these appears satisfactory as an explanation of the problem of acid precipitation depends on how we frame the question. What question we ask determines the line between potential causes and causal field and the importance of the distinction between triggering causes and permissive causes (Brady and Seawright, 2004). If we ask why acid rain was a significantly greater environmental problem in the 1960s in Europe than in Latin America, for example, the differences in levels of economic development and levels of environmental concern capture our attention. But if we ask why acid precipitation was addressed in the 1970s while marine oil pollution was addressed as early as the 1920s (Mitchell, 1994a), differences in knowledge and concern about – and differences in the legal and institutional infrastructure for addressing – atmospheric *vs* marine environmental impacts might become preferred causes. In short, what emerges as a cause and what becomes the relatively silent causal field of permissive conditions depends on how we ask the causal question (Brady and Seawright, 2004: 9).

Developing a satisfactory explanation of an international environmental problem, or any phenomenon for that matter, also depends on distinguishing between necessary and sufficient conditions and between strong and weak causes. As already noted, a distressing multifinality pervades international environmental problems: most international environmental problems can emerge under many conditions and in varied contexts. Put differently, relatively few conditions appear necessary for their emergence (or, alternatively, those necessary conditions are distressingly common). Thus, river pollution occurs when riparian states are democratic, autocratic, or both; when they are highly developed or relatively undeveloped; when they have highly interdependent or relatively independent relationships; and when they have market economies or command economies (Conca, 2006). One of the few truly necessary conditions for the emergence of an international environmental problem is that aggregate human pressures on a resource exceed that resource's ability to continue providing the environmental service demanded of it. But even this excessive demand can result from a large population making relatively low per capita demands or from a small population making relatively large per capita demands.

That said, there appear to be some 'strong' or sufficient conditions (or combinations of conditions) under which international environmental problems emerge, or are likely to emerge. Thus, international environmental problems will almost certainly emerge if an activity causes environmental harm but humans are ignorant of that harm. They also will emerge whenever environmental concern is low, since efforts to investigate environmental impacts and to constrain economic and technological development to avoid such impacts will be rare. They tend to emerge in contexts involving either Tragedies of the Commons or upstream/downstream situations. Knowledge, environmental concern, and certain incentive structures thus seem to be 'strong' causes, operating in a relatively independent fashion from other factors. These causes produce international environmental problems in a wide range of settings including those in which other factors militate against problem emergence. Thus, ignorance that an economically advantageous activity is environmentally harmful almost always leads to environmental problems, although that linkage is not logically necessary since, as the precautionary principle highlights, a burden of proof of 'no environmental harm' could be placed on those seeking to engage in new behaviors. Likewise, rules allowing unrestricted common access (which generate Tragedy of the Commons situations) are intellectually compelling precisely because they have been shown consistently to generate overexploitation that persists even in the face of high levels of knowledge and concern about a problem.

By contrast, other variables tend to be weak causes, leading to international environmental problems only when aligned with other conditions. These variables generate problems in multi-causal or conjunctional settings. Just as lumber, tinder, and sparks must all be present for a forest fire to occur, certain causes tend to generate international environmental problems within a context of other facilitating variables. As already noted, the six perspectives tend to highlight causes that are necessary and enabling rather than sufficient and proximate, and so most causal stories of particular environmental problems involve reference to several causes existing simultaneously. The overappropriation of most international fisheries can be seen as dependent, simultaneously, on the high seas being treated as an international commons, on the existence of technologies that allow the harvesting of fish in large quantities on the high seas, and on the absence of a deep ecological norm of ecological egalitarianism – 'the equal right [of all species] to live and blossom' (Naess, 1973: 96). Remove any one of these causes and, counterfactually, over-appropriation would become unlikely. Likewise, cultures and deep-seated value structures can provide considerable freedom or room for maneuver and can underdetermine environmental problems. Differences in the priority placed on environmental protection – whether evident in the variation between indigenous and modern cultures or in progressive changes within modern cultures – presumably make environmental degradation more or less common. Yet, it seems unlikely that environmental degradation has been absent in any cultural tradition or value system. Within any culture or value system, other variables determine whether environmental degradation occurs.

With respect to probabilistic causation, it is worth noting simply that, for both ontological and epistemological reasons, it is likely 'that social science relationships will appear probabilistic even if they are deterministic' (Brady and Seawright, 2004: 14; see also Marini and Singer, 1988). To identify Tragedy of the Commons or upstream/downstream situations as the causes of international environmental problems does not require that such problems always emerge when those situations exist and that they always be absent when they do not. Precisely because of the existence of conjunctional causation, where an effect depends on two or more causes occurring simultaneously, 'causes can happen without leading to a specific effect if other features of the situation are not propitious for the effect' (Brady and Seawright, 2004: 18). We should not ignore the explanatory power of particular variables simply because they do not work under all conditions. Explanations are most satisfactory when the factors alleged as causes are strong causes in the sense of leading international environmental problems to emerge much more frequently when those causes are present than when they are absent, with that evidence being particularly compelling if it comes from a relatively broad range of circumstances including many in which other permissive causes are not propitious.

## Conclusion

This chapter has identified an array of variables and perspectives that explain why humans generate environmental damage, and why such damage is likely to be more common in international settings than domestic ones. The IPAT identity provides a useful, if limited, starting point for understanding why international environmental problems emerge. Environmental degradation is, to be sure, caused when each of a large number of people has access to large amounts of resources and has technological options that are pollution intensive or otherwise impose significant environmental damage.

But the insights derived from the IPAT identity can be considerably extended by viewing environmental degradation as the result of the interplay between six different sets of factors: values, knowledge, law, incentives, capacity, and power. Explanations of the overarching environmental predicament we find ourselves in or specific international environmental problems depend on variables drawn from one or more of these six perspectives. Our overarching environmental predicament results from the fact that environmental degradation exhibits a distressing multifinality: numerous causes, both individually and in combination, can produce environmental degradation across a range of contexts. There appear to be relatively few necessary conditions for international environmental problems to emerge and those that do exist appear to be relatively common. Hence, we find ourselves facing a wide variety and increasing number of international environmental problems. Producing an intellectually satisfying explanation of why any specific international environmental problem emerges depends (a) on whether the explanatory goal is a full and rich explanation of an individual case or identification of a relatively few causes that explain a large number of cases, (b) on whether carefully selected comparative cases and carefully developed counterfactuals provide compelling evidence and arguments that the problem would not have emerged had the alleged causes been absent, and (c) on the degree to which logical theoretical predictions regarding the causal mechanisms involved can be empirically verified.

# THE INTERNATIONAL EMERGENCE OF ENVIRONMENTAL PROBLEMS

Given the myriad impacts humans have on the environment, what determines which ones become topics for international discussion? On what basis and by what social processes do some anthropogenic (human-caused) environmental impacts emerge on the international stage as soon as they are identified while others languish for years with little or no international attention? This chapter explores the processes, actors, variables, and conditions that foster the emergence of certain environmental impacts on the international agenda. Although issue emergence is not sufficient for an environmental problem to be addressed internationally, it is certainly necessary. International action on a problem requires the prior discussion of that problem. And the factors that influence whether issues emerge onto the agenda or not are crucial because they determine which issues are 'organized into politics' and which 'are organized out' (Schattschneider, 1975 [1960]: 71).

This chapter contends that international environmental issue emergence involves three transitions: from environmental impact to problem; from problem to discussion item; and from discussion item to action item. The states of three large-scale variables explain whether and when these transitions occur: knowledge, concern, and urgency. Impacts become problems when actors who already have a general concern about environmental issues gain knowledge about a specific anthropogenic environmental impact. Problems become discussion items either when those initially concerned succeed at persuading the relevant international actors that levels of knowledge and political concern warrant international discussion or when the relevant international actors already concerned about environmental issues gain new knowledge about anthropogenic environmental impacts. Finally, discussion items become action items by 'catalytic' or 'focusing' events making action appear more urgent, by the discovery that new or existing alternatives are cheap enough to undercut prior resistance to action, by gradual increases in concern and knowledge that make important actors deem action as now warranted, or by institutional pressures and inertia increasing the difficulty of continuing to merely study and discuss the issue.

## Definitions

Discussing international issue emergence and agenda setting can benefit from some terminological clarifications. Questions of why certain issues are discussed but others are not traditionally have been discussed in terms of agenda setting or 'the process of raising issues to salience among the relevant community of actors' (Livingston, 1992: 313).

So what is the *international agenda*? Even more so than in other arenas, 'the lack of an agreed-upon agenda locale, let alone an explicit document, frustrates the analysis of international agenda-setting' (Livingston, 1992: 314–15). It is tempting to think of the international agenda as a list of issues on the agenda of the next meeting of some international organization. But it proves more useful to conceptualize the international agenda broadly, to view it as that set of topics which are of sufficient concern to relevant national governments that they decide to take them up for discussion. In bilateral settings, the pollution of a river or the overexploitation of a fishery becomes part of the international agenda if, when one country raises the issue, another country responds. In multilateral settings, the international agenda consists of those issues that some subset of states engages with on an ongoing basis. Although the international agenda is dominated by states, it is not theirs exclusively. Deforestation, habitat preservation, and even climate change have been kept on the international agenda not only via intergovernmental discussions but also through discussions among nongovernmental organizations (NGOs) and multinational corporations, and between those sectors and governments (see, for example, Ceres: Investors and Environmentalists for Sustainable Prosperity, 2008; Leon H. Sullivan Foundation, 2008).

The emergence of issues on the international agenda reflects three transitions between four stages. Potential issues start in a 'pool' of *anthropogenic environmental impacts,* that myriad of ways in which humans alter the environment. This phrase distinguishes *environmental* impacts from the many influences humans have on other humans and *anthropogenic* impacts from natural variation, even though the latter may prompt human responses. Anthropogenic environmental impacts are *international environmental problems* to the extent that some set of individuals are aware of them and perceive them as negative. If knowledge and the negative perceptions of an impact by a few individuals come to be shared by a sufficiently large or influential set of people to then become 'politically significant', it is deemed an environmental problem, even if we cannot define how many – or which – people must share that perception (Davies, 1974: 157). An international environmental problem becomes an *international environmental discussion item* if it generates enough concern for an important set of international actors to give it 'active and serious consideration' (Davies, 1974: 158). A discussion item becomes an *international environmental action item* if it generates sufficient concern that international actors decide it warrants some form of action beyond discussion, often but not only consisting of the negotiation of some form of international policy.

Given this terminology, we can rephrase this chapter's main questions. What causes certain anthropogenic environmental impacts, but not others, to emerge as international environmental discussion items or action items? Why do certain environmental problems receive significant and prompt international attention while others receive little, late, or no attention? What actors, processes, variables, and conditions foster these transitions from an impact into a problem, a problem into a discussion item, and a discussion item into an action item?

## Variation in the International Agenda: What Needs Explanation?

As noted throughout this book, explaining why something happens as it does requires that we first clearly identify what is actually happening. This chapter describes some of the variation in the international environmental agenda before examining those factors that may explain that variation. Certainly, the international community engages and takes remedial action far more promptly with respect to some environmental impacts than others. Various governments had begun discussing international wetlands degradation in the 1960s and had signed a wetlands protection treaty in 1971 even though most people at that time still considered wetlands to be wastelands (Matthews, 1993). Discussions to protect the stratospheric ozone layer began as early as the 1977 International Conference on the Ozone Layer, even though the linkage of chlorofluorocarbons (CFCs) to ozone depletion was only identified in 1974 and remained unconfirmed until the late 1980s (Haas, 1992a: 197–200). Other anthropogenic environmental impacts become international discussion items relatively quickly while remedial action is delayed for years. Thus, deforestation has been a topic of international discussion since at least the 1980s but an international treaty to redress it has yet to be signed. Yet other anthropogenic environmental impacts remain undiscussed by the international community long after they have been identified. For example, the vast amounts of nitrogen- and phosphorus-based fertilizers annually applied to soils around the world is known to have significant environmental effects but has received little international environmental attention (Vitousek et al., 1997).

Why does the list of problems addressed internationally and those not addressed bear so little resemblance to those lists of 'environmental severity' reflecting expert judgments or public opinion polls? Environmental problems known to kill millions of people each year – the lack of potable water or indoor air pollution – receive relatively little attention while others whose impacts are less severe, far off in the future, and influence fewer people – like stratospheric ozone depletion – receive significant attention (Young, 1998: 56). Similarly, why do environmental problems that the scientific community knows exist, knows the causes of, and has solutions for, remain unaddressed for years and then rapidly become an international subject of regulation? Why did climate change only become a significant topic of international policy discussion in 1988, despite the fact that scientific assessments had been confident of the likely impacts of human carbon emissions since at least 1979 (Torrance, 2006)? Why did the continuing and regular marine oil spills that occurred in the Russian north during the 1980s and early 1990s 'suddenly burst onto the scene as a matter of international concern toward the end of 1994' (Young, 1998: 57)?

Why do countries in some regions sign treaties on environmental problems long before they have even prompted discussion in other regions? Despite widespread knowledge, understanding, and empirical evidence that unregulated international fisheries tend towards overexploitation, some international fisheries were regulated in the 1940s while others were regulated only recently – and some remain unregulated. European states adopted policies to improve the enforcement of marine environmental protection rules in 1982 while Latin America and Asia did so in 1992 – other regions did so only in the late 1990s (Kasoulides, 1993; Plaza, 1997; DeSombre, 2006). Acid precipitation became a discussion item in Europe in the 1970s and in Asia in the 1990s – but has yet to receive significant attention elsewhere in the world (Wilkening, 2004). The treatment of sewage and industrial wastes before discharge into rivers is well-documented – but has also received little international attention (Conca, 2006).

These examples highlight that variation in issue emergence does not simply reflect variation in the severity of environmental problems. Environmental degradation is not included on the international agenda 'automatically or spontaneously following the emergence of problems that are important in some objective sense' (Young, 1998: 56). What does appear on the international agenda is the product of a range of processes, variables, and conditions as well as the serendipity of catalytic events, making issue emergence, at times, challenging to predict.

## Explaining Issue Emergence: Knowledge, Concern, and Urgency

An environmental impact becomes an international discussion item when relevant actors have sufficient knowledge that human activities are causing, may be causing, or may in the future cause that impact, and then collectively share sufficient concern about that impact to initiate discussions to address it. More briefly, discussion items emerge when there is sufficient knowledge of and concern about some anthropogenic environmental impact. High concern but limited knowledge about the magnitude of some environmental impact, about which human activities cause those impacts, and/or about potential solutions to a problem can make actors willing to discuss the problem without committing to taking action on it. As knowledge increases and concern becomes more urgent – whether because the issue 'matures' or because of exogenous events – actors may become willing to move beyond discussion to taking action.

An explanation of issue emergence as the result of a confluence of sufficient knowledge, concern, and urgency is unsatisfying, however, since their influence can only be recognized post hoc. We can only recognize levels of knowledge, concern, or urgency as 'sufficient' to cause emergence by examining whether the issue actually emerged on the international agenda. We are stuck with a tautology in which we use the same evidence to identify whether an issue has emerged and whether there was *sufficient* knowledge, concern, or urgency to cause it to emerge. However, we can make the concepts of knowledge, concern, and urgency analytically useful by thinking of them as intervening variables that rise and fall in response to changes in other variables. Thus, we can reframe the analytic task as identifying the variables, conditions, and processes that cause increases in the knowledge, concern, or urgency that relevant actors have about some anthropogenic environmental impact. Those seeking to have an environmental problem discussed internationally must raise knowledge, concern, and urgency above a certain – albeit unspecified – threshold.

Even this brief introduction clarifies that ideas play a prominent role in agenda setting. To be sure, material power cannot be ignored if we want to explain why some issues are discussed internationally and others are not. Yet whether actors recognize an environmental problem and consider it serious enough to address has more to do with what those actors think than what they do. Hence, in this policy phase, more than during the negotiation or implementation of international environmental policies, ideas and persuasion play greater roles than power and coercion.

# Processes of International Agenda Setting

Issue emergence progresses through three relatively sequential processes: an identification and recognition of the problem and its causes; diffusion of that knowledge and mobilization of concern; and prioritization of the issue on the international agenda. A fourth process, framing the issue, cuts across and links together the other three. Taken together, these processes define the problem, demonstrate its political importance, and gain support for particular ways of discussing the issue that influence whether and when the issue will be taken up for discussion or action.

## Recognizing the problem

For an anthropogenic environmental impact to appear on the international agenda, it must be a 'problem'. That is, some set of individuals must know – and be concerned – about that impact. Human impacts cannot emerge on the agenda until they are known. As the stratospheric ozone case mentioned previously illustrates, issue emergence often begins when a behavior previously considered benign is thought to have unexpected but real environmental impacts. And such impacts, once known, will not emerge on the international agenda unless they evoke concern. For example, humans consciously try to reduce bacteria, viruses, and other human health threats. Such efforts clearly alter ecosystem processes and – as in the eradication of smallpox – may reduce biological diversity. Yet few, if any, people would consider these environmental impacts a problem. But once some set of actors both knows and cares about some anthropogenic environmental impact an environmental 'problem' then exists, creating the possibility for it, at some future time, to emerge onto the international agenda.

Ignorance regarding anthropogenic environmental impacts can take three forms, any of which can prevent issue emergence: causal ignorance, effect ignorance, and total ignorance. *Causal ignorance* exists when environmental changes have been observed but their human causes, if any, have not been determined. Recent examples include the discovery of various frog mutations, the decimation of bee populations by 'colony collapse disorder', and massive die-offs of bats (United States Geological Survey, 2001; Gill, 2007; Minkel, 2007; New York State Department of Environmental Conservation, 2008). In such 'whodunnits', problems emerge as the certainty grows that human activities are causing an environmental decline.

*Effect ignorance* exists for those activities suspected of harming the environment but where the impacts are unknown or uncertain. We know relatively little about the environmental impacts of many human activities such as the application of agricultural fertilizer, the coverage of large fractions of the Earth's land surface with buildings and roads, and the discharge of such micro-pollutants as human and veterinary pharmaceuticals (Vitousek et al., 1997; Daughton and Ternes, 1999; Elvidge et al., 2007). International fisheries have often remained unregulated because of uncertainty about – and excessive optimism regarding – whether catch levels are exceeding the carrying capacity of the fish stock. In effect ignorance situations, the actors most suspicious of the activity have incentives to collect evidence of the behavior's harmful effects. Bringing such evidence to light can initiate a political-scientific interchange between concerned actors who seek more evidence of the suspected activity's environmental damage and those who benefit economically, politically, or socially from the activity and seek to refute that evidence. Eventually, that debate may resolve whether the behavior is causing environmental damage or not. But before that, those concerned may have mobilized enough political pressure to get international discussions started about whether to regulate suspect activities. Indeed, the precautionary principle consists of precisely the prescription that we should take action to constrain those activities suspected of causing environmental damage even before such damage is certain.

*Total ignorance* exists when the impacts of non-suspect human activities are unknown. For many human activities that we have assumed are environmentally benign, we usually have little reason to re-examine that assumption. Yet that assumption may prove wrong. CFCs were initially embraced because their chemical properties suggested they were environmentally-benign: they were non-carcinogenic, non-toxic, and inert. For decades, there seemed no reason to worry about or investigate their environmental impacts. Total ignorance involves 'unknown unknowns'. In the cases of causal ignorance and effect ignorance, we have some knowledge about the type and extent of our ignorance and can try to correct it. But in the case of total ignorance, we are not even aware that we need to be concerned about human activities that are having real and significant environmental impacts. By definition, we cannot know which of the human activities that we currently assume to be benign actually are. But it seems likely that, in the decades ahead, we will discover that our assumptions about at least some of those activities are wrong, causing a transition to a causal ignorance state if environmental impacts are found or an effect ignorance state if scientific insights suggest those activities are environmentally harmful. Indeed, individual scientists, governments, and the United Nations Environment Programme (UNEP) often monitor 'emerging environmental issues' that include both suspect human behaviors and troubling patterns of environmental change (United Nations System-Wide Earthwatch, 2007).

Issue emergence begins with the recognition that certain human activities may have environmental impacts that are considered harmful. In one mode, issues may emerge when scientists identify environmental problems and bring them to the public's attention. Individual scientists and epistemic communities of scientists often identify which human behaviors are harming the environment; the type, magnitude, and scope of those harms; the sectors or countries responsible for a problem; and any potentially effective solutions (Haas, 1989). Scientific research relies on systematic methods and instrumentation that allows for the identification of many environmental changes that simply could not be observed otherwise. Equally important, scientists are interested in and have developed methods specifically designed to distinguish 'true' causes of environmental changes from the many 'spurious' factors that covary with those changes but are not their causes. Thus, efforts to identify historical greenhouse gas levels and global average temperatures from ice cores, corals, and tree rings have been crucial in identifying both that climate change is occurring and that humans are a major contributor to it. Likewise, neither the depletion of stratospheric ozone nor its cause in the release of CFCs could have been identified without significant scientific efforts.

Scientific research contributes to issue emergence in different ways. In some cases, the causal links between human behavior and environmental conditions are straightforward but scientists clarify the size of human impacts. Thus, both harvesting and habitat loss clearly harm the stocks of particular species. Yet scientists play crucial roles in identifying the not-so-readily-observed size of, and trends in, those impacts. Likewise, even for clearly harmful pollutants, only scientific studies can clarify the levels of damage caused by aggregate human pollution and the levels the environment can absorb without damage. In other cases, theoretical insights may make a particular activity environmentally suspect, with scientists then gathering evidence to assess that theory's accuracy. Thus, scientists took years to find evidence validating theoretical claims about the environmental damage caused by acid precipitation and CFCs (Levy, 1993; Parson, 2003). In yet other cases, scientists seek out the causes of observed environmental changes. Those changes may be identified through long-term scientific monitoring programs or by non-scientists identifying 'clusters' of disease (like those at Love Canal: see Kuran and Sunstein, 1999) or dramatic changes in species with which they work closely (as with beekeepers' identification of colony collapse disorder). Even if non-scientists have initially identified such changes, scientists often quickly undertake research into the reasons for such changes.

Environmental problems are not exclusively identified by scientists. Indeed, some features of scientific culture make scientists unlikely to observe or investigate certain types of environmental impacts. Unusual or unexpected events that are the first signal of an environmental problem may be disregarded as anomalies or outliers. Phenomena that can be readily observed and measured with existing instruments may distract attention from other phenomena that may better show environmental impacts. Non-scientists may be more aware of and have greater stakes in resolving certain local environmental impacts, impacts that 'disinterested' scientists may overlook or de-prioritize (Tesh and Williams, 1996). The dominance of international science by scientists living and trained in industrialized countries can focus research on environmental impacts of concern to industrialized rather than developing countries (Biermann, 2006b). Scientists may favor cutting-edge research questions over more 'mundane' problems of greater environmental importance (Kammen and Dove, 1997). Indeed, many governments create scientific academies and agencies to balance curiosity-driven and problem-driven research better. National governments can channel research toward some environmental problems and away from others. Increasingly in the international arena NGOs have adopted science as a source of influence and have hired scientific staffs to investigate their particular environmental concerns.

## Getting on the agenda: knowledge diffusion, concern mobilization, and issue framing

Knowledge of environmental changes and their human causes is often sufficient to make some individuals concerned. The next stage of issue emergence requires that their knowledge and concern be diffused among more – and more politically significant – international actors. This transition from environmental problem to international discussion item involves 'agenda advocacy': initially concerned actors try to make key individuals and groups aware of, concerned about, and engaged with particular problems; the mass media publicizes efforts by those actors generating further support; efforts to engage policy-makers begin; and 'the opinions of the general public both influence and are influenced by these activities' (Davies, 1974: 158).

Knowledge diffusion can occur in various ways. The incorporation of new scientific information can be part of institutional processes and culture. Many environmental treaties have subsidiary scientific bodies or links with external scientific advisory bodies to improve 'the understanding of the participants regarding the issues at stake' (Young, 1998: 68). Many fisheries treaties, for example, have established scientific committees to provide regular stock assessments that can make already-concerned policy-makers aware of new problems and threats. Other fisheries regimes and marine pollution regimes rely on either periodic or 'on request' assessments by expert working groups of the International Council for the Exploration of the Sea, while UNEP, the Convention on International Trade in Endangered Species (CITES), and the Convention on the Conservation of Migratory Species of Wild Animals (CMS) rely on scientific advice from independent organizations like the International Union for the Conservation of Nature and the World Conservation Monitoring Centre. Many international environmental institutions have institutionalized commitments to addressing any threats to the regional sea, habitat, or species that they seek to protect and therefore may be quite receptive to taking up an issue as soon as scientists bring it to their attention.

International organizations can facilitate the diffusion of knowledge and the mobilization of concern simply by providing a forum 'where an issue may be legitimately raised' (Livingston, 1992: 316). The discovery of a new greenhouse gas, a newly endangered species, or a new pollutant harming the Mediterranean can readily be added to the next meeting of the United Nations Framework Convention on Climate Change (UNFCCC), CITES, or the Convention for the Protection of the Mediterranean Sea (MEDPlan). By contrast, the discovery of a problem – such as agricultural nitrogen fixing or transboundary air pollution in Africa or Latin America – for which no corresponding forum of concerned actors exists is less likely to receive attention. Indeed, international institutions that hold annual meetings may foster the emergence of issues simply by

providing an agenda onto which pro-change actors can place their concerns. In most international organizations, representatives from any
member state can place any item on the agenda for discussion by request.
Knowing this, activists can prompt such a discussion simply by identifying an appropriate organization and a sympathetic member state.

International organizations also have bureaucratic incentives to
expand the range of topics they engage (Weber, 1957 [1922]). Institutions may foster issue emergence in realms in which 'policies are
advanced by technical experts acting on their sense of the public interest, not by interest groups or elected officials acting on behalf of public demands for improved policy' (Birkland, 1998: 67). In such
'policies without publics' (May, 1990), an institution may be able to
focus government attention on an event even without focusing events
or strong political pressure for action (Birkland, 1998). The environmental agenda of the International Maritime Organization (IMO) initially focused on oil pollution but, over time, has expanded to include
almost any environmental impact of shipping, including air pollution,
ballast water, shipwrecks, and salvage. The Convention on Long-
Range Transboundary Air Pollution (LRTAP) initially regulated sulfur
dioxide but has since regulated several additional pollutants.
Incentives may lead institutions to resist adding new issues when
their 'plate is full' but to search out 'new worlds to conquer' at other
times. Thus, the CMS regime has progressively expanded the list of
species it addresses, discussing new species each time negotiations on
previously-discussed species succeed. Institutions may sequence their
attention, with some being taken up for action, others for discussion,
and yet others tabled or ignored until later.

When those initially aware of a problem consider policy-makers
insufficiently concerned about it and likely to rebuff their pressures
for its discussion, they will seek to increase public knowledge of the
problem's magnitude, causes, and solutions and mobilize concern.
Pro-change NGOs and transnational networks of such NGOs often
try to 'broaden the scope of conflict' (Schattschneider, 1975
[1960]). Doing so increases 'the likelihood of more influential and
powerful actors entering the conflict on the side of policy change'
(Birkland, 1998: 55). Tactics here may include publishing reports,
holding press conferences, advertising, writing op-eds, and direct
mail campaigns, as well as direct action, civil disobedience, and
eco-sabotage. The mass media often facilitate knowledge diffusion
and mobilization by reporting on such actions (Davies, 1974: 170).
Pro-change groups are constantly seeking 'opportunities to advocate policy change based as much on advocacy opportunities as on
technically superior analysis' (Birkland, 1998: 55). In the international setting, their success generally requires mobilizing concern

in many countries, including politically significant ones, to create both domestic and international political climates in which policy-makers find it less costly to discuss an issue than to ignore it.

This diffusion of knowledge and mobilization of concern can be fostered by a leader or 'champion' taking up an issue (Davies, 1974: 170). Indeed, Young argues that 'the emergence of a champion is a necessary condition for an issue to move to the top of the political agenda' (Young, 1998: 53). Champions are those 'altruistically motivated' individuals, groups, or states who 'lobby to draw awareness to an issue' (Carpenter, 2007: 104). NGOs often take the lead in urging the international discussion of environmental problems, although powerful 'gatekeeper' NGOs appear more effective at garnering the media coverage and 'traction' that influences government officials than smaller, less well-known, or less-respected NGOs (Carpenter, 2007: 103). But champions can also come from governments or international organizations. Mostafa Tolba, as executive director of UNEP, was a strong advocate for action on the ozone layer, climate change, and regional seas protection, helping to bring 'scientists and policy-makers together in dialogue and exploration of the issues and options' (Hempel, 1996: 130). The Intergovernmental Panel on Climate Change (IPCC), established by the World Meteorological Organization and UNEP (while under Tolba's leadership), has become a major and ongoing champion for the discussion of climate change science and policy. Government officials from Sweden, Norway, and Finland took leadership roles in promoting international discussions of acid precipitation (Patt, 1999: 110). Although champions can focus attention on an issue, their success depends not only on being 'taken seriously, as an expert or a leader' but also on being 'persistent and wait[ing] for the opening of a policy window' (Pollack, 1997: 126). Other forces, including both the efforts of the scientific community and the constellation of political forces, often determine whether efforts to champion an issue succeed.

Governments sometimes need little prompting from NGOs to put environmental issues on the agenda. Indeed, at times non-state actors appear to play a scant role in that process (Young, 1998: 75–6). Environmental problems that threaten important national values can prompt governments to move quickly without significant political pressure. European governments responded almost instantaneously in demanding improved international nuclear regulations after the Chernobyl accident. When environmental problems threaten key military or economic goals, affected governments will often place the issue on the agenda before public concern kicks in. And, at times, mobilizing knowledge and concern in a single, powerful, state can move an issue onto the international agenda. Many environmental issues have appeared on the international agenda due to American unilateralism (DeSombre, 2000). If domestic pressures are strong enough that the US government seems likely to adopt costly domestic restrictions, American companies may fear a 'patchwork quilt' of international regulations and support international policies that would apply American rules to their international competitors and may, in the process, reduce their stringency.

Whether governments are receptive to international discussions of an environmental problem depends on the levels of political support which, in turn, depends on the costs of action and inaction, who is likely to pay those costs, the precedents for action, and the competition with other issues for attention. In some cases, both action and inaction with respect to an environmental problem have clear costs and benefits. States, and influential domestic or international actors, whose interests are threatened by action on certain issues will oppose efforts to discuss them (Young, 1998: 62). When such interests are clear, the persuasion necessary to evoke concern may simply fail (Risse, 2000). But on other, especially emerging, problems, states may be less clear about what their interests are and, therefore, more open to listening to concerns raised by NGOs, other states, or multinational corporations (Zürn, 1998). And even in cases in which 'interests are real', how those interests are understood may be influenced 'not only by factual information but also by the organizing concepts policy-makers adopt in thinking about' the issue (Young, 1998: 63).

## Moving up the agenda: prioritizing the issue and the transition to 'action item'

When and why do international environmental discussion items become action items? How does an international environmental problem gain 'sufficient momentum to graduate to the stage of explicit negotiations' (Young, 1998: 72)? That transition involves an increase in urgency that can occur through three pathways. In the first, existing levels of knowledge and concern are sufficient to get an environmental impact discussed but not acted on. In such cases, 'catalytic' or 'focusing' events can increase the perceived urgency of the problem, prompting international action. In a second pathway, important actors who are aware and concerned resist calls to move beyond discussion because effective and economically-attractive responses are unavailable. In these cases, the discovery of new alternatives – or that existing alternatives are cheaper than previously thought – can remove obstacles to shifting from discussion to action. In a third pathway, a gradual maturation in levels of concern and/or knowledge may lead important actors to shift their views and accept action as warranted. Institutional inertia and pressures create a natural progression and inherent logic that make arguments for the indefinite continuation of research and discussion untenable. A problem should either move off the agenda if evidence shows the problem no longer exists or should become an action item once sufficient knowledge about the problem, its causes, and its solutions becomes available.

Indeed, agreement to discuss an environmental problem tends to involve rhetorical entrapment, with a strong presumption that, if the problem is shown to exist, it should be addressed (Keck and Sikkink, 1998). A decision to participate in discussions of an environmental problem may appear 'uncontroversial' but 'enmeshes the participants in a web of institutionalized activities from which they cannot easily extricate themselves, ... lends credence or authority to a set of broader principles, ... [and keeps the issue] before national policy-makers in a politically potent manner' (Young, 1999c: 266–7). All of these pathways couple knowledge and concern with urgency in ways that motivate relevant actors to move beyond discussion to action.

If champions strive to raise knowledge and concern to prompt discussion of a problem, they also strive to make that problem appear urgent. A champion's influence depends on persuasion more than coercion, and derives from references to ideas and values more than material sources of power. Although intergovernmental action is often assumed to be the response of reluctant state governments to activist environmental NGOs, there are still many instances in which states are 'in the driver's seat' when getting issues prioritized on the international agenda (Young, 1998: 62). Certainly, governments whose citizens experience severe impacts from some environmentally-harmful behavior have incentives to call for international action. Thus, the US government sued Canada for pollution from the Trail Smelter (Bratspies and Miller, 2006) and Nordic countries that were bore the brunt of acid precipitation from other states consistently pushed for action within LRTAP (Levy, 1993; Sprinz and Vaahtoranta, 1994). Indeed, nominally weak states can sometimes get stronger states to discuss action on an environmental problem simply through the intensity of their interest (Young, 1998: 73, 184).

As noted above, governments facing pressure for unilateral domestic action may prefer joint international action as a way to address the problem more completely without burdening domestic industries with competitive disadvantages. Structural power and interdependence can provide such states with enough leverage to urge other states to action. If states share valued trade or other linkages, then one side may be able to prompt the other to action. In the ozone case, the United States 'directly manipulated its unparalleled bilateral ties to flood other states with arguments and scientific information' to make action appear more urgent (Livingston, 1992: 316). The United States also has threatened to close certain markets in response to whaling and fishing problems, creating linkages that make international action more attractive than the alternative (DeSombre, 2000). In upstream/downstream problems, an upstream state has no incentives even to discuss action unless the downstream state creates positive linkages that make addressing the problem worthwhile (Mitchell and Keilbach, 2001). Governments may also strive to prevent international action on environmental issues. Between 2000 and 2008, the United States expended considerable effort to shift climate change from an action item back to a discussion item. At (and since) the 1992 UNCED conference, Malaysia and other countries have prevented any efforts to transition deforestation from discussion to action. The greater success in the latter case highlights that powerful states are not always more successful than weak states in such efforts.

International institutions can also prompt the transition from discussion to action. Indeed, bureaucratic incentives may well prompt international organizations not only to add discussion items to agendas but also to move them toward action. Organizational leaders and staff, on their own initiative or requested by member states, may analyze alternative strategies for action or generate initial negotiating texts in preparation for when most states become open to taking action. An organization's mission and the commitments of its personnel may lend value to research and discussion only to the extent that it is moving toward real environmental action. The international agenda exhibits both inertia and momentum, with issues remaining on the agenda until they gain sufficient momentum to be resolved (Wood and Peake, 1998: 174, 182; Young, 1998: 79–80). Issue maturation – a steady growth in concern and knowledge – may lead to a shift in favor of action over discussion. The efforts at persuasion that discussion entails may lead to a convergence of views about the problem, its causes, any solutions, and the need for action. Particularly when governments 'are uncertain of their own policy preferences [...] entrepreneurial institutions may provide focal points around which the uncertain preferences of the member governments can converge' (Pollack, 1997: 130). Yet international organizations do not always facilitate the discussion-to-action transition. International organizations are agents of states and may be captured by the industries they regulate. Thus, both an organization and its staff at times will be more reluctant than those in the pro-change community to take up controversial agenda items. Also, these organizations must balance environmental concerns against economic and other concerns and so will have incentives to initiate negotiations only once they seem likely to succeed and may resist calls for action on controversial topics that could disrupt otherwise-friendly relations.

International institutions also may prompt discussion-to-action transitions by example. Issues in one arena often gain urgency from negotiation successes in related arenas that show that progress can and should be made. The Helsinki Convention on the Protection of the Marine Environment of the Baltic Sea Area provided a 'demonstration effect' that increased the efforts Arctic countries made to create a regime to protect the Arctic (Young, 1998: 78). The Montreal Protocol became both a model and the impetus for many agreements, including the UNFCCC. Diplomatic successes at addressing particular environmental problems in one region may lead other regions to initiate parallel action out of a sense that 'that's what's done' even if those impacts are not a major current concern in that region (Livingston, 1992: 316; Finnemore, 1993). The 1982 Memorandum of Understanding on Port State Control among European states to improve their enforcement of, inter alia, international marine pollution rules was duplicated in the early 1990s in Latin American and the Asia-Pacific region, and in the late 1990s in the Caribbean, the Mediterranean, the Indian Ocean, the West and Central African region, and the Black Sea.

The urgency of action is often prompted by a 'catalytic event [that is] not part of the stream of conscious efforts to form a regime' (Young, 1998: 53). Although such events are not 'driving forces like material conditions, interests, or ideas, ... [they] need to be taken into account in any effort to make sense of the creation stories of specific international regimes' (Young, 1998: 78). A major environmental accident can, by itself, prompt action. The Chernobyl nuclear accident, the Sandoz pollution spill in the Rhine, and the *Exxon Valdez* oil spill are just three, of many, examples of 'powerful, focusing, and galvanizing events that led to abrupt shifts in national and international policies, priorities, and actions' (Leiserowitz et al., 2006: 437; see also Davies, 1974: 165). Events that are sudden and infrequent, involve large 'harms that are concentrated in a particular geographical area or community of interest', and are 'known to policy-makers and the public simultaneously' tend to receive considerable international attention (Birkland, 1998: 54). A single, relatively small, environmental accident may be followed quickly by another, or a string of such accidents, thereby sustaining media, public, and stakeholder attention and pressure on policy-makers to take action.

Scientific breakthroughs can also put issues on the agenda or increase their urgency (Keohane, 1996: 27). The discovery of significant stratospheric ozone loss over the Antarctic contributed to the perceived urgency of regulating CFCs. Reports that documented the effects in Finland of massive sulfur dioxide emissions from Soviet nickel smelters were central to prompting international engagement with Arctic environmental issues (Young, 1998: 54). Scientific findings also may build, with each new finding suggesting the problem is more severe, extensive, and costly, with predictions of future impacts and their costs becoming increasingly pessimistic, and with an increasing certainty that humans are causing the problem. Such developments foster calls for a transition to action. Alternatively, events may lead to a sense that the issue is less important than previously thought, leading to a predictable fall-off in attention or to attention being diverted to other arenas (Wood and Peake, 1998: 178). Indeed, the transition from discussion item to action item cannot be 'taken for granted' since it can be derailed by major changes in the scientific understanding of a problem or by larger geopolitical events – imagine the issues that were on the verge of significant action on 9/10/2001 (Young, 1998: 77). States may resist addressing an environmental problem when issues considered more important crowd the agenda (the Cold War, the War on Terror, global recession) but may be more receptive as those other issues wane in importance.

Catalytic events are best understood as 'proximate' causes of action, with their influence depending on deeper conditioning causes being in place (Nye, 2000). Consider, for example, the plausibility of counterfactuals related to claims that 'the end of the Cold War caused regime X to form' and that 'the wreck of the *Exxon Valdez* caused regime Y to form'. It is much more plausible that 'regime X would not have formed had it not been for the end of the Cold War' than to claim that 'regime Y would not have formed had it not been for the wreck of the *Exxon Valdez*'. In the latter case, we believe that the regime would have formed, but simply later and in some different way than it actually did, because the regime was formed to address an underlying and ongoing problem of ship wrecks causing environmental damage of which the *Exxon Valdez* wreck was simply one example. If deep conditions are in place, an issue is likely to be taken up as an action item either without a triggering event (through slow yet progressive efforts) or in response to whatever triggering event becomes available. Metaphorically, during a drought, any lightning strike or tossed cigarette can start a forest fire but, during the rainy season, even large sparks cannot start one (Nye, 2000). Catalytic events will prompt action only when deeper causal conditions are in place, when relevant actors have known about and been concerned about an issue for some time (Haas, 1992b: 14; Livingston, 1992: 325).

## Framing the issues

Precisely because the questions of whether an international environmental problem exists, what the problem is, and how urgently it should be addressed are 'up for grabs', framing plays a central role in which issues are seen as problems which are discussed, and which are taken up for action (Young, 1998: 23, 83). Frames are 'specific metaphors, symbolic representations, and cognitive cues used to render or cast behavior and events in an evaluative mode and to suggest alternative modes of action' (Zald, 1996: 262). Efforts at framing include the strategies and processes by which pro-change actors select ways to discuss an environmental problem to better diffuse knowledge, mobilize concern, and generate urgency and thereby prompt relevant international actors to consider it a problem, discuss it, and act to address it (Stone, 1989: 281–2). 'Brute facts' constrain how a problem can be defined and possible solutions, scientists, NGOs, and governments can wield considerable influence within those constraints (Litfin, 1994: 9). Problems can be framed as regional or global, as a symmetric Tragedy of the Commons (with all parties both victims and perpetrators) or as asymmetric externalities (with some parties the victims, others the perpetrators), as stand-alone problems or ecosystemic ones, or as warranting little regulation or complete bans. Which of various proposed framings comes to dominate the debate, in turn, influences whether the problem garners attention, how the problem is defined, and whether, when, and which responses get considered. Thus, chloride pollution was 'persistently ... framed as an individual issue, not as an integral part of Rhine pollution' both to ensure that complex and contentious negotiations on other pollutants did not prevent easy-to-achieve progress on chlorides and to avoid the financial transfers considered for chlorides becoming the precedents for other pollutants (Bernauer, 1996: 206, 219–20). Likewise, negotiators framed solutions to chloride pollution in 'Coasian' terms – with downstream victims paying upstream polluters to reduce their pollution – rather than in more adversarial 'polluter pays' or 'legal liability' terms that would have delayed or altogether precluded successful negotiations (Bernauer, 1996: 203–5).

Framing involves efforts to define a problem, its causes, and its potential solutions in ways that are calculated to gain support for the position of the actor doing the framing. Efforts at framing are contested precisely because they 'assign responsibility' and so point to which actors must change their behavior and incur corresponding costs (Stone, 1989: 283). Framing by groups pressing for action often mobilizes alternative framings from other stakeholders with 'information beget[ting] counterinformation' (Litfin, 1994: 8, 13; Stokke, 1997: 135; Young, 1998: 64). The 'discourse' surrounding an issue (the way it is discussed) emerges and changes as a result of the dynamic political struggle between such stakeholders, with the relevant actors evaluating competing frames and selecting all or parts of some while rejecting others. Indeed, all stakeholders have interests in and cannot be prevented from entering their preferred framing into this competition. Powerful states or weak states; NGOs, corporations, and other non-state actors; and even individuals can put forth compelling ideas. Many view Rachel Carson's *Silent Spring* as having launched the environmental movement in the United States by re-framing environmental degradation as the result of human pollution rather than natural processes (Stone, 1989: 290). The Brundtland Report's notion of 'sustainable development' reframed environmental problems as incapable of being resolved independent of considerations of economic development. The process of frame contestation is evident in the debate over which states are (and will be) responsible for climate change and, by implication, who should pay the costs of addressing it. That debate involves a competition between those who seek to make industrialized states responsible by discussing greenhouse gas emissions in terms of historical contributions, per capita emissions, and survival *vs* luxury emissions and those who seek to have developing states also considered responsible by discussing emissions in terms of future contributions and national aggregate emissions (Biermann, 2006b: 96).

Persuasion and argument play important roles in this process, a process which 'exhibits a life of its own that is hard to control through the exercise of power in the material sense' (Young, 1998: 189). Particular framings tend to succeed and 'become the dominant belief and guiding assumption for policy-makers – if the proponents have visibility, access to media, and prominent positions; if the theory accords with widespread and deeply held cultural values; if it somehow captures or responds to a "national mood"; and if its implicit prescription entails no radical redistribution of power or wealth' (Stone, 1989: 294). Whether a framing becomes the dominant way that people, and particularly relevant actors, discuss and perceive an environmental problem depends on how much it resonates not only with their interests but also with existing cognitive, normative, and discursive contexts.

The cognitive or scientific context matters for the framing of an issue and its acceptance on the international agenda because most environmental problems will necessarily involve claims about cause-and-effect relationships. Issues are difficult to get on an agenda without 'supportive consensual knowledge' about a problem, its causes, and its potential solutions that meets accepted standards of scientific credibility (Livingston, 1992: 325). Large uncertainties – about the existence and significance of environmental changes, about the responsible human activities, and about potential solutions – will work against those framings that urge immediate action. As such uncertainty begins to resolve, framings by pro-change groups that encourage discussion of the issue, and eventual action on it, may gain traction. Indeed, even groups seeking to ban the killing of particular species, such as whales, on moral grounds often include questions regarding scientific certainty in their framings of that issue (Mitchell, 1998a).

Existing normative and discursive contexts also influence whether and how an issue is discussed on the international agenda. Leaders and advocates can increase the chances of getting an issue on that agenda by linking the new problem to 'preexisting moral standards' and making it 'resonate' with perceptions and actions taken on other problems (Carpenter, 2007: 103–4; see also Florini, 1996). Thus, the increasing use of a precautionary discourse on international environmental problems has helped to move specific problems onto the international agenda and toward policy action more quickly than traditional discourses that require scientific certainty before taking action (Litfin, 1994: 10). Because international action generally involves the development of international law, those seeking to promote action also must ensure their framings mesh with the existing legal 'rules of the game' (Jasanoff, 1990, 1995). States more readily engage new environmental issues when these are framed to follow existing legal precedents. CITES created three appendices to allow for the regulation of endangered species, threatened species, and those of concern to individual governments, a precedent that made it easier to raise the plight of individual species and subpopulations within CITES as well as within other international contexts.

During issue emergence, the contestation over framing focuses considerably on whether the problem is anthropogenic or natural and whether environmental damages are a necessary or acceptable price to pay for the economic or other benefits of the responsible activity. Thus, those seeking to get an issue on the international agenda highlight evidence that the observed changes are human-caused and that substitute activities can be cheaply and easily adopted (Birkland, 1998: 67–8). In 1998, the Media Research Center, an American pro-status quo group, fought against efforts to keep climate change on the international agenda by arguing that 'there is no convincing scientific evidence' of catastrophic global warming, that such warming as was occurring was economically beneficial, and that remedial actions would be costly, ineffective, and harmful to American security and economic interests (Media Research Center, 1998). International organizations can play a powerful role in how problems and their solutions are framed. Thus, the IMO frequently used the urgency generated by the catalytic events of major oil spills to focus regulatory attention on the more common and widespread problem of intentional operational discharges (Mitchell, 1994a).

Issues tend to move onto, and up, the international agenda to the extent that actors can generate a coalition of support for a single frame, either by offering frames that reflect 'matters of interest to different players' or by articulating 'a coherent vision' and then selling that vision to others (Young, 1998: 53). In both modes, pro-change actors make conceptual linkages between the environmental problem and other issues in an effort to convince those actors who initially resist calls for action (Young, 1998: 64). The 'sustainable development' frame linked industrialized states' desires for environmental protection with developing states' desires for economic development to convince both sets of states to address both sets of issues. Framings often succeed by forging alliances among different victims of a problem (Stone, 1989: 295). Those concerned about a particular environmental impact of a behavior may highlight evidence of other environmental impacts. Alternatively, 'Baptist/bootlegger coalitions' can form when environmentally-concerned actors highlight the economic benefits of international action, as was evident when environmental advocates framed dolphin protection in ways that coincided with the American tuna industry's interest in protectionism (DeSombre, 1995). Debt-for-nature swaps also illustrate how one individual can offer a new framing that builds on the existing interests of relevant actors and succeeds at mobilizing action, notably action that was international but not intergovernmental. In a 1984 *New York Times* editorial, Thomas Lovejoy proposed that NGOs seeking habitat protection should purchase the bad debt of those defaulting governments who were seeking to regain access to international credit markets from banks interested in recouping their potential losses in exchange for those governments protecting certain endangered habitats (Lovejoy, 1984). By 2007, over 40 debt-for-nature swaps had 'generated more than an estimated $117 million in local currency for conservation projects', a transfer of wealth that would have been unlikely had Lovejoy not successfully framed the issue in ways that met the interests of different actors simultaneously (Sheikh, 2007: 3–4). Thus, framing involves 'interactions between interests and ideas' in which ideas suggest 'new ways to pursue familiar interests' (Young, 1998: 82).

## The Actors Involved

Much, though not all, of the development of knowledge, concern, and urgency about certain environmental impacts reflects conscious efforts to influence the international agenda. As already alluded to, 'pro-status quo' groups support existing policies and are content with the existing international agenda while 'pro-change' groups look at current policy negatively and seek to get new issues onto that agenda (Birkland, 1998: 62). Issues then emerge in response to the competition between these groups over the scarce resource of governments' attention (Wood and Peake, 1998: 174).

States dominate what is on the international agenda if only because the collective agendas of governments are 'where the agenda is' (Livingston, 1992: 315). But states also can actively seek to influence the international agenda (Davies, 1974: 164). Certain states (such as Sweden and Norway) view themselves, and are viewed, as environmental leaders generally while others choose to champion particular environmental problems, either because they are victims of the problem or because they face domestic pressures for action. International organizations, as noted above, can also play key roles in moving particular problems onto the international agenda.

Scientists can foster issue emergence both by increasing knowledge about an environmental problem among relevant actors and by signaling how concerned those actors should be, how much urgency they should feel, and what actions they should take. Scientists – as individuals and as members of epistemic communities – can 'provide complex technical information that is indispensable for policy-making on issues marked by both analytic and normative uncertainty' (Hisschemöller et al., 2001 cited in Biermann, 2006a: 244). They clarify the magnitude, type, geographic and temporal scope, and future trends in environmental problems that other actors cannot credibly provide. The societal tendency to make science 'the arbiter of empirical questions' (Stone, 1989: 294) leads policy-makers to grant those scientists with relevant scientific expertise considerable power over what is allowed on, and what is kept off, the international agenda (Haas, 1989, 1992b).

Unlike governments that must balance competing policy concerns, environmental NGOs and transnational networks of such organizations can focus exclusively on environmental issues. This makes them more likely to become aware of environmental changes, to be concerned about them, and to support placing them on the international agenda (Betsill, 2006: 182). The success of NGOs or transnational networks in placing issues on the international agenda depends on 'their perceived legitimacy' or 'their claim to represent civil society' as a means 'to *persuade* states to adopt particular policies and practices' (Betsill, 2006: 182).

By contrast, the influence of multinational corporations (MNCs) and business interests on the international agenda derives from their direct economic power and the 'tacit power' they gain as sources 'of economic growth and the production of energy' (Newell,

2000: 159; see also Chatterjee and Finger, 1994). Business interests often benefit from existing patterns of regulation (or non-
regulation) and therefore often oppose placing those environmental problems on the international agenda that seem likely to lead to
costly regulatory changes. However, the competitive disadvantage
of one state's unilateral regulation, the patchwork quilts of different
states' regulations, the opportunities in new 'green' markets, and
some corporate philosophies can create incentives that lead some
corporations and corporate networks to support and even initiate
efforts for international action on environmental problems (Betsill,
2006: 176–7).

Individuals, as 'policy entrepreneurs' who champion specific environmental problems, help issues to emerge on the international stage
(Carpenter, 2007: 104). Presidents and prime ministers as well as the
heads of international organizations that make personal commitments to an issue can combine their position and persuasive powers
in ways that lead others, at a minimum, to discuss an issue and, at a
maximum, to take that issue seriously. Although climate change was
on the international policy agenda long before former American Vice
President Albert Gore drew attention to it, his efforts in 2006 and
2007 clearly heightened the perceived concern and urgency regarding the problem. James Hansen, a climate expert working for the US
government, also brought considerable attention to the climate
change issue through statements made to Congress back in 1988.

Finally, the media serve both as communicators of knowledge and
as promoters of concern about environmental problems. 'What the
television news covers influences what citizens think is important
and how they evaluate their leaders' (Wood and Peake, 1998: 175).
The media report on but also mediate catalytic events, with 'news-
worthiness' determining whether an environmental accident or
scientific report is headlined, backpaged, or ignored and how the
problem is framed. Certain focusing events are, or can be made,
'symbolically rich' with 'easily understood and vivid images'
(Birkland, 1998: 68). Thus, dramatic decreases in stratospheric
ozone became the 'ozone hole' in the media. The media can also
serve as a conduit by which pro-change activists can convince policy-
makers, directly or through the public, to take up an issue (Betsill, 2006:
182). The media can influence the international agenda by whether, and
how, they cover catalytic events (Birkland, 1998: 56). They can also
hinder promote or hinder pro-change. Attention to non-environmental
issues (such as the events of 9/11/2001) and to particular types of
environmental issues (such as whales, polar bears, and other
'charismatic megafauna'), the value of 'news' over the repetitive
reporting of a long-standing problem, and the biases introduced by

giving equal attention to 'both sides' in unequal scientific debates can all inhibit the emergence of environmental issues on the international agenda (Boykoff and Boykoff, 2004: 125).

# Variation in the Nature of the Problem

To claim that social processes designed to increase knowledge, concern, and urgency explain why environmental impacts become problems and then discussion items and then action items is not to imply that all environmental impacts have an equal chance of doing so. The inherent characteristics of two problems cannot, by themselves, explain why one emerges on the international agenda and the other does not (Carpenter, 2007: 103). However, those characteristics can facilitate or hinder efforts to develop knowledge, concern, and urgency around that problem. Human perceptions, understandings, and framings of a problem are central to whether an issue is addressed. This section examines how those subjective perceptions, understandings, and framings are constrained by certain relatively objective characteristics of an environmentally-harmful behavior's impacts, causes, and solutions.

## Types of impacts

The features of anthropogenic environmental impacts and their causes make some more likely to emerge on the international agenda than others because they influence the changes that people know and care about regarding those impacts. Although perceptions of impacts matter, it is the facts, at least to some degree, that shape perceptions about a given impact and constrain the degree to which other actors can alter and frame those perceptions.

The perpetrator-victim relationships of some environmentally-harmful behaviors constrain which actors become aware of environmental impacts and the behaviors causing them and which actors have incentives to act on that knowledge. Perpetrators know what behaviors they engage in and at what levels. Victims may or may not know about those behaviors or their environmental impacts, either because the behaviors and impacts are hard to observe or because the impacts are hard to link to the behaviors. But when perpetrators are also victims of their own collective behavior, they then have incentives to track the known – and investigate the suspected – impacts of their behaviors. Thus, in most Tragedy of the Commons situations, some perpetrators of a problem experience sufficient costs as victims of the problem to seek international discussion of the issue.

By contrast, in upstream/downstream situations, perpetrators and victims are distinct, non-overlapping, groups. Having access to clean water and clean air is often a negligible concern to companies that discharge large quantities of pollutants into rivers and lakes or the atmosphere. Ocean transporters of oil, chemicals, and hazardous waste value the ocean as a medium for transportation, a value that is uninfluenced by pollution levels. In such cases, potentially-concerned victims often lack information about environmental impacts or the behaviors causing them. The perpetrators who have information about their behaviors and may know the actual or suspected impacts of those behaviors may be unconcerned about those impacts and, if eliminating those impacts is costly, have incentives to prevent such problems from coming to light. In such cases, issue emergence will be delayed until its victims, or the individuals who share their concerns, uncover both the perpetrators' behaviors and their impacts.

Environmental problems also emerge on the international agenda more readily when environmental impacts and their anthropogenic causes are visible, immediate, and clear, when they patently answer the questions of 'what happened and why'. With environmental impacts that are difficult to observe, that are distant in time or space from their causes, and that arise through mechanisms or in contexts in which their anthropogenic causes are ambiguous or indirect, there will be more uncertainty among scientists, the lay public, and policymakers about whether an observed environmental change is occurring and whether it stems from human (anthropogenic) actions or natural variation. An oil spill's environmental impacts do not require the insights of scientists for us to understand: spilled oil floats, coats feathers and fur, and causes birds, seals, otters, and other animals to die. By contrast, the impact of fossil fuel consumption on sea–level rise (leaving aside other impacts) does require scientific insight to understand: burning fossil fuels increases atmospheric heat retention which increases the average global temperature which, over decades, leads to the warming and expansion of ocean water as well as increased ice cap melting, which leads to higher sea levels. Many (though not all) oil spill impacts are directly visible whereas average global temperatures and average sea levels involve cognitive constructs (global averages) that must be mediated through measurements and statistics. The impacts of oil spills are immediate (and can be measured in days) whereas those of fossil fuel use occur decades after such use. Finally, there are fewer alternatives to the oil spill as the cause of the death of oil-soaked seabirds and seals than to fossil fuel use as the cause of warming temperatures and sea-level rise.

Whether known environmental impacts are perceived as needing urgent attention depends, in turn, on perceptions regarding the salience, acceptability, and availability of the risks. Environmental harms tend to appear on the international scene when the salience of a 'local or geographically delimited' problem is linked with 'larger, more generic concerns' (Young, 1998: 53). Impacts that are strictly local 'do not warrant serious consideration at the international level ... but broader issues that cannot be linked to or represented in terms of more specific concerns are unlikely to achieve sufficient focus to show up as action items on the international political agenda' (Young, 1998: 57). Events like major oil spills or the travels of the *Khian Sea* waste barge capture international attention because they draw attention to the immediate and local problems generated by more widespread and common patterns of behavior. People also view certain risks as more acceptable than others based on criteria other than the likelihood of their occurrence and the magnitude of their impacts. Thus, environmental impacts become more threatening when they are new, irreversible, uncontrollable, have known and immediate impacts, and receive heavy media attention and are more readily tolerated and accepted otherwise (Kuran and Sunstein, 1999: 709).

Environmental impacts also vary in how amenable they are to 'availability heuristics'. People's assessments of how likely something is to occur depend less on the frequency with which it occurs than with 'the ease with which we can think of relevant examples' (Kuran and Sunstein, 1999: 685). 'If people can easily think of such examples, they are far more likely to be frightened' (Sunstein, 2006: 198). Pro-change groups seeking to increase concern about, and the urgency of addressing, a problem will try to increase the availability of information about a problem to boost its perceived magnitude and decrease its acceptability (Kuran and Sunstein, 1999: 712). Some environmentally-harmful behaviors 'are prone to sudden, dramatic events' that are 'newsworthy' and that capture the attention of relevant actors and the public (Birkland, 1998: 61). Catalytic events can transform obscure, causally-attenuated, distant, and 'technical and probabilistic' harms into 'obvious, and visible' harms (Birkland, 1998: 55, 70). Thus, nuclear pollution and marine and river pollution are arenas in which environmental impacts sometimes result from accidents whereas most behaviors that contribute to climate change or to acid rain involve steady and ongoing emissions. To be sure, environmental impacts in which accidents play little or no part still frequently make it onto the international agenda. But those issues might make it onto that agenda sooner if major accidents highlighted the problem and made action seem more urgent. When major impacts of behaviors, like those causing climate change, are gradual or unlikely to be experienced in the near future, those impacts will tend not to be 'cognitively available' to people who, therefore, 'will not "see" those harms until it is too late' (Sunstein, 2006: 200).

The costs of reducing environmental risks, and hence the likelihood of calls for international action, also vary in their 'availability' and vary over time and across countries. Even if people are aware of environmental risks, 'if the costs of reducing the risk are also "on screen", and if they seem high, then people will not be so enthusiastic about extensive precautions' (Sunstein, 2006: 200). Levels of concern also are influenced by the types of costs involved (Cobb and Elder, 1972). Some environmental impacts have direct and immediate economic costs, others have clear impacts on human health that are less readily translated into economic costs, and yet others have impacts on important but not readily monetizable human values. An upstream country's pollution of a river can increase the costs for downstream countries of providing clean drinking and agricultural water, can decrease the health of those citizens that bathe or fish in the river, and can threaten aquatic species living in the river. Discharges of pollutants that have only the last of these impacts, however, are less likely to emerge on the international agenda than those which have only the first of them.

## Magnitude and scope of impacts

Although behaviors with larger impacts are not always addressed before those with smaller impacts, the magnitudes of environmental impacts do influence levels of concern and urgency. As the IPAT identity clarifies (see Chapter 3), a behavior's environmental impacts can vary because of how often (and how many) people engage in it or because of its 'impact intensity', defined as the environmental damage per unit of the activity. Many behaviors have a range of environmental impacts, some large and some small. Certain pollutants have major and immediate effects on some species but smaller and more delayed effects on others. Equally important, the magnitude of both previously observed impacts and of predicted future impacts influences levels of concern and urgency. With climate change in particular, scientists increasingly have identified potential future non-linearities in which small increases in – or the continuation of – existing levels of an activity may generate disproportionate increases in environmental impacts, such as the collapse of the ocean currents responsible for our current patterns of regional climatic conditions.

If impact magnitude matters, so too does geography. The greater the geographic scope of impacts, the more likely it is that those impacts will be observed and that a larger set of actors will be affected by and concerned about those impacts. Geographic location as well as scope matters. Impacts that occur in remote locations may go unrecognized for some time. Thus, we remain more ignorant about whether (and which) human activities damage the deep ocean than about whether (and which) damage lakes and rivers. 'Where' also matters with respect to whether the environmental impacts are of concern. As a result, the location of oil spills has tended to influence when oil pollution emerges on the international agenda more than the size of those spills. Very few people would recognize the names *Atlantic Empress*, *ABT Summer*, and *Castillo de Bellver* as the tankers responsible for the three largest oil spills in history because they all occurred off the coasts of African countries and generated little international attention. By contrast, smaller spills off France (the *Amoco Cadiz*), the United Kingdom (the *Torrey Canyon*), and the United States (the *Exxon Valdez*) received significant attention and promptly led to international action.

Finally, temporal scope matters. Temporal scope refers to both how long environmental impacts last and how long they are visible. These characteristics influence how likely it is that impacts will be observed and how concerned people will be about those impacts. Environmentally-harmful behaviors which leave only relatively short-lived evidence (for example, releases of chlorine gas or marine chemical spills), are more difficult for people other than those responsible to observe, and those who are responsible may have few incentives to report such events. Behaviors that have long-lived environmental effects are easier to link to those effects and are more likely to evoke greater concern than comparable behaviors that have relatively short-lived effects.

## Behavioral causes

If 'brute facts' about impacts influence knowledge and concern, so also do 'brute facts' about the behaviors causing those impacts. Levels of concern are influenced by the degree of conflict between environmental and other values and the extent to which impacts are considered intentional and avoidable (Kuran and Sunstein, 1999: 709). At one extreme, humans sometimes self-consciously modify the environment in pursuit of other goals. Humans build cities and dams, introduce alien species, remove predatory animals, eradicate mosquitoes, and drain wetlands. Closely related are activities with inherent and recognized environmental consequences that, historically, have been considered acceptable. Fishing and hunting, the conversion of land to agriculture use, and similar activities have goals that cannot, for a given level of activity, be accomplished with less environmental harm. Such activities present stark conflicts between environmental protection and other human values, conflicts that often involve treating their impacts as acceptable costs of the pursuit of other social or economic goals. By contrast, the environmental impacts of other activities are unintentional and avoidable, with those impacts arising either from a lack of knowledge or concern or a lack of alternatives considered viable. Pollution often arises as an unintended, even if recognized, by-product of activities engaged in for other reasons. Those responsible for air, water, or marine pollution are often amenable to adopting less polluting alternatives so long as they can still achieve their economic (or other) goals. Not surprisingly, environmental protection that requires foregoing other human values tends to evoke more resistance than that which does not.

The environmental impacts of new activities also tend to evoke more concern than those of long-standing or recurring activities (Cobb and Elder, 1972: chapters 6 and 7; Davies, 1974: 153; Kuran and Sunstein, 1999: 709). The environmental impacts of new activities are unknown – and known to be unknown – whereas the environmental impacts of long-standing activities are, or are assumed to be, both known and acceptable given the perceived benefits of those activities. Concern about the environmental impacts of activities previously considered acceptable is lower, and harder to generate, than that surrounding the impacts from new activities, even if the latter are fewer or less serious (Davies, 1974: 153).

## Availability of viable solutions

Finally, the availability of viable solutions influences levels of concern and hence the pressures to discuss and address a problem internationally. 'Difficult conditions become problems only when people come to see them as amenable to human action' (Stone, 1989: 281). Pro-change groups can generate more support for international discussion and action and will face less resistance when solutions are available and cheap than when they are not. That said, such problems often show up as discussion items during a 'known problem, unknown solutions' stage, precisely because of the value of international cooperation in pooling and focusing research and development efforts to identify solutions. If relevant international actors acknowledge an environmental impact as a problem, they may take up that problem when research is thought likely to generate viable solutions.

Indeed, a lack of capacity – rather than a lack of concern – may best explain why industrialized states tend to take up more environmental issues sooner than developing states. Environmental issues are not absent in the bilateral and regional cooperation among Latin American, African, and Asian states but they have tended to appear less frequently and later than in corresponding efforts among European states. This does not appear to reflect less concern – as argued by proponents of the environmental Kuznets curve hypothesis (Grossman and Krueger, 1995) – since survey evidence suggests that the citizens of developing and industrialized countries are equally concerned about environmental degradation (Inglehart et al., 2002; Leiserowitz et al., 2006). Regional variation in the degree of engagement with environmental issues may reflect less a lack of concern than constraints on the capacity to address them.

## Conditions for Issue Emergence

As suggested throughout the foregoing discussion, contextual conditions influence issue emergence. Although efforts to champion ozone protection by the US government (and individuals within it) helped move beyond discussion to action in the form of the 1985 Vienna Convention and the targets and timetables of the 1987 Montreal Protocol, that shift also reflected the influence of UNEP which held 'an almost continuous series of international meetings on the topic; a scientific consensus ... [that] enabled advocates to launch vigorous warnings from an authoritative, shared knowledge;' and shifts in the views of key companies engaged in CFC production (Livingston, 1992: 316; Haas, 1992a; Parson, 2003). The political, institutional, and normative climate can influence when and whether environmental issues emerge internationally.

Political and economic contexts can either foster or inhibit an environmental problem of concern to a few from becoming an international environmental agenda item of concern to many (Young, 1998: 83). Although efforts to preserve wildlife entered the international scene in the late 1800s (Giordano, 2002a), environmental concern has become increasingly intense and widespread, especially since the 1960s. Increased environmental awareness and the rise of 'post-material values' in many states have expanded the number, type, geographic scope, and time horizon of environmental problems being addressed (Inglehart, 1995; Meyer et al., 1997). These environmental trends, coupled with trends in economic, cultural, and informational interdependence and in views regarding the appropriate role of government, have made environmental issues more central to the international agenda (Davies, 1974: 155). Trade liberalization, the 1987 Brundtland report, the Gorbachev-era shifts in Soviet foreign policy, the end of the Cold War, and the events of 11 September 2001 have all created conditions and 'opportunity structures' that influence how willing relevant actors are to add environmental issues to their agendas (Young, 1998: 21, 58–9).

At times, governments place environmental issues on the international agenda as attractive and relatively uncontroversial ways to initiate cooperation with previously-hostile states (Young, 1998: 170). Cooperation on environmental issues avoids the spillover effects of economic cooperation, the high risks of security cooperation, and the ideological obstacles to human rights cooperation. Thus, in the 1970s, the Soviet Union and the United States consciously turned to European air pollution as a low risk means of promoting détente (Levy, 1993).

The influence of structural power is evident in how the environmental concerns of powerful states dominate the international environmental agenda while those of less powerful states receive far less attention. Even environmental problems with readily-available solutions often remain unaddressed if their costs, however great, are borne by developing countries. A lack of fresh water, the indoor air pollution created by cooking fires, and pollution-related illnesses kill millions of people annually in the developing world but remain unaddressed while international policy focuses on ozone depletion, wildlife protection, and other issues that pose smaller and more distant risks. Environmental problems tend to garner international attention only when people in powerful, 'agenda-setting' states become concerned about them.

Institutional climate and context also matter. States engage environmental problems internationally more quickly when an appropriate institutional forum exists for doing so. Environmental problems related to Antarctica are readily raised within the Antarctic treaty system. Ship-related marine pollution problems are readily raised in the IMO's Marine Environment Protection Committee or one of UNEP's Regional Seas programs. European air pollution problems are readily raised at LRTAP meetings. Existing institutions provide agendas on which issues can emerge, whereas problems that are sufficiently 'new' or different from earlier problems may well require the creation of new institutions. Such new institutions may prove attractive if existing ones are unreceptive to discussing or acting on an environmental problem, as evident in the unwillingness of most deforestation advocates to work within the International Tropical Timber Organization. But existing institutions usually lower the obstacles to the international discussion of an issue and can 'use focusing events to dramatize the need for improved policy' (Birkland, 1998: 67).

The normative climate surrounding environmental issues also influences how readily they arise – or at least how they must be framed to arise – on the international agenda (Cass, 2007). International actors are more receptive to engaging environmental problems today than 100 or even 50 years ago, simply because the view that 'humans should dominate nature' has been replaced by one that favors 'a more equal relationship' (Leiserowitz et al., 2006: 421). The Brundtland report on sustainable development both reflected and strengthened the norm that economic growth should be consistent with environmental protection, thereby creating a normative context in which the World Bank, International Monetary Fund, World Trade Organization, and the North American Free Trade Agreement accepted environmental concerns as appropriate agenda items (World Commission on Environment and Development, 1987). Similarly, efforts to preserve habitats rather than individual species reflect not only a scientific recognition of the relationship between ecosystem and species preservation but also a normative shift in which habitats, per se, deserve our attention and protection.

## Conclusion

The international policy agenda is neither a systematic ranking of global environmental risks nor a list of problems whose resolution provides large benefits and entails few costs. What issues emerge internationally depends on the success of usually self-conscious efforts by various actors to generate and diffuse knowledge, mobilize concern, and to frame the environmental problem in ways that make relevant international actors likely to recognize the problem, to take it up for discussion, and to begin taking action to address it. The magnitude of environmental harms certainly matters, but so do the types of environmental impacts involved, the scope of those impacts, their behavioral causes, and the availability of solutions. How receptive international actors are to engaging problems depends on the relative effectiveness of the pro-change actors seeking engagement and the pro-status quo actors opposing engagement. However, their receptiveness also depends on subtle and deep biases in the political, economic, scientific, institutional, and normative context. Which environmental issues appear on the international agenda, which do not, and how issues are prioritized for discussion or action reflects not only the interests of states in addressing these problems but also the influence of multiple groups, the characteristics of the problem involved, the background context, and the influence of catalytic events.

# 5

# NEGOTIATING SOLUTIONS TO INTERNATIONAL ENVIRONMENTAL PROBLEMS

A consensus about the existence, causes, and importance of an environmental problem does not always produce a consensus among states on whether, let alone what, international action to take. Even after an environmental change becomes a topic for international discussion, highly concerned states may fail to prompt international action. This chapter focuses on the background conditions, negotiation processes, and institutional provisions that facilitate or hinder intergovernmental regime formation. It addresses two questions central to the study of international environmental politics: regime formation and regime design (see Young and Osherenko, 1993c: vii). With respect to regime or institutional formation, when are states likely to succeed in negotiating solutions to identified problems? Why do states reach agreement on addressing some international environmental problems but not others (Hasenclever et al., 1997: 1)? Why do states address some problems promptly but others only after decades of discussion? Why have states negotiated numerous protocols and amendments to some agreements but left others unchanged? With respect to regime design, why do some agreements have more specific and stringent provisions than others? Why do some carefully monitor and sanction violations, others seek to facilitate compliance, and yet others pay little attention to compliance?

## Definitions

Scholars have engaged such questions in terms of both regimes and institutions (Krasner, 1983; Keohane, 1988; Taylor and Groom, 1988), examining both their formation and their design (Young and Osherenko, 1993a; Koremenos et al., 2004). To clarify these questions, this chapter focuses on that subset of international regimes and institutions comprised of formal intergovernmental agreements – international environmental agreements (IEAs). Countries some-times cooperate through informal or tacit understandings without formalizing their understandings. And when states choose to coop-erate through formal legal agreements, those agreements may not shape the expectations and social practices considered to define international regimes and institutions (on the regime/institution distinction, see, for example, Lipson, 1991; Keohane, 1993: 28; Hasenclever et al., 1997: 19–20). And, even when legal agreements shape expectations, they may not significantly alter behavior (Keohane, 1993: 28; Hasenclever et al., 1997: 9–10). Yet, consid-erable evidence exists that negotiations that eventually produce treaties, conventions, and other agreements are the likely and 'nor-mal' outcome of intergovernmental efforts to resolve international environmental problems (Young and Osherenko, 1993a: 225). I use 'regime' and 'institution' interchangeably in this chapter and adopt Keohane's definition of international agreements as 'institutions with explicit rules, agreed upon by governments, that pertain to particular sets of issues in international relations' (Keohane, 1989: 4). There are, of course, many alternative mechanisms by which governments, nongovernmental organizations (NGOs), and multinational corpora-tions (MNCs) address international environmental problems.

Following the prior chapter's structure for discussing issue emer-gence, this chapter categorizes the influences on intergovernmental environmental negotiations as including relatively passive 'back-ground conditions' that, even if not necessary, make it possible or likely that states advocating action will succeed as well as more active 'proximate determinants' that more often appear as direct and immediate influences on the formation and design of intergovern-mental agreements.

## Background Conditions that Support International Action

Many factors create background conditions that foster interna-tional environmental negotiations. Some factors relate directly to the environmental problem at hand while others are exogenous fac-tors that, although unrelated, facilitate or inhibit international efforts to cooperate on that problem. The former category includes the type and number of actors relevant to addressing the problem, those actors' interests and motivations, the distribution of power among them, and the availability of an appropriate institutional forum. The latter cate-gory includes broader interdependencies among states and long-term policy trends.

## Relevant actors

To understand success in negotiating IEAs for some environmental problems but not others, start by considering which, and how many, actors are relevant to resolving a problem. Although victims and perpetrators dominate the issue emergence stage (see Chapter 4), negotiations often expand the pool of relevant actors to include a third group, potential contributors.

As discussed previously, victims are defined as those that perceive it as costly to leave a problem unaddressed or as beneficial to address it. States materially harmed by environmental degradation are, to be sure, more likely to consider themselves victims than those that are not. Yet, some states that *are* materially affected may not view those effects as negative – or as sufficiently negative to require their resolution. Both political rhetoric and scholarly analyses identify most problems as Tragedies of the Commons, implying that all states are victims and would benefit from the problem's resolution. Yet often this is not the case. Thus, concerns about deforestation are not shared by some governments that view logging as an engine for economic growth rather than an environmental problem. And, states that are *not* materially affected by some environmental degradation may nonetheless perceive themselves as victims. Many non-whaling, and even non-ocean-bordering, states are active members of the International Convention for the Regulation of Whaling (ICRW). Negotiations commence only after at least some states perceive themselves as victims and international action as warranted.

Perpetrators are those whose actions – or inactions – contribute to causing an international environmental problem. Some problems involve few actors whose actions unambiguously cause a problem, for example, nuclear weapons testing or nuclear weapons waste disposal. Some involve many actors whose actions can be clearly identified as causing the problem, including many types of marine, atmospheric, or freshwater pollution. Some impacts can be attributed to specific states' or individuals' actions, such as oil or chemical spills and other accidents, while others are the aggregate result of individual actions, such as overfishing or climate change. In these latter cases, causal responsibility can be shared relatively equally among states or can be dominated by a few states. And which states are considered responsible reflects competing efforts at framing designed to blame certain actors and not others (Stone, 1989).

Efforts to resolve a problem may involve identifying potential contributors who are neither perpetrators nor victims. Resolving environmental problems does not always require restricting the activities that cause it. Environmentally-harmful activities can continue or even increase if technological or behavioral strategies for offsetting impacts can be developed. Such strategies may engage actors who are not responsible for the problem but see attractive economic opportunities in resolving it. 'Green technology' companies recognize that international regulation can create new markets and stimulate existing ones. Thus, climate change negotiations have bolstered various efforts to develop solar and wind energy as well as hybrid vehicles, have revived the prospects for nuclear energy, and have fostered research into carbon sequestration technologies. Resolving some environmental problems can generate non-environmental benefits, as when the international protection of reefs, wetlands, or forests promotes eco-tourism. And, actors may self-consciously devise linkages between environmental progress and economic benefits, as in debt-for-nature swaps. In all these cases, actors who are neither perpetrators nor victims may have incentives that make them willing to contribute to resolving a problem.

For any problem, the number of victims, perpetrators and potential contributors who must be engaged affects the ease of negotiating international agreements. International negotiations depend on concerned states and non-state actors convincing other states to perceive themselves as victims and crafting an agreement that can induce enough, even if not all, perpetrators and/or potential contributors to take enough action that an agreement is worth having. The number of actors who must be engaged to address a problem to the satisfaction of concerned states influences the ease with which a problem can be resolved (Koremenos et al., 2001). Generally, the more countries that must be 'at the table', the more difficult and time-consuming it will be to reach agreement, since more interests must be integrated into that agreement's terms (Young and Osherenko, 1993b: 12; Koremenos et al., 2001). That said, regional agreements with 30 to 40 governments and global agreements with over 100 countries are not uncommon and bilateral negotiations sometimes fail to produce an agreement (Young and Osherenko, 1993b: 12).

## Interests and motivation

States' interests are major influences on regime formation and design. Scholars have proposed various typologies of interest configurations and conflict types to explain the chances for success of international negotiations (Young, 1998, 1999a; Miles et al., 2002).

Scholars often argue that negotiations succeed only if the relevant states 'share common interests which they can realize only through cooperation' (Hasenclever et al., 1997: 30). Such a view obscures, however, that 'common interests' are not necessarily an inherent and fixed trait of a problem but, as often, reflect the efforts of concerned states and other actors to convince states to become concerned or to alter their behavior even if they remain indifferent to the problem. To be sure, when environmental problems reflect Tragedy of the Commons situations or arise from incapacity, concerned states accept the environmental problem and the need for action. But even in many Tragedy of the Commons cases, some states reject the view of concerned states that a problem requires action. States can more easily – and hence are more likely to – resolve Tragedy of the Commons cases than upstream/downstream problems if only because, in the latter case, the perpetrators of a problem can reject the notion that a problem exists. Thus, consider two countries that pollute and take water from both a transborder lake and a transborder river. Although both countries have incentives to negotiate to reduce lake pollution, the upstream state has no incentive to negotiate to reduce river pollution (Hasenclever et al., 1997: 53).

A necessary condition for successful environmental negotiation is one state having sufficient concern that it seeks to cooperate with others to address it. If no state views – or is convinced by non-state actors to view – environmental degradation from some human activity as warranting resolution, then international negotiations will not commence. Although only one concerned state is needed, IEA formation becomes more likely as the fraction of relevant actors increases. Before negotiations can begin, various state and non-state actors must try to generate concern among initially indifferent states. This can involve scientific or interest-based arguments that clarify the effects and implications of the environmental problem, as exemplified by the Intergovernmental Panel on Climate Change (IPCC) reports or in early LRTAP scientific efforts (see Levy, 1993). But it can also involve value-based arguments, as was evident in the success of concerned governments and NGOs in garnering support for the adoption and continuation of a commercial whaling moratorium within the ICRW based on the notion that whaling is no longer an 'appropriate' form of the exploitation of natural resources. Regardless of the process involved, increasing the number of states that view themselves as 'victims' increases the likelihood that an IEA will form.

The magnitude of international concern, rather than the number of concerned states, may better predict the prospects for IEA formation. The notion of 'magnitude' captures the idea that what matters is the number of concerned states as well as the strength of each state's concern. A few states, or even a single state, when strongly concerned about a problem may have the motivation and resources to generate concern among many other states. And even if they fail to generate sincere concern, strongly motivated states may be willing to expend resources and make linkages with other issues that induce states that remain unconcerned about an environmental problem to negotiate for instrumental reasons.

A state's level of concern depends on its view of the costs and benefits of addressing a problem compared to those of not addressing it. State positions in environmental negotiations depend on their ecological vulnerability and the abatement costs they would face under proposed rules (Sprinz and Vaahtoranta, 1994). States with high ecological vulnerability and low abatement costs will be 'pushers', leading negotiation efforts. Those with low ecological vulnerability and high abatement costs will be 'draggers' or 'laggards', resisting international efforts. States with high ecological vulnerability but high abatement costs will be 'intermediates', supporting international agreement but negotiating to minimize the costs they will bear. And states with low ecological vulnerability and low abatement costs will be 'bystanders', being indifferent to whether such an agreement is negotiated.

If such underlying incentives influence states' negotiation positions, those positions also reflect policy styles, party politics, bureaucratic structures, industrial interests, NGO influence, and transnational linkages (Schreurs, 1997; DeSombre, 2000; O'Neill, 2000). Under certain conditions, these forces can lead states to enter negotiations looking for integrative solutions and to compromise to address a problem. Indeed, negotiations appear to succeed 'only when integrative bargaining or a search for mutually beneficial solutions assumes a prominent role in the process' (Young and Osherenko, 1993b: 13). Negotiation success does not depend on a problem being a high priority for relevant states: a low priority may allow states to avoid fractious politicization by treating negotiations as 'technocratic' issues (Young and Osherenko, 1993a: 15). Nor does negotiation success depend on states acting altruistically (Young and Osherenko, 1993b: 16). The predictable self-interest-seeking negotiating positions of states do not preclude them from identifying solutions that will meet the needs of all self-interested parties.

## Power

As in most of international relations, power influences whether pushers succeed in establishing an IEA. International treaties are voluntary contracts among sovereign states. States cannot be forced to participate in negotiations or join IEAs once they are formed. They must be convinced that it is in their interests to do so. International negotiations consist of those who would benefit most from resolving a problem attempting to raise concern and to craft agreement terms so that those who can contribute most to resolving the problem will either view it as in their interests – or can be convinced by other means – to participate.

The interaction of power with interests becomes evident by considering two extreme cases. In one, a single state experiences considerable immediate and tangible costs from some form of environmental degradation. In the other, a single state that is a major source of the environmental problem would face significant costs to reduce their contribution to the problem and would benefit little from the problem's resolution. Clearly, the former would be a pusher and the latter a dragger. But to know whether an IEA is likely to form requires that we also know how much power these states have. Pusher states that are powerful – in the sense of controlling various resources capable of influencing other states – can use their resources to induce draggers to negotiate and can also design institutional provisions to make participation rewarding and non-participation costly. If pusher states lack such resources, they will have fewer ways of engaging perpetrating states. Likewise, powerful dragger states can more readily resist, delay, or simply ignore calls from less powerful states to alter their environmentally-harmful behaviors.

Structural power – as embodied in military hardware and economic prowess – surely matters in international environmental affairs. IEAs are more likely to emerge when five members of the G-8 are pushers than when five developing states are. Yet structural power provides less explanatory leverage than realists might have us believe (Zürn, 1998: 625). The general unwillingness of states to deploy military or even significant economic resources to pressure others on environmental issues means that structurally powerful pusher states usually rely on persuasion more than coercion and that structurally weaker dragger states can and will resist such pressures if doing so would be viewed as bowing to external pressure or if more powerful states fail to offer attractive incentives to forego the activities in question. Issue-specific power (a state's ability to influence outcomes if no agreement is reached and their voting and bargaining power within international environmental institutions) gives states considerable power over what gets done, when, and how. Brazil can effectively block progress to protect tropical rainforests just as Botswana, Namibia, and Zimbabwe can to protect elephants.

American opposition to the Kyoto Protocol after 2000 illustrates that IEAs can develop despite the opposition of powerful states. Yet powerful states, in particular the USA, have used their power to induce recalcitrant states to take environmental concerns seriously, influencing the timing and content – and membership – of several international environmental regimes (Young and Osherenko, 1993a: 230; DeSombre, 2000). And, while American

unilateralism drew initial international attention to the ozone protection issue, China and India later used the power of 'their growing demand for CFCs' to resist pressures to participate until
industrialized countries amended the Montreal Protocol to cover
their costs of compliance (Young and Osherenko, 1993a: 231;
Gruber, 2000).

## Science

Science has received particular attention as a force promoting
international environmental cooperation. Although expertise is
crucial to the negotiation of arms control, trade, and human rights
treaties, scientific expertise wields greater influence in environmental negotiations because of science's central role in understanding the magnitude, causes, and solutions to environmental
questions. As with the need for concern in at least one country, scientific evidence *suggesting* that humans are contributing to some
form of environmental degradation is a necessary condition for
negotiations to commence. Cooperation becomes easier 'to achieve
once a common or widely shared (though not necessarily accurate)
understanding of the problem, its causes, and its solutions arises'
(Young and Osherenko, 1993b: 19). When knowledge is uncertain
but inaction threatens high costs, policy-makers may turn to scientists in 'epistemic communities' to help them identify the nature of
the problem and whether, when, and what type of action to take
(Haas, 1992a: 188 and 215, 1992b; Young and Osherenko, 1993b:
20). Epistemic communities concerned about an environmental
problem can be particularly influential – even without strong public awareness or concern – if their attempts to foster international
policy do not engender strong interest-based opposition. Thus, scientists convinced governments to negotiate and adopt the
Convention on Wetlands of International Importance (Wetlands
Convention) in 1971, long before the development of public concern about wetland loss (Matthews, 1993).

  States often grant scientific arguments more legitimacy in negotiations than interest-based arguments and, hence, can prove quite
influential (Jasanoff, 1990, 2004; Young and Osherenko, 1993b: 16).
Scientists' methods and rules of discursive legitimacy provide an
alternative to typical interest-based and power-based bargaining. In
environmental negotiations, informal norms generate expectations
that states should support their positions with empirical evidence
and scientific research. Indeed, the international whaling regime
and many other IEAs require that protocols and amendments
'be based on scientific findings' (International Convention for the
Regulation of Whaling, Art.V.2.b). Scientific evidence need not be

overwhelming, non-controversial, or even widely accepted to have influence. Governments sometimes act before scientific knowledge fully consolidates. Various states negotiated the 1985 Vienna Convention for the Protection of the Ozone Layer before the most compelling evidence identified CFCs as the source of ozone depletion; 'the real decisions' underlying the 1987 Montreal Protocol were made before a scientific consensus emerged (Haas, 1992a: 224). In other cases, public concern develops despite scientific uncertainty. When governments commence negotiations in such settings, scientific findings that magnify a problem or identify cheaper ways to address it can foster international agreement by altering states' calculations of their ecological vulnerability or abatement costs while contrary findings can reduce pressure for agreement.

However, scientific arguments can also be ignored, obscured, or manipulated in the service of interest-based positions (Young and Osherenko, 1993a: 233). International fisheries agreements routinely ignore or override the recommendations of their own scientific advisory bodies (Walsh, 2004). And although scientific norms and training usually lead scientists to resist pressure from governments or others to generate science to fit policy positions, unconscious and implicit biases can influence the questions asked, the interpretation of results, the communication of uncertainty, the options considered, and the policy conclusions offered. Indeed, values and power that are embedded in scientific information can rationalize or reinforce rather than reduce political conflict (Jasanoff, 1990; Litfin, 1994: 186). And even if scientific research could be made objective and impartial, policy-makers could still selectively use or ignore science to support interest-based positions.

## Institutional forums

States expend time, take risks, and incur costs to create international institutions. Therefore, having a pre-existing institution in which to negotiate can facilitate IEA creation (Keohane, 1984). For bilateral problems or those involving only a few states, the 'institution' may consist simply of interactions between a few government representatives who document their agreements in an 'exchange of notes' or 'exchange of letters'. When more states are involved, a more formal negotiating forum is usually established. In new areas of international environmental cooperation, such forums are often created by a particularly concerned government hosting a conference and inviting relevant countries. At such initial meetings, states engage in 'constitutional' negotiations over the rules for subsequent substantive negotiations including whether to make decisions by unanimity, consensus, or qualified majorities. Over time, meta-norms for international environmental negotiations have developed, with those rules being understood and accepted by all participants and modified, if needed, to fit the vagaries of the specific context.

In many areas of international environmental law there are decades of negotiating experience and many pre-existing forums for negotiation. Many international environmental institutions hold regular meetings to review progress under existing agreements, to discuss proposed revisions, or to negotiate new ones. Such regular meetings can foster negotiations by providing both a ready-made discussion forum and a foundation for mutual knowledge, understanding, and trust among the negotiators. Most fishery commissions meet annually to adopt catch quotas. The regular meetings of the Marine Environment Protection Committee of the International Maritime Organization and of the Alpine and LRTAP Conventions have fostered adoption of numerous conventions, protocols, and amendments, many that are far afield from the initial topics of negotiation. The Convention on the Conservation of Migratory Species of Wild Animals (CMS) encourages member states to conclude additional agreements. UNEP provides a forum for negotiation on regional seas issues and the European Union provides a forum for European environmental issues. Such forums remove the mundane but important obstacle to resolving a problem, namely, having an established place and time to talk about it. And they also have bureaucratic incentives to avoid 'going out of business', leading them to promote new areas for negotiation once existing ones have been addressed. They also place states reluctant to take action on an issue in the awkward position of either discussing the problem or actively, and publicly, opposing its discussion. Thus, such institutions favor the interests of those states seeking to have an environmental problem recognized and addressed. Indeed, the availability of institutional forums explains why problems in some environmental sectors are more readily resolved than in others. It seems hard to imagine that as many conventions, protocols, and amendments addressing marine pollution and fisheries would have been negotiated in the absence of ongoing institutions in which to negotiate them.

## Long-term interdependencies

Environmental negotiations are more likely to succeed when states – and among those states that – interact frequently, have a dense set of interactions, have generally cooperative relationships, and have issue-specific power resources that foster interdependence (Keohane and Nye, 1989; Hasenclever et al., 1997: 54–5). Interdependence strengthens incentives to cooperate and provides more opportunities for each state to know that other states may be watching their environmental behaviors and that those behaviors may influence, implicitly or explicitly, their ability to cooperate in other, more important, arenas. Upstream or upwind states may find that downstream or downwind states raise pollution issues in economic or other forums. Thus, the dense interdependence among European states helps explain the greater number and range of IEAs in Europe than in other regions. More direct interdependencies between environmental and other issues can enhance international cooperation, as was evident in the negotiation of the North American Agreement on Environmental Cooperation as part of the North American Free Trade Agreement negotiations.

## Trends in environmental concern

Long-term trends in environmental concern also play a role. The prospects for negotiating an IEA have increased as environmental concern has grown. Thus, the rate of one IEA per year before the Second World War became 10 per year in the 1960s and 20 per year in the 1990s (Mitchell, 2003). Beyond such long-term trends, negotiations can be fostered or inhibited by more short-term changes in the international setting: 'Larger national and world events which, though far removed from the subject matter involved in specific cases of regime formation, can and do significantly affect both the timing and content of regime formation' (Young and Osherenko, 1993b: 20–1). The importance of the environment relative to other concerns can mean the difference between the successful conclusion of negotiations or delay, continuation, or termination. Thus, the negotiations regarding Svalbard Island were interrupted by the First World War, but were taken up by 'the Paris Peace Conference ... even though the question of Svalbard had not figured in any way in the war' (Young and Osherenko, 1993a: 255). Likewise the international regulation of whaling, institutionalized in agreements in 1931 and 1937, was interrupted by the Second World War but recommenced directly thereafter. The end of the Cold War allowed environmental issues to move up many states' (including the superpowers') lists of international priorities while the events of 11 September 2001 pushed environmental concerns down those same lists.

# Processes of International Negotiation

As with most realms of international relations, outcomes reflect both structure and agency. Structural forces like interests, power, institutional forums, and interdependencies may promote or inhibit, but do not determine, negotiation success. Within structural constraints, actors' choices can have a significant influence on whether an IEA forms, when it forms, and what form it takes.

Much scholarship has highlighted the influence of states, epistemic communities, NGOs, domestic political constituencies, and individuals (Young, 1991; Haas, 1992b: 18; Raustiala, 1997a ; Betsill and Corell, 2001; Corell and Betsill, 2001). The influence of such actors is best understood in terms of how well they perform certain functions that foster or inhibit IEA formation. However 'ripe' structural conditions may be for agreement, reaching such agreement depends on the efforts and skill of various actors in performing certain tasks (Zartman, 1985).

## Background on negotiation processes

Intergovernmental negotiations can proceed in various ways but do tend to have common features. First and foremost they are negotiations among governments, with negotiations conducted by executive branch officials. In high-visibility multilateral negotiations, large developed countries may send national delegations consisting of more than 50 people, including executive branch political appointees and staff as well as experts and advisors from the national legislature, academic institutions, or NGOs. Small developing countries, on the other hand, may be represented by a foreign national negotiating on behalf of several countries or may not be represented at all. Negotiation rules usually allow only government representatives to speak during negotiating sessions, with others allowed to speak only if invited. Some negotiating forums grant NGOs – whether representing scientific, economic, or environmental interests – observer status that allows their representatives to attend some or all negotiating sessions. Although much early international environmental diplomacy was conducted with scant public attention, environmental negotiations now receive significant attention from NGOs and the international media. As negotiations have become more multilateral, public, and complex, much of the 'real action' has moved out of the formal sessions into smaller 'working groups'. These working groups can draft particular provisions and include negotiators from a subset of countries considered representative of, or sensitive to, the interests of all relevant states. The exclusion of lobbyists from negotiation and working-group sessions does not preclude lobbying, of course. Conference hallways, local restaurants, and hotel lobbies have become places where government representatives seek input from scientists, NGOs, and business interests and where the latter lobby the former to propose particular treaty language or to support, reject, or change proposals made by others.

Precisely because all governments can object to specific provisions or reject, in toto, any agreement arrived at, negotiations 'normally operate under consensus rather than majoritarian rules' (Young and Osherenko, 1993a: 227). This generates dynamics that combine efforts to find collectively acceptable – and sometimes 'least ambitious program' (Underdal, 1980) – provisions that address all states' interests, to persuade other governments to reassess their initial position, to engage in log-rolling and linkage, to make otherwise-unacceptable provisions acceptable, and to use pressure tactics and side-payments. International negotiations can also reflect the tension between the integrative bargaining needed to get agreement from other governments and the distributional bargaining needed to meet the interests of one's own government (Raiffa, 1982).

## Continuing to build knowledge, concern, and urgency

The fostering of knowledge, concern, and urgency that is central to getting environmental problems on the international agenda does not end once negotiations start. Activist NGOs and leader states must continue their efforts to get more states to the table, to transform reluctant states into leaders, and to get leader states to take more aggressive positions. Improved understanding by negotiators of environmental problems and their causes – whether requested from or provided by scientists and NGOs – can foster negotiations by leading states to revise their estimates of the costs of reaching, or failing to reach, agreement. Global environmental assessments (evaluations of the status, trends, causes, and impacts of an environmental problem undertaken by international groups of government and independent scientists) especially when picked up by the media, can increase pressures on negotiators. Findings from groups like the IPCC can be quite influential with those governments that view them as credible (scientifically 'accurate'), salient (relevant to current decisions), and legitimate (reflective of their interests and perspectives) (Mitchell et al., 2006b).

Before negotiations can start, interest groups must make constituencies aware of a problem, mobilize pressure on governments, and make taking action seem urgent. Once negotiations do start, environmental NGOs and corporate actors provide conduits that can keep constituencies informed about negotiation progress and negotiators informed about constituency preferences (Lipschutz and Conca, 1993; Princen and Finger, 1994: 217; Lipschutz and Mayer, 1996; Wapner, 1996). Scientists, corporate representatives, and environmental activists also can 'infiltrate' governance, joining national delegations or working directly with the bureaucracies of international organizations (Haas, 1992b: 27; Raustiala, 1997b: 730). These dynamics matter because, while interest groups try to influence negotiators' views on ecological vulnerability and abatement costs, they also try to convince them that, regardless of such vulnerabilities and costs, the political costs of opposing a group's views are greater than those of adopting its position.

## Generating mutually acceptable goals and policies

Once governments have 'come to the table' (Stein, 1989), they shift their attention to defining mutually acceptable goals and to identifying policies for achieving those goals. Although states must already share an understanding of an environmental problem to start negotiations, to reach agreement they must create a shared understanding of the appropriate solution to it, despite their varying levels of concerns and their often competing interests. Even before a range of policies – and their corresponding costs and risks – has been specified, differing levels of state concern will generate differing views of what and how much should be done.

The first several paragraphs (or preamble) of most IEAs usually lay out the problem at hand and a mutually acceptable, if not always shared, vision of the goal of resolving the problem. Preambles are often laundry lists of varied – and sometimes contradictory – goals that reflect, without resolving, the different interests, perceptions, values, and objectives of the states involved. Thus, the 1992 Convention on Biological Diversity's (CBD) preamble links protecting biological diversity to its intrinsic value and value in maintaining Earth's 'life sustaining systems', to states' 'sovereign rights over their own biological resources', to precautionary approaches and technology transfer, to the concerns of indigenous communities and women, to economic development and 'poverty eradication', and to meeting human food and health needs. Such language in IEA preambles illustrates that states can reach agreement through two different processes: compromises and 'horse-trading'. In the former, states reach agreement by identifying a middle ground among their positions that, at its best, resolves contradictions in those positions to the satisfaction of all parties. In the latter, states reach agreement by combining their positions in ways that, at the extreme, merely 'paper over their differences' (Mitchell, 2005: 205). States make international policy either through compromise or by 'avoiding making decisions when none of the participants in the deliberations is willing to compromise' (Mitchell, 2005: 205).

Even when states share a motivation to take collective action and develop a consistent vision of the goals of such action, significant obstacles may arise with respect to what actions to take. Agreement on the need for action need not imply agreement on many institutional design elements, including how much action to take, how quickly, by which actors, and with which actors bearing the costs. Environmental problems that require ongoing management rather than one-shot solutions (see below) may generate significant disagreement over decision making procedures (like voting) that will be used in revising institutional rules. What pollutants are banned and which restricted, what species are listed as endangered and which merely as threatened, or when and how fish stocks are protected can all become crucial aspects of negotiations that can then become deal-breakers. When environmental protection entrains high economic costs, transparency about the actions of all relevant states and sub-state actors may become crucial and devising acceptable inspection procedures may slow or prevent agreement.

Negotiation progress is fostered by 'deft diplomacy' that involves the ability to 'add and subtract issues to facilitate the bargaining process, craft the terms of negotiating texts, and broker the deals needed to achieve consensus' (Young, 1998: 23; see also Sebenius, 1983). Although material resources are helpful, diplomats, bureaucrats, or NGO and corporate representatives can often facilitate agreement without them (Young, 1998: 23). Good diplomacy often entails getting states with competing positions to focus on the underlying interests they seek to promote through the negotiations, thereby shifting from positional, distributive, or zero-sum bargaining to interest-based, integrative, or win-win bargaining (Fisher and Ury, 1981). The former tends to produce failed negotiations or agreements that incorporate suboptimal compromises, whereas the latter, though harder to achieve, tends to produce agreements that simultaneously address the concerns and interests of all relevant actors (Fisher and Ury, 1981: 5). Integrative bargaining also increases the support of participating states for an agreement and – because it reflects and meets those interests – makes it more likely that they will find it in their self-interest to fulfill their treaty obligations (Humphreys, 2001: 125).

Negotiation success involves not merely identifying a zone of possible agreement (the intersection among the pre-existing interests of the states involved) but also in convincing states to clarify and/or re-evaluate their interests (Raiffa, 1982). When states rely on distributive bargaining or efforts at integrative bargaining fail to identify mutually acceptable solutions, negotiations may fail altogether or produce 'least ambitious program' solutions in which countries agree to do little more than what they would have done anyway (Underdal, 1980; Hovi and Sprinz, 2006).

Assuming that bargaining generates mutually acceptable – if not the best possible – provisions, a second phase of building support for the negotiated agreement commences. Countries that have accepted existing terms must be prevented from re-opening provisions for negotiation and other countries must be convinced to accept existing agreement terms without adding or changing provisions that would make the agreement unacceptable to existing supporters. Joint agreement on a treaty text does not preclude states from reverting to distributive bargaining strategies designed to improve the benefits they receive from the agreement even if this is at the expense of other parties. And consensus among those states most active in negotiations must be broadened to those that may have had less say in designing certain provisions but are still crucial to the final success of the negotiations. Those seeking to foster IEA formation must convince all relevant states – mutually and simultaneously – to accept the agreement's current terms rather than to continue negotiating for better terms or to walk out of the negotiations (Ikle, 1964: 59–60).

The willingness of states to accept the set of provisions that constitute an international treaty also reflects what Putnam calls 'two-level games' (Putnam, 1988). Negotiations among governments are conducted in a context in which each government's representative recognizes that they must find positions that are simultaneously acceptable to other governments and to their own domestic constituencies. NGOs and the media can serve as communication channels by which negotiators learn about the preferences of their constituencies and those constituencies learn about the proposals and likely actions (or inaction) of their governments, with negotiations involving a process in which governments may 'discover' their interests as much as they attempt to further those interests.

## Discourse, framing, and negotiation dynamics

Negotiations involve both rationalist elements in which 'identifiable and fixed' preferences are inputs to the process and constructivist elements in which preferences develop during and through the process, leading to outcomes that may differ significantly from what any participant would have predicted at the outset (Zürn, 1998: 627). The inability of those involved, let alone others, to predict negotiation outcomes highlights the influence of the process on those outcomes.

Often states have 'well-developed conceptions of their own interests' with respect to an environmental problem (in terms of ecological vulnerability, abatement costs, etc.) that they bring to, and maintain during, negotiations (Young, 1998: 97). And in such cases, states attempt, offensively, to promote their interests through institutional design and, defensively, to protect their interests from institutional encroachment. However, international environmental negotiations are not merely venues for governments to lay out their positions to determine if an area of agreement exists or to bully or entice others to accept their positions. Negotiations include such dynamics but can also include 'communicative action' in which governments attempt to argue and persuade and, to varying degrees, are open to the arguments and persuasion of others (Risse, 2000).

States' interests and preferences tend to be less clear and less stable when issues are complex, knowledge is uncertain, and material interests are 'weakly or ambiguously affected', features that are typical of many environmental problems (Stokke, 1998: 132–3; Zürn, 1998: 629–30). States may have insufficient information to know what is in their own interests and, even if they do, may not know which of various possible agreements would best promote those interests. Mutual agreement is created not by formulaically mapping the intersection of states' pre-existing interests but through a dynamic process in which negotiators initially 'focus on a few key issues and then ... [develop] a negotiating text setting forth proposed provisions relating to these issues' (Young and Osherenko, 1993b: 12). States do not just restate their positions but listen to the arguments of and respond to proposals from other states, non-state actors, or individuals, looking for creative, integrative solutions that promote their interests *and* those of others.

Long-term trends in the scientific framing of environmental issues and international political and legal norms influence what problems negotiations attempt to address and what types of solutions agreements create. On the scientific side, IEAs in the early twentieth century were primarily bilateral and regional efforts to protect individual species as natural resources to facilitate continued human harvest, while agreements today address a much wider array of issues including pollution and habitat degradation, adopt a much more ecosystemic approach, and are often global in character (Mitchell, 2003). Modern environmental treaties often reference non-environmental issues, such as economic development and the rights of women and indigenous communities. IEAs also reflect legal norms and precedents. Negotiators do not create agreements from 'scratch' but look instead to prior agreements for both general strategies and specific provisions. At a broad level, successful prior institutions have provided models – for example, framework-protocol approaches or calls for the use of precautionary measures – that have become increasingly common in environmental treaties (List and Rittberger, 1998: 70–1). At a narrower level, the non-substantive parts of agreements including amendment, entry into force, and withdrawal clauses are often treated as boilerplate, reading almost identically across a wide range of agreements (Depledge, 2000).

## Maintaining momentum and prompting action

Precisely because of the complexity of addressing many environmental problems, negotiations are fostered by actors committed to successful conclusion of the negotiations rather than to ensuring that a particular nation's interests are furthered by an agreement. Representatives of international organizations such as UNEP, of particular states, or of NGOs often take actions that are designed simply to maintain momentum. Obstacles to agreement always arise. Conferences end before agreement is reached. External events may focus policy-makers on other issues. When such forces make reaching agreement more difficult or less urgent, maintaining 'political momentum' becomes crucial (Young, 1998: 87–8). NGOs, for example, can mobilize international opinion when agreements are nearing completion or require ratification. Entrepreneurial leaders will often prepare proposals in advance, waiting for the political conditions to ripen, as was evident in UNEP executive director Mostafa Tolba's proposals on ozone negotiations (Keohane, 1996: 26; Young, 1998: 119).

External events also can increase the prospects for success (Young and Osherenko, 1993b: 14; Hasenclever et al., 1997: 54–5). Large-scale conferences or agreements in one arena can spark interest in negotiating other IEAs. The 1972 UN Conference on the Human Environment and the 1992 UN Conference on Environment and Development reflected existing environmental concern but also reinforced and heightened that concern, with governments signing several agreements at, and subsequent to, both conferences. Governments may favor continuing to negotiate on a problem until new scientific evidence or increased public pressure makes reaching agreement a more attractive strategy (Young and Osherenko, 1993b: 15). Focusing events can put environmental problems on the international stage (see Chapter 4) but also can foster agreement after negotiations have begun. Especially when dramatic environmental problems affect powerful countries, they can 'engender a sense of urgency that spurs quick action to conclude international agreements' (Young and Osherenko, 1993b: 15). Focusing events cannot generate agreement out of thin air but, if negotiations have made enough progress, such events can generate domestic political pressures that may lead a range of governments to accept agreement terms that were previously unacceptable or to negotiate more flexibly. However, focusing events are not necessary for negotiation success; IEAs are often signed through the mundane but sustained efforts of committed countries and negotiators finding agreements that meet all the relevant countries' interests.

## The role of leadership

All the foregoing dynamics, in turn, are fostered by actors who provide leadership. In trying to move negotiations along, leaders use various resources to increase knowledge, raise concern, design provisions, or maintain momentum. Structural leaders use material power, entrepreneurial leaders use negotiating skill, and intellectual leaders use ideas to resolve conflicts and disagreements in ways that relevant actors are willing to accept (Young, 1991). Negotiations often succeed only 'when effective leadership emerges' (Young and Osherenko, 1993a: 233). Though it may be difficult to identify independently and beforehand what leadership is, certain traits seem to promote negotiation success. Structural leadership often plays an important role in negotiations, when powerful states want agreement to be reached and are willing to expend resources to get otherwise-reluctant actors to come to the negotiating table and to accept agreement terms (Hasenclever et al., 1997: 77). For example, the United States has used its economic and diplomatic power to get both reluctant states to participate in environmental negotiations and already participating states to accept regulatory proposals that they might otherwise have found unattractive (Barkin and DeSombre, 2000; DeSombre, 2000).

Intellectual leadership also can foster international environmental negotiations (Young, 1991). Diplomats skilled at introducing new ideas, re-framing existing ideas, or shaping the discursive context can facilitate agreement by identifying realms of common interests or by getting actors to reevaluate their interests and positions.

Entrepreneurial leaders can use their personality, personal credibility, political capital, and material resources to convince various actors to accept the current terms of an agreement as, if not the best possible terms, at least the best that are likely to be available. The leaders or foreign ministers of individual countries, the heads of UNEP, and the Secretary-Generals of many international environmental secretariats have dedicated their time, resources, and reputations to keeping such negotiations going and bringing them to fruition. Individuals can become 'determined champions' who promote certain proposals and stage focusing events to prompt action at crucial junctures (Haas, 1992a: 222; Young and Osherenko, 1993b; Young, 1998). By creating a conducive negotiating forum and having a draft text 'ready to go', entrepreneurs can take advantage of the 'policy windows' that open up when focusing events occur (Kingdon, 1995: 165).

# Influences on Institutional Content

The previous section outlined factors that influence whether an IEA *forms*. This section outlines factors that influence their *content*. IEAs vary in choices as fundamental as the specificity and ambitiousness of requirements to those as mundane as official languages and which country or organization will be the depository for official documents. The theoretical and empirical foundation for explaining institutional variation, although weak, sheds light on why some institutions contain certain features and others do not.

## Fundamental institutional form

IEAs vary in their fundamental institutional form. Young classifies IEAs as regulatory, programmatic, procedural, or generative (Young, 1999b). Regulatory institutions proscribe or prescribe actions; procedural institutions establish procedures for regular collective decision making; programmatic institutions allow states to 'pool resources' for projects that would not be undertaken unilaterally; and generative institutions create new and 'distinctive social practices' (Young, 1999b: 28–31). These categories are ideal types, with some real-world institutions fitting neatly into these categories while others include elements from each. Various aspects of problem structure (see Chapter 2) make the choice of one or another of these alternatives more likely.

Generative institutions reflect efforts by 'a community or a collection of groups that join forces ... to promote a particular set of activities ... [by] structuring the way parties think about problems' (Young, 1999b: 40–1). Not surprisingly, then, such institutions are common during the early stages of an international environmental problem's lifecycle when the definition of the problem is still in a state of flux. Indeed, they are most common during the issue emergence stage discussed in the previous chapter (and therefore they receive little further discussion here).

Programmatic institutions tend to appear when states want to foster scientific progress on problems that are poorly understood or that few countries have developed plans to address. Collaborative research efforts can generate more and higher quality data, monitoring, analysis, and insights that can produce a more complete picture of complex environmental problems than any country can generate alone. LRTAP's protocol for a program to monitor and evaluate air pollution in Europe (known as EMEP), for example, standardized and expanded environmental monitoring and sped up cooperative research that produced Europe-wide models of the sources and recipients of acid rain precursors. States tend to develop such scientific programs early on in an environmental issue's lifecycle to reduce uncertainty about the magnitude and trajectory of an environmental problem, its causes and impacts, and the availability and effectiveness of potential solutions. Such institutions may also serve the more cynical purpose of 'buying time', allowing states to quell demands to 'do something' with research rather than action. States may also pool resources into programmatic institutions to provide both incentives and resources for states to undertake local environmental remediation. The Global Environment Facility provides one example, with states contributing resources to carefully screened projects that facilitate environmental improvements that developing country governments would not take without such assistance (Sharma, 1996; Young, Z. 1999).

Among environmental problems that are well understood and on which states are ready to take action, regulatory and procedural institutions predominate. Reading IEA texts clarifies the distinction between these two institutional forms. Regulatory IEAs specify behavioral proscriptions and prescriptions while procedural IEAs create organizations to negotiate such proscriptions and prescriptions in the future. Thus, the Kyoto Protocol and the Montreal Protocol required certain member states to reduce their emissions of greenhouse gases and ozone-depleting substances by certain dates. What makes these and similar institutions regulatory is not whether the treaty language requires or merely encourages certain behaviors but the fact that they specify the behaviors that states are expected to take. By contrast, the texts of procedural IEAs include no rules on behaviors that states must avoid or undertake but instead delineate the institutional structures by which member countries can generate such rules. Fisheries treaties rarely explicitly ban or restrict fishing but, instead, identify a mandate and tasks for decision making institutions including such things as the frequency, representation, and voting rules for meetings. The 1973 Convention on International Trade in Endangered Species of Wild Fauna and Flora (CITES), like many IEAs, blends these strategies, specifying sets of rules that states must follow to protect species facing different levels of endangerment and appendices of species to which each set of rules apply while also creating a Conference of the Parties to allow for the regular revision of those appendices.

Both regulatory and procedural institutions usually emerge when states agree that a problem warrants resolution. States tend to prefer procedural to regulatory institutions in three situations: when the problem requires management rather than resolution, when scientific uncertainty is high, and when political will is low. First, environmental problems differ in whether they can be solved or only managed, with states tending to create regulatory institutions for the former and procedural institutions for the latter. The nature of some problems allows states to establish one-time, static rules which, if followed, would address the problem to the satisfaction of the states involved – those rules require revisiting only if states become more (or less) ambitious in their desire to resolve the problem. States may establish institutions to allow for such revisions but those institutions tend to focus on the implementation of existing rules rather than the formulation of new ones. In such settings, states can establish bans or fixed limitations on some activity and feel that the problem has been addressed. By contrast, the nature of other problems dictates the need for ongoing management, with procedural institutions being required to allow for adaptive regulation. Of course, whether a problem can be solved or only managed depends on social definitions and framings. Consider international whaling: early on, the 'whaling problem' was a Tragedy of the Commons among whaling states who sought international cooperation to foster mutual restraint to ensure the 'orderly development of the whaling industry'. Whaling states could not 'solve' this problem through a regulatory agreement specifying a particular level of catch for the indefinite future. Instead, as with most international fisheries, states created the International Whaling Commission as a procedural institution that was mandated to meet annually to set quotas. By the mid-1980s, however, the 'whaling problem' had become a power struggle between whaling states and anti-whaling states about whether to allow whaling at all. By 1986, the procedural institutional structure remained but the challenge had become one that anti-whaling states, at least, thought could be solved by banning commercial whaling. Although annual meetings continue, the politics involved have changed this procedural institution into a regulatory one.

Second, scientific uncertainty also predisposes states toward procedural rather than regulatory institutions. The increasing adoption of framework-protocol strategies in IEAs reflects the desire to initiate international cooperation through procedural frameworks when uncertainty is large (and states are either reluctant to accept regulation or unclear as to what the best regulatory strategy is) and to establish regulatory protocols as the problem and concern about it became clearer. Thus, the 1985 Vienna Convention for the Protection of the Ozone Layer required only that states 'cooperate in the formulation of agreed measures, procedures and standards'. States established clear targets and timetables for the phasing out of ozone depleting substances (ODSs) in the 1987 Montreal Protocol and revised those targets and timetables in subsequent amendments, with each modification reflecting greater certainty about the magnitude and causes of the problem, the costs of solutions, and the willingness of states to accept regulation. Those changes have transformed the ozone regime from procedural to regulatory as the complete phasing out of many ODSs became technically, politically, and economically possible. Procedural institutions are designed to foster just such modifications of regulations in response to new knowledge. The United Nations Framework Convention on Climate Change (FCCC) has adopted a similar institutional form but, unlike the ozone regime, is unlikely to become a regulatory institution. Like the Vienna Convention, the FCCC itself established only vague requirements but did create a Conference of the Parties tasked with, inter alia, negotiating more substantive protocols. However, unlike the ozone regime, the climate change regime is likely to remain procedural since the economic processes that produce greenhouse gases have few technologically available and economically attractive alternatives and therefore climate change is much more likely to require long-term management than one-off solutions. As with climate change, international fisheries involve environmentally harmful behaviors that states are unwilling to wholly ban and, hence, require adaptive management with regulations revised in response to environmental, economic, and political feedback (Arvai et al., 2006).

Third, states prefer procedural to regulatory IEAs when there is sufficient political will to take joint action on some but not all aspects of a problem. The CMS agreement is designed precisely to address this dynamic. Appendix I of the CMS convention lists migratory species that are endangered, whereas Appendix II lists migratory species that are threatened and that require or would 'significantly benefit from' international agreement. When the CMS agreement was signed, Appendix I listed those species that all member states viewed as endangered and banned all killing of such animals. Appendix II listed those species over which member states disagreed about the status, need for action, and type of action that should be taken. For Appendix II species, the parties created a procedural strategy of requiring only that relevant states 'endeavour to conclude Agreements' for the conservation of those species. Notably, those provisions have generated six treaties and eight Memoranda of Understanding that do delineate specific rules for protecting particular Appendix II species.

## Incorporating science

Regardless of the institutional form, addressing environmental problems effectively usually dictates the establishment of mechanisms to incorporate scientific advice into policy-making. States may create procedural institutions for problems that are known to require adaptive management. But even in IEAs addressing well understood problems, states may establish mechanisms to ensure a ready forum for the discussion of new science about related problems. Such scientific 'institutions' may involve simply coordinating existing national research programs or exchanging data, scientific findings, and scientific personnel. But states may establish deeply collaborative monitoring and research that could not go on otherwise. LRTAP's EMEP program, noted above, dramatically expanded the network of European monitoring stations and improved data collection, analytic techniques, and national research capabilities. Many international environmental treaty organizations rely on subsidiary scientific bodies. Others rely on scientific advice from independent scientific bodies. The International Council for the Exploration of the Sea, the Scientific Committee on Antarctic Research, and the IPCC are international institutions that provide unsolicited reports and solicited advice on existing (and emerging) environmental problems. These institutions reduce scientific uncertainty but also help generate a commonly accepted body of knowledge and perceptions of a problem. They can transform a patchwork of national scientific research into a single international 'understanding' of a problem. Such common understandings, in turn, facilitate agreement on substantive and regulatory provisions, by making the problem seem larger, more urgent, or easier to resolve, and by reducing disagreement over what the problem is.

## Allowing flexibility

Beyond scientific uncertainty, states are concerned about interest uncertainty, that is, the uncertainty they have about the current and future interests of their own and other states with respect to an environmental problem. Such uncertainty leads states to negotiate flexibility into international institutions (Koremenos et al., 2001).

Even problems whose nature and causes are clear may leave states behind a 'veil of uncertainty' with respect to who will be 'losers' and who will be 'winners'. Such uncertainty may make states more cautious in reaching agreement or, alternatively, may lead them to negotiate agreements that maximize their flexibility to revise or legally renege on their commitments if these prove more costly than expected.

Creating procedural rather than regulatory institutions allows states to adopt and modify commitments progressively as the costs of those commitments become clearer. Alternatively, if states have enough environmental concern and political will to adopt regulatory rules, they may create 'relief valves' to avoid institutional conformance becoming too costly (Rosendorff and Milner, 2001). Almost all international treaties contain standard provisions that allow states to withdraw after notifying other states and waiting for a specified period of time. IEAs often provide additional and more ad hoc means of avoiding treaty obligations. IEAs allow states to join 'with reservations', to continue otherwise-banned practices if these are undertaken in certain ways, or to file 'objections' or opt out from particular provisions. Thus, having objected to the 1986 ICRW moratorium on commercial whaling, Norway has killed numerous whales commercially while remaining a treaty member in good legal standing. Although such flexibility provisions are often viewed as 'loopholes' by environmental activists, they are often included precisely because, without them, states central to an institution's success would choose not to join.

## Variation in regulatory institutions

Unlike variation within procedural, programmatic, and generative institutions, variation within regulatory institutions has received considerable scholarly attention and is therefore discussed more fully here. Regulatory institutions attempt to induce behavioral change through their primary rule systems, their information systems, and their response systems (Mitchell, 1996).

### Primary rules
International institutions exhibit considerable variation in their central prescriptions and proscriptions or primary rules. Because most environmental problems can be addressed through various alternative regulatory strategies, decisions about which activity to regulate and how to regulate it will dictate which actors with what interests and capacities must change their behavior, how large and costly those changes will be, and whether other factors will

reinforce or undercut subsequent incentives to meet agreement obligations. Negotiators pay particular attention to variation across strategies in the costs their country will incur, the benefits they might receive, and the likelihood that other states will fulfill the commitments involved. Four characteristics of primary rules that are often central to international negotiations are concerns about ambitiousness, specificity, common *vs* differentiated obligations, and equity.

The primary rules or obligations states accept vary considerably in how ambitious they are, that is, in the 'depth' of required behavioral changes (Downs et al., 1996). Theory suggests that states accept only 'shallow' agreements involving few, if any, costs for member states. Empirical evidence, however, shows that sometimes states do create IEAs that prove costly, sometimes with the states being aware of those costs at the time and sometimes with those costs only becoming evident later. The strength of state preferences, and conflict among those preferences, will influence the ambitiousness of institutional goals. Weak concern may cause negotiations to fail. But when it doesn't, states may start small with framework conventions, cooperative research programs, or nonbinding agreements. Such outcomes may reflect universally low concern, an inability to resolve conflict between concerned and unconcerned states, or high concern but uncertainty about the best way to address a problem. Indeed, the nature of solutions shapes support and opposition as much as the nature of the problem. Proposed IEAs that are not ecologically ambitious may, nevertheless, generate resistance if their design involves high costs or imposes costs on powerful economic sectors. Thus, the FCCC and its Kyoto Protocol have evoked considerable resistance even though emission reduction goals fall far short of what climatologists consider necessary to prevent climate change. Regimes that seek deep cooperation, provide little flexibility, or involve stringent enforcement will evoke resistance unless states see sufficiently large offsetting benefits (Downs et al., 1996). Notably, framework-protocol approaches work precisely because states will accept non-ambitious collective decision making rules with the hope that they will produce more ambitious regulatory rules later.

In general, more international concern generates more ambitious primary rules. The greater the share of relevant actors who are leaders rather than draggers, the more ambitious the agreement will be. Ambitiousness is properly evaluated not by simply looking at the constraints or requirements placed on states but also by comparing those constraints and requirements to the counterfactual of what states would have done otherwise. Thus, an agreement requiring the stabilization of emissions of some pollutant within 10 years may be more ambitious than one requiring a 50 per cent reduction within five years if the states in the former all had increasing emissions while those in the latter either had already made, or were on emission trajectories that would have lead them to make, large reductions. Thus, an IEA's ambitiousness is the degree to which states agree to take actions when matched by others that they would not take on their own.

A tradeoff also exists between ambitiousness and participation. Common wisdom suggests that successful negotiations require involving all states that have an interest in a problem (Young and Osherenko, 1993b: 16). Yet a set of 'contingent leaders' – each of whom is willing to take meaningful action but only if others do – can pursue more ambitious goals if they exclude recalcitrant draggers. Scandinavian states often have established high environmental standards even though other major contributors to the problem are unwilling, at least initially, to agree to those terms. States may create institutions that address only a fraction of a problem or engage only a fraction of the perpetrators, either because a partial solution is better than no solution or because they believe some initial steps will foster conditions that will lead currently-reluctant states to participate. This 'go it alone' power can allow an activist subset of states to reach an agreement despite the opposition of powerful states that are contributing to a problem (Gruber, 2000). Just as the six states that initiated the creation of the European Union did so over strong opposition from the United Kingdom, so too did states bring the Kyoto Protocol into existence despite clear opposition from the United States. Institutions that 'go it alone' are weaker than they might be but can still allow committed states to initiate international action without being held hostage by powerful dragger states.

IEAs also vary considerably in specificity, with some containing only vague provisions and others detailing pages of rules, requirements, conditions, targets, and timetables. When states are unconcerned or uncertain about how an environmental problem is affecting their interests, they are more likely to generate vague provisions in unambitious agreements. This lack of specificity can arise when a consensus regarding the need for action is not matched by a consensus on what to do. Vague provisions can also arise when states that have not found real compromises respond to pressure to reach an agreement – such as happens at the end of a diplomatic conference – by 'papering over' their differences (Mitchell, 2005). But a lack of initial specificity can provide the foundation for greater specificity over time. Thus, the Wetlands Convention includes many quite vague rules, one of which requires only that states promote the 'wise use' of wetlands in their territory. However, since 1971 the Conference of the Parties has made considerable progress in attaching substantive meaning to this vague phrase.

IEAs also vary in whether they contain common or differentiated obligations. Traditional international law has relied on 'common' obligations in which each member state accepts the same regulatory requirements. Several recent IEAs, however, have adopted 'differentiated' obligations in which different groups of states or even individual states are treated differently. As an extreme, in the Kyoto Protocol 39 developed countries committed to country-specific emission limits or reductions that ranged from 8 per cent decreases to 10 per cent increases. A less extreme variant is more common, as was evident in the Montreal Protocol's granting developing, but not developed, states a 10-year 'grace period' with respect to the ODS phase-out timetable. Other agreements' rules involve nominally common obligations that were known at the time to distribute the behavioral burden unevenly. States collectively committed in the Second Sulfur Protocol to the LRTAP Convention, for example, to prevent sulfur *depositions* from exceeding certain levels but that commitment was known to require much larger emission *reductions* from some states than others. These examples are exceptions, however, and most IEAs still adopt common obligations that, nevertheless, impose different costs in practice.

What accounts for this difference in approach? Certainly the norm that agreements should impose equal obligations on all parties makes common obligations the default model. But states now appear to strive toward common obligations while being open to accepting differentiated obligations to get agreement among states with divergent interests and levels of concern. Those interests may divide states into two groups, as in the Montreal Protocol, or may leave states far more differentiated, as in the Kyoto Protocol. Differentiated obligations appear to be more a last, than first, resort, if only because they can easily be framed as politically meaningless, shallow agreements that codify states' planned behaviors rather than prompt new ones.

All three types of obligations present problems: nominally equal requirements can impose quite unequal costs in practice; considerable variation within groups of developed or developing countries means that some will benefit far more than others within either group; and allowing the self-selection of commitment levels may mean that states agree only to those actions they would have taken anyway. Yet all three have the virtue of simplicity, considered crucial to negotiation success, and parties appear more willing to accept obligations of these three types than the range of alternatives involving more complicated formulas (Young and Osherenko, 1993b: 14, 233).

Finally, negotiations 'succeed only when all the major parties and interest groups feel that their primary concerns have been treated fairly' (Young and Osherenko, 1993b: 14, 233; see also Young and Wolf, 1992). By definition, negotiations succeed only when relevant parties accept their terms. Indeed, it becomes tautological to contend that equitable solutions foster agreement if we define an agreement as 'equitable' so long as all the negotiating states accept it. Yet, we can distinguish here between agreements that all relevant states consider as in their interests and those they see as equitable. States are unlikely to accept agreements that do not reflect their interests and may accept agreements that further their interests even if the costs involved, or the benefits of, the agreement appear inequitable. However, they are more likely to accept agreements that further their interests and that also meet 'identifiable community standards of equity' (Young and Osherenko, 1993b: 14). Such standards do not require equal treatment, only that differential treatment be based on criteria that each state views as appropriate.

## Information systems: environmental and behavioral monitoring

Regulatory IEAs also vary in their information systems. Some IEAs encourage countries to exchange the environmental information they already collect while others provide for extensive new environmental monitoring. Some IEAs coordinate and standardize data collection to foster the development of higher quality information about the magnitude, causes, and impacts of a problem. Others have created networks of scientists and monitoring stations and have pooled funding so that countries with more advanced monitoring programs help other countries develop theirs. IEAs also treat the information they receive differently. Some IEA secretariats simply archive the information they collect, while others organize, analyze, and disseminate the data to foster better environmental management. What explains such variation? As with ambitiousness, the level of concern and the magnitude of potential impacts play important roles. When states share significant concern about a poorly understood environmental problem, they will invest more in gathering information that can help them take action early enough to avert those impacts. To the extent that such impacts are thought to be small or of little concern, committing such time and resources becomes less attractive.

Beyond environmental monitoring, IEAs also vary in their concern with behavioral monitoring and transparency. With respect to regulated behaviors and compliance, most IEAs rely almost exclusively on countries providing self-reports. Recognizing both the practical obstacles to reporting and that states are unlikely to engage in 'self-incrimination' if sanctions are the likely response, some IEAs establish reporting systems that provide positive incentives for, and build the capacity to, report (Mitchell, 1998b). Several IEAs have held workshops to help states develop the infrastructure needed to provide high quality information on their country's performance. Although intrusive monitoring systems are still rare, rising environmental concerns may make these more common in the future.

Whether IEA provisions focus on compliance information depends on the 'violation tolerance' of members regarding the problem. When states believe that the failure of other parties to meet their obligations will harm their interests, will alter their own interests in meeting their own obligations, or will undercut the IEA's ability to achieve its objectives, they are likely to demand relatively intrusive inspection procedures. Some institutions rely on proactive monitoring to identify behaviors that might not otherwise come to light ('police patrols') while others rely on passive strategies that assume that environmentally harmful activities will harm certain actors enough to lead them to report them ('fire alarms') (McCubbins and Schwartz, 1984; Raustiala, 2004). Most violations of marine pollution agreements, for example, occur in ways that are difficult to detect or difficult to link to the perpetrating actor. In response, some states have established regional 'port state control' agreements to coordinate and encourage aerial surveillance and the in-port monitoring of international shipping (Kasoulides, 1993). Likewise, CITES established an elaborate system of species import and export certificates (Reeve, 2002). By contrast, the Convention on Early Notification of a Nuclear Accident that arose in response to the Chernobyl incident relies on self-reporting by the state in which an accident occurs. Yet other IEAs involve NGOs in the institutional structure as actors who have both incentives and resources to serve as 'police patrols', watching out for the behaviors of governments and sub-state actors who may violate IEA rules. Choices among monitoring systems depend on evaluating the perceived need for monitoring and then looking for strategies that can meet that need.

## Response mechanisms

Finally, regulatory IEAs vary in how they respond to regulated behaviors. Scholars have identified various institutional design implications based on distinctions in the constellations of states' interests, including distinctions among assurance, coordination, collaboration, and suasion games; coordination and incongruity problems; symmetric and asymmetric problems; conflicts over values, means, relatively assessed goods, and absolutely assessed goods; and commons problems, shared natural resource problems, and transboundary externalities (Martin, 1992b; Hasenclever et al., 1997; Underdal, 2002). The direct tit-for-tat that can discourage violations of trade and arms control treaties proves less useful in environmental realms where states that support IEAs are generally unwilling to harm the environment as a retaliatory sanction and, even if they did, would fail to influence perpetrating states unconcerned about the environment. Recognizing this, many scholars have stressed the need to couple economic sanctions with monitoring mechanisms that trigger them (Bernauer, 1995a: 363; Downs et al., 1996; Wettestad, 1995). Others argue that such an enforcement model is less effective than a more 'managerial' model of diplomacy, norms, and rewards (Chayes and Chayes, 1995). Indeed, rewards appear to be the only option for inducing 'upstream' actors to alter their behavior (Mitchell and Keilbach, 2001).

IEAs also attempt to induce behavioral change through 'systems of implementation review' and 'sunshine methods' involving reporting, monitoring, and review without any explicit or direct response (Brown Weiss and Jacobson, 1998; Victor et al., 1998a). Ecolabeling, certification, and prior informed consent rules may induce behavioral changes via marketplace incentives. IEAs also incorporate norms, argument, and persuasion in their efforts to influence behavior by altering notions of appropriate and inappropriate action (Finnemore, 1996; Risse, 2000). Thus, general norms regarding the appropriate relationship between environmental protection and development or regarding the precautionary principle can, over time, significantly alter how states respond to environmental problems, even if that causal influence may prove hard to demonstrate.

Choices as to how an international environmental institution should respond when states do, or do not, alter their behavior to meet IEA commitments are influenced by the underlying problem structure. IEAs addressing upstream/downstream problems do not include sanctions because upstream states will not accept agreements that legitimize the right of other states to sanction them for behaviors that, pre-institutionally, the other states could not legitimately sanction (Mitchell and Keilbach, 2001). The Montreal Protocol illustrates that 'upstream' states which contribute to – but view themselves as unharmed by – an environmental problem will not participate without some reward: India, China, and other developing countries that contributed to, but were unconcerned about, ozone loss joined the Protocol only after industrialized and concerned (that is, 'downstream') states compensated them for the costs of phasing out ODSs.

In the 1976 Convention on the Protection of the Rhine against Pollution by Chlorides, the French agreed to reduce their chloride pollution of the Rhine only in response to payments by the downstream Dutch government, with contributions from Germany and Switzerland. Notably, institutional inertia also influences institutional form, with the burden-sharing in that agreement incorporated in subsequent agreements on Rhine pollutants that had few similarities (Bernauer and Moser, 1996). Rewards may, however, make potential donors more reluctant to join the institution even as they attract potential recipients.

Although sanctions are a non-starter in IEAs addressing upstream/downstream problems, states must choose between rewards and sanctions in Tragedy of the Commons situations. In some cases, states can use the threat of mutual retaliation to support cooperation. Thus the underlying, if often implicit, incentive for states to stay within international catch quotas is the threat that excessive violations by one party will lead others to do the same and, hence, a reversion to the no-institution baseline of unrestrained fishing. Particularly in situations involving over-appropriation of an environmental resource, such retaliatory threats may help sustain international cooperation, though the poor track record of most fishery IEAs demonstrates that they do not always do so. In most cases, however, states adopt more diffuse, indirect, and unspecified reciprocity as an 'enforcement' mechanism. For example, the United States has frequently used the removal of fishing rights as a response to behaviors by whaling states that it viewed as undermining the effectiveness of the IWC (DeSombre, 2000). In such contexts, states recognize that they may avoid the 'unraveling' of cooperation that tit-for-tat sanctioning would produce by providing states that are supportive of an IEA with mechanisms for them to take actions that harm an initial violator's interests without asking them to engage in environmentally-harmful activities, which they would be unlikely to adopt in any event (Axelrod and Keohane, 1986). However, states can use rewards as well as sanctions to address Tragedy of the Commons situations. Coase (1960) argued that externalities can be resolved by victims paying perpetrators to halt harmful activities. Thus, in response to the overharvesting of North Pacific fur seals, Canada, Japan, Russia, and the United States agreed in 1911 that the former two countries would stop all seal harvesting in exchange for the latter two countries compensating them in the form of 15 per cent of their seal harvests every year (Dorsey, 1998).

Response strategies can also include capacity building. IEAs increasingly seek to influence non-compliant countries by making it easier for them to fulfill their obligations. Negotiators increasingly recognize that non-compliance for certain states can arise as much from incapacity and inadvertence as from intention (see Chapter 6). They also recognize that sanctions are neither appropriate nor effective if states cannot, rather than will not, meet their obligations. Non-compliance is necessarily intentional in many IEAs: consider the trade in endangered species; the harvest of fish, whales, or polar bears; or river or ocean pollution. In others, however, IEAs require the deployment of financial resources or technical expertise that developing states may not have available. When an IEA requires states to protect fragile ecosystems from large-scale socio-economic forces or to provide high quality environmental monitoring, both developed and developing states may support establishment of mechanisms that urge non-compliant countries to identify the causes of non-compliance so other countries can facilitate that compliance.

Violation tolerance also influences the strength of the responses adopted. States tend to be relatively 'violation tolerant' early on in an environmental problem's lifecycle, if only because that is the status quo situation (Young, 1999b; Chayes and Chayes, 1993). Response mechanisms may be relatively weak or non-existent. But as the issue's importance or institutional developments make states more sensitive to whether other states are fulfilling their commitments, response mechanisms tend to become stronger.

In short, states build responses into IEAs that reflect the expected sources of, and harm of, non-compliance. Where those sources are seen as intentional, they are more likely to adopt sanctions. Where those sources are seen as predominantly due to incapacity and inadvertence, they are more likely to adopt some form of facilitative approach. Where the possibility exists for both types of shortcoming, they are likely to create institutions that begin by investigating their sources and then allow for different types of responses, an approach adopted in various amendments to the Montreal Protocol.

# Negotiation Participation and Institutional Membership

Before an IEA can come into existence, negotiators must sell the agreement to domestic constituencies. Negotiators may need to convince their prime minister or president that their concessions were more than offset by those of other countries and that the agreement is in their country's interests. Although uncommon, examples do exist of states refusing to sign the very agreements they helped negotiate. And countries involved in negotiations can always reject the terms of a 'final' agreement in the hopes of re-opening negotiations to achieve better terms (Ikle, 1964: 59–75). For most countries, international treaties do not become legally binding or enter into force without legislative branch ratification of executive branch negotiations. The two-level games mentioned above require that negotiators convince domestic political actors – including both legislators and citizens – with diverse interests and perspectives that an agreement's benefits exceed its risks and costs and that no better agreement can be negotiated (Putnam, 1988). Not infrequently, government executives sign agreements that their legislatures refuse to ratify, either because the executive misjudged their domestic constituencies' interests or because those interests had shifted. Thus, the American government signed the UNFCCC and its Kyoto Protocol, and ratified the former, but has refused to ratify the latter. Many IEAs also have been signed but have not taken effect because too few countries ratified the agreement. The unwillingness of many states to ratify the 1973 MARPOL convention, for example, led to the negotiation of a 1978 Protocol that revised provisions that otherwise would have precluded the agreement from taking effect. While negotiators often feel pressure to reach 'some agreement, any agreement' by the end of an international conference, legislatures may feel no such pressure and can then take years to consider whether to ratify an IEA.

## Conclusion

Whether environmental negotiations end in agreement depends on the constraints and opportunities created by structural factors, more direct forcing or inhibiting events related to the influence of particular actors and the negotiating process, and the influence of external factors and prior conditions. Young and Osherenko have called interests, power, and knowledge 'social driving forces', while leadership, context, and other variables are 'cross-cutting factors' that influence the negotiations (Young and Osherenko, 1993a: 247). It is the interaction among these factors that helps to explain whether negotiations succeed and what form any agreement takes. This chapter has delineated the factors that make states willing to engage in negotiations, the factors that influence the content of agreements, and the factors that influence whether states become members of such agreements. The next chapter takes up the questions of whether and when these efforts at negotiation lead states to take actions that are any different from those they would have taken in the absence of such agreements.

# EVALUATING THE EFFECTIVENESS OF INTERNATIONAL ENVIRONMENTAL INSTITUTIONS

When are international environmental institutions effective? When do international environmental agreements (IEAs) work? When do they accomplish, or at least promote, the environmental goals that motivate the states that create them? States spend considerable time and resources negotiating intergovernmental environmental agreements. They have signed hundreds of environmental treaties, protocols, and amendments and continue to do so at rates averaging 20 multilaterals and 30 bilaterals per year (Mitchell, 2003: 438–9). People often assume that the treaties that states sign to address environmental problems will reduce, if not eliminate, those impacts. Indeed, our interest in issue emergence and treaty negotiation only make sense if IEAs 'work', if they lead states to change their behavior with corresponding environmental benefits. Yet, even a cursory assessment suggests that many IEAs come up short and that some fail altogether. This chapter explores the factors that explain what types of IEAs influence behavior, differences in the types of influence they have, and how the conditions under which IEAs operate affect their influence. It engages questions of effectiveness, of when, why, and to what extent international environmental institutions achieve their environmental objectives.

## Compliance, Effectiveness, and Effects

When evaluating IEAs, international lawyers and legal scholars often focus on compliance, defined as the extent to which state behaviors conform to institutional rules. International relations scholars, by contrast, usually focus on effectiveness, defined as the extent to which state behaviors reflect institutional influence. This

Table 6.1   The relationship of compliance and effectiveness

|  | **Effectiveness: Behavior influenced by IEA** | **Non-effectiveness: Behavior NOT influenced by IEA** |
| --- | --- | --- |
| Compliance: Behavior meets agreement standards | Treaty-induced compliance | Coincidental compliance |
| Non-compliance: Behavior does NOT meet agreement standards | Good faith non-compliance | Intentional non-compliance |

interest leads them to ask why states behave as they do, whether IEAs play any part in that behavior, and, when they do, what features of an IEA's design are responsible. In focusing on effectiveness, international relations scholars make notions of causation and influence central to their research and, thereby, allow an engagement with many questions that go beyond compliance.

The dichotomy of the legal concept of compliance (compliance or non-compliance) obscures much of analytic interest that the causal concept of effectiveness (or institutional influence) captures. To see this, consider the four categories of behavior depicted in Table 6.1: treaty-induced compliance, coincidental compliance, good faith non-compliance, and intentional non-compliance. Focusing on compliance creates two analytic problems. First, interpreting compliance as effectiveness overstates the latter by conflating coincidental compliance with treaty-induced compliance. As developed below, states comply with IEAs for many reasons, some of which are unrelated to their influence. Agreements may demand only those actions that member states would have taken anyway. They may require actions that leader states have already fulfilled in an attempt to get laggard states to alter their behavior. Economic recessions may reduce production that, in turn, leads to reductions in emissions of regulated pollutants for reasons unrelated to institutional influence. Interpreting compliance as influence or effectiveness is analytically misleading because compliant behaviors may have occurred even without the IEA.

Second, interpreting non-compliance as the absence of institutional influence also misleads. Like a smoker who only halves their cigarette use in their efforts to stop smoking completely, states may engage in good faith non-compliance, making sincere efforts to promote an agreement's goals but still falling short of its legal standards. In response to ambitious targets and timetables, states may undertake various environmentally-beneficial behaviors that fall short of compliance but involve more behavioral change than would have occurred under less aggressive rules. Thus, it seems plausible to argue that the frequent violations of the trade bans enacted under CITES have still produced lower trade levels than would have occurred under low, but non-zero, trade limits that exhibited higher compliance rates.

Given this, the rest of this chapter adopts the view that questions of compliance form a subset, but only a subset, of the questions central to evaluating IEA effectiveness. Evaluation of institutional influence or effectiveness (I will use the two terms interchangeably below) focuses on two key questions: did actors behave differently than they would have done without the IEA and why did they behave as they did? These questions then prompt several subsidiary questions, as detailed in the following sections.

## Identifying an indicator of IEA influence

To evaluate an IEA's influence, we must first ask: what should be evaluated? Where should we look for an IEA's effects (Underdal, 2002)? We need an indicator of influence – that is, some phenomenon that we would expect an IEA to influence. Three potential indicators are implied by the public policy trichotomy of outputs, outcomes, and impacts (Sabatier, 2007). Outputs include the laws, policies, and regulations that states adopt to transform an IEA from an international agreement into national law. Using national laws and regulations as evidence of IEA influence has the advantage that the adoption of public rules is easily identified and that this is a necessary precondition for behavioral changes in most countries. In addition, IEA 'fingerprints' are often evident in legislative or regulatory language that quotes or references an IEA. As important, we would be rightly skeptical of claims that an IEA caused reduced emissions in states that had never passed laws designed to encourage such reductions. Yet new laws and policies seem incomplete indicators of IEA influence, since they are necessary but certainly not sufficient as evidence of meaningful behavioral change.

Most scholars look for IEA influence in outcomes – that is, in changes in how governments or sub-state actors behave. Behavioral change is valuable since IEAs almost always identify behavioral changes that must occur to achieve agreement goals. Making a case for institutional influence is challenging if those, or related, behaviors cannot be shown to have changed. But evidence that behaviors *have* changed does not, by itself, constitute evidence of institutional influence given the number of other potential explanations of such change. Using behavior as an indicator presents other problems, including that many behaviors cannot be readily observed, especially when those responsible have incentives to keep them secret, and that demonstrating IEA influence on a particular behavior convincingly is usually more difficult than demonstrating such influence on legislation or regulations. Behavior is also unsatisfactory as an indicator of IEA effectiveness in cases in which even significant behavioral changes would be insufficient to generate a visible environmental improvement.

We can look for IEA influence in impacts – that is, in changes in environmental quality. Environmental improvement focuses attention on what is usually the ultimate object of concern that, at least nominally, motivates those negotiating IEAs. Equally important, the absence of environmental improvement provides valuable feedback to IEAs: if environmental quality is not improving, this suggests a need for different or more aggressive efforts. The disadvantage of using environmental quality as an indicator is that so many factors other than IEAs (and even other than human behaviour) influence environmental quality, including natural variation, thereby presenting challenges to accurately isolating IEA influence.

Finally, beyond the choice of laws and regulations, behavior, or environmental quality, an analyst must choose whether to look at the indicators defined by negotiators as important or at other indicators. We can evaluate CITES in terms of the trade in endangered species, the hunting and harvest of such species, or our efforts to protect such species. We can evaluate the International Convention for the Regulation of Whaling (ICRW) in terms of its effects on the whaling industry, the whale population, or the legal standing of whales. We can assess pollution agreements through ambient pollution levels, reduced cancer rates, or reduced resource use.

## Identifying a comparator of IEA influence

Beyond an indicator of influence, one needs a point of reference or 'comparator' against which observed outputs, outcomes, or impacts can be compared. Three types of comparators are possible: the legal standard established in the IEA, the 'counterfactual' of what would have happened without it, or some goal as defined by the IEA or by an analyst.

### Assessing IEA compliance

Assessing compliance involves adopting an IEA's legal standards as the comparator. For those IEAs that require the passage of particular implementing legislation; that ban, limit, or require specified behaviors; or that specify environmental quality targets and timetables, we can compare, respectively, actual legislation, behaviors, or environmental quality to those standards and identify which actors complied with particular provisions of an agreement. Indeed, once an agreement takes effect, the relevant questions for many people are 'which actors complied with, and which violated, their legal obligations?' and 'what can be done to make actors more likely to comply in the future?' Many IEAs have a subsidiary compliance body or the secretariat assess compliance or treat it as a recurring agenda item at their meetings. NGOs also undertake compliance assessments at times. Such assessments often evaluate current compliance and also identify non-compliant states and the reasons for their non-compliance and states that have complied despite obstacles. Both types of findings can foster the development of responses that make agreements more effective over time. Focusing on legal standards has the advantage of providing a comparator that usually can be identified by reading the IEA. Yet IEAs often incorporate vague or ambiguous standards, posing challenges to identifying what the standard is let alone whether states complied with it or not. Even when the standards are clear, accusations and determinations of non-compliance often involve highly-charged and political dynamics that reflect factors far broader than those implied by a dispassionate analytic evaluation of whether actual behavior met a specified standard. The biggest problem with using compliance as a comparator, however, is that even perfect levels of compliance may tell us little about IEA influence.

## Assessing IEA goal achievement

Environmental advocates and many scholars also assess IEAs in terms of environmental goals. Environmental advocates frequently criticize IEAs because behaviors fall short of their goals or because behaviors achieve those goals but the goals themselves fall short of an adequate response to the problem. Some scholars evaluate IEAs against the goals that motivated negotiators to create the institution (Young and Levy, 1999). Others evaluate them against some ideal or 'collective optimum' solution to the problem as identified by experts (Hovi et al., 2003a, 2003b; Young, 2003). Indeed, whether an IEA achieved an environmental goal, however defined, is central to what most people think of when they ask whether an agreement 'succeeded'. But even during treaty negotiation, a significant gap can develop between the lofty goals countries will accept in a preamble and the more limited proscriptions and prescriptions they will accept in substantive articles. Evaluating IEAs against publicly delineated environmental goals avoids using standards that are more ambitious than negotiators were willing to accept, often because they recognized they could not be achieved. And evaluating IEAs against their own goals, when it shows them falling short, can foster the renegotiation of existing – and the negotiation of new – agreements. International environmental progress often results from assessments which, when they show environmental progress has been made, identify how to 'move the bar' to maintain environmental progress.

## Assessing IEA effects using behavioral change and counterfactuals

Yet, assessing compliance or goal achievement can lead to insufficient care in assessing whether (or how much of) what occurred was caused by an IEA. Compliance and goal achievement can be 'happy coincidences' that have occured for reasons completely unrelated to an IEA's influence. To attribute compliance or goal achievement to an IEA – that is, to identify IEA effects – requires counterfactuals. A counterfactual is an analytically established baseline of 'what would have happened otherwise' (Fearon, 1991; Biersteker, 1993). Counterfactuals identify IEA influence by asking whether and how the legislation or regulations passed, the behaviors undertaken, or the environmental quality experienced would have been different had the IEA not existed. Comparing what *did* happen to what *would have* happened otherwise allows for the identification of various institutional effects that escape notice when using IEA legal standards or goals as comparators. A counterfactual or 'effects-oriented' approach allows the identification of those cases in which states or sub-state actors have responded to an IEA by changing their behavior but have done so in ways that fall short of, exceed, or differ from the IEA's rules. Counterfactuals can inform the renegotiation of existing agreements by identifying which IEA features or which external factors have led to particular effects, be they better, worse, or simply different than expected. Counterfactuals can also help identify forces that inhibit IEA influence by examining those cases in which we expect IEA influence but do not see it. In addition, counterfactuals allow us to derive insights from the many IEAs that lack the clear legal standards or clear goals that are requisites for assessing compliance or goal achievement. The major challenge of using counterfactuals, of course, is to estimate convincingly what laws, behaviors, or environmental quality would have existed in an IEA's absence, so that that estimate can be used to infer the IEA's influence.

Whether a compliance, goal achievement, or counterfactual approach is most appropriate depends on the analyst's goals. In the policy realm, identifying compliers and violators – even if we cannot determine whether their actions reflect IEA influence – can highlight ways to induce more compliance. Likewise, identifying those goals that have been achieved and those that have not can motivate greater efforts and identify what efforts to make. Assessing which states and sub-state actors have been influenced by an IEA and which have not, as well as which IEAs have had significant influence and which have not, sheds light on how to design IEAs to increase their influence. It is this last, counterfactual, approach on which the balance of this chapter focuses.

## Selecting the level of analysis

Our analytic goals shape both the level at which we assess an IEA, the questions we ask, and the indicators we use. We may want only to know how a particular IEA influenced a particular country. But we may want to compare the influence of one IEA on different countries. We may want to compare performance across agreements, examining either an IEA's average or total influence across many countries. We may want to compare the effects of different rules within an agreement. Or we may want to assess a rule that is common to several IEAs to determine how sensitive its effectiveness is to contextual factors.

The choice of level of analysis also entrains particular analytic obstacles. Consider an effort to assess how a particular developed country was influenced by an IEA that required developed countries (1) to reduce pollutant levels by 20 per cent; (2) to contribute annually to a pollution reduction fund; (3) to collaborate with other countries in scientific research; and (4) to provide annual emission reports. How do we assess IEA influence if that country reduces its emissions by 12 per cent, does not contribute to the pollution reduction fund, promotes extensive collaborative research, and provides annual reports only in alternate years? We might disaggregate the analysis, looking at behavior with respect to each of the four requirements separately. But consider other issues here. How do we compare the IEA's influence on this country with its influence on another that did more on two of the requirements but less on the other two? How do we compare this IEA's influence to that of another that involved only developing country parties or that required a smaller reduction in a pollutant that was much harder to control? How, if at all, do we compare the effects of pollution-regulating IEAs to wildlife-preserving IEAs? These questions highlight how plausible claims about IEA performance often entail analytic choices, assumptions, and judgments about aggregation and comparison that are, when examined, neither obvious nor straightforward.

# IEA influence, endogeneity, and selection effects

Assessing IEA influence also requires addressing endogeneity and selection effects (Mitchell, 2009). Endogeneity problems arise when the causes of a problem also influence the policies adopted to resolve it. In the domestic sphere, endogeneity poses less of an analytic problem since the actors adopting regulations are rarely the targets of regulation. However, treaties require collective efforts by actors who are simultaneously regulators and targets of regulation. As a result, the forces that influence environmentally-related behaviors also influence the design of agreements and which states become parties. This creates two challenges to assessing IEA influence. First, it reminds us that agreements are often agreed to only when states (and by those states that) are ready to limit environmental harm. IEAs exhibit 'selection effects' in which they clarify whether countries are laggards or leaders, 'screening' them *as* the former or the latter rather than influencing them to *become* the latter (Simmons and Hopkins, 2005; von Stein, 2005). Therefore, the usual evidence of IEA influence – how the post-agreement behavior of parties differed from their own pre-agreement behavior or from the post-agreement behavior of non-parties – may not confirm IEA influence. Such comparisons may simply indicate that, when states' interests become more environmental, they negotiate and/or become parties to agreements that require them to take actions they would have taken anyway, and that those states whose interests have not changed will remain non-parties.

Second, the possibility of endogeneity clarifies that comparing the influence of different IEA strategies requires surmounting the methodological problem that such strategies are not 'randomly assigned' to IEAs but are selected through processes that make certain strategies much more likely in response to certain problems. For example, we cannot assess the relative effectiveness of sanctions *vs* rewards by simply comparing the average performance of sanction-based IEAs to reward-based IEAs because states accept sanctions in IEAs under systematically different conditions than those under which they accept rewards (Mitchell and Keilbach, 2001). And those systematic differences also influence how much or how little states change their behavior in response to the IEA. These methodological problems can be surmounted (for example, by only comparing IEAs that are independently identified as addressing the same problem type), but ignoring them is a recipe for drawing inaccurate conclusions about what makes IEAs work well.

# Understanding the Influence of IEAs: How and Why do They Make the Differences They Make?

To be convincing, claims of IEA influence must demonstrate that the IEA caused the observed changes in outputs, outcomes, or impacts and must identify how and why those IEAs had the influence they had. Most IEAs have received little if any analytic attention and those that have been analyzed often have not received such critical evaluation (Mitchell, 2003). Of those that have, agreements on stratospheric ozone, waste dumping in the North Sea, and the dumping of radioactive wastes have been deemed effective; those addressing the trade in endangered species, the world's natural heritage, tropical timber, and many fisheries regimes have been deemed less effective (Peterson, 1993; Brown Weiss and Jacobson, 1998; Miles et al., 2002). Yet such judgments depend considerably on whether one is most concerned with compliance, goal achievement, or counterfactual behavior change. We can better understand when, why, and how IEAs influence behavior and why different analyses of a single IEA often reach different conclusions by considering two models of why states behave as they do and, hence, why states are more responsive to some IEAs than others.

## Two models of actor behavior

International relations scholars view the behavior of actors – whether individuals, corporations, or states – as resulting from one of two distinct logics: a logic of consequences or a logic of appropriateness (March and Olsen, 1998). These logics, which correspond approximately to 'rational actor' and 'normative' models respectively (Wendt, 1999; Fearon and Wendt, 2002), put forth different explanations of why actors comply with or violate international law and, in turn, what institutional features are most likely to induce them to adjust their behaviors.

The dominant understanding of why states behave as they do reflects a logic of consequences. Within this logic, states behave as they do as a result of explicit, instrumental calculations of how the consequences of the behaviors available to them will influence their interests. Actors have clear and well-established goals and interests and choose behaviors based on 'what is best for me'. In this 'rational actor model', actors focus on how different courses of action will affect their interests. They gather information about available alternatives and their consequences – including the likely responses from other actors – to calculate relative costs and benefits and identify which will maximize their chances of achieving their goals. Realist scholars believe that states' concerns about survival produce an exclusive focus on relative gains and how international cooperation will affect their power. These scholars expect international institutions, including IEAs, to have little influence on state behaviors (see, for example, Waltz, 1979; Strange, 1983; Mearsheimer, 1995). Institutionalist scholars contend that states, while concerned about security and their relative position in the international system, are also concerned about improving their economic, political, and social well-being and thus operate under constraints imposed by the preferences of their citizenries and domestic bureaucracies (Keohane, 1984, 1988; Keohane and Martin, 1995; Milner, 1997). The realist view suggests a healthy skepticism about whether post-institutional behavior is institution-induced behavior. It implies that the post-institutional world differs from the corresponding 'no-regime counterfactual' world only rarely and that claims to the contrary reflect misestimation of that counterfactual. The institutionalist view suggests that IEAs can alter the expected consequences of engaging (or the ability to engage) in certain behaviors in ways that change a state's decisions about what choices best suit their interests. Institutionalists (as a subset of rationalists) do not contend that institutions always influence behavior. Rather, they argue that assessing institutional influence requires empirical assessment of which institutions influence behavior, under what conditions, and how. Both views build on a logic of consequences in which institutions work through instrumental mechanisms such as sanctioning bad behavior; rewarding good behavior; redressing incapacities; undertaking joint scientific, financial aid, or technology transfer programs; increasing knowledge and concern about a problem; and so on.

The constructivist alternative to this rationalist perspective views behaviors as responses to the interplay of norms and identity operating within a logic of appropriateness (March and Olsen, 1998). States do not calculate how the available options help or harm their interests, but instead choose among behaviors by assessing 'what is the "right" thing to do in this situation for someone like me' (Finnemore, 1993; Finnemore and Sikkink, 1998). IEA influence stems from their ability to establish, strengthen, and codify norms of 'right' and 'wrong' behavior, whether 'universally', or in particular situations for particular actors. Agreements influence decisions by signaling that certain behaviors are 'appropriate' and others are 'inappropriate', or by signaling that an actor's behavioral choices will lead other actors to consider them as being a particular type of actor. For example, legal proscriptions and prescriptions transform what was, prior to successful negotiations, an undifferentiated spectrum of behaviors into the dichotomous categories of compliance and violation. Even if, as with many IEAs, the consequences for compliance or violation are unspecified and rarely implemented, simply placing behaviors in these socially-important categories may influence some actors some of the time.

From this perspective, actors respond to IEAs based on their current or desired social identities. They do not ask 'what is in my interests?' but 'how do I want to see myself?' and 'how do I want others to see me?' IEAs, for example, help define what a state must do to be considered 'environmental' or 'green'. More broadly, they define what a state must do to be considered a 'law abiding' state. What 'does the work' is not instrumental threats of sanctions or promises of reward but social processes that identify what is right, what is required, or what is expected and then socialize actors to accept and abide by those norms (Checkel, 2001, 2005; Zürn and Checkel, 2005). Norms can operate through different pathways. Strongly socialized actors may accept either the broad legal meta-norm of *pacta sunt servanda* (that legal agreements are to be obeyed) or the increasingly general norm that states should 'protect the environment'. For states or sub-state actors that internalize such norms, law assumes a 'taken for granted' character in which behaviors reflect little if any calculation. Upon the creation of a new IEA, such states accept as a foregone conclusion that they should strive to meet its commitments. Such states identify what behaviors are legal and give little thought to engaging in those that are not. Such actors are driven by an internal commitment to particular identities.

Consider a set of states or corporations generally committed to either environmental protection or law conformance but that are engaged in behaviors that a new IEA has now banned. If those actors promptly bring themselves in line with the agreement, especially if doing so is costly or if they do not seriously consider the costs, we can assume that these actors are operating according to a logic of appropriateness. Thus, judges and lawyers in states with strong rule-of-law traditions tend to 'import' international environmental law into domestic legal decisions with little consideration for the economic impacts of such rulings (Koh, 1997; Alter, 1998; Raustiala and Slaughter, 2002).

Less strongly socialized actors engage in a calculus about their behavioral choices, but it is a calculus in which the perceptions of others, rather than their material responses, are central. Governments may choose to violate an environmental agreement but cannot choose to do so while having other states or their own domestic audiences continue to consider them 'green' and 'law-abiding'. The desire to be viewed by such audiences as good environmental citizens may lead some governments to exclude violating an IEA as an option. This logic helps to explain why states that lodge objections to or withdraw from an IEA may still continue to behave in line with their rules. Thus, Norway, Japan, and Iceland all opposed the ICRW's 1986 moratorium on commercial whaling but each has since pursued whaling in ways that keep it in compliance with the ICRW's provisions: Iceland by withdrawing from the agreement; Norway by remaining a member but using ICRW procedures to 'opt out' from the moratorium's application; and Japan by issuing scientific permits for annual whale kills (Sand, 2008). And all three countries have kept whaling below pre-moratorium levels and have selected catch levels and hunting techniques using scientific principles delineated in the agreement. Thus, even cases that demonstrate the inability of international environmental law to achieve certain goals may demonstrate the power of its norms to produce outcomes that we would not expect otherwise.

This intellectual distinction between a logic of consequences and a logic of appropriateness helps us assess both whether and how IEAs can influence the behavior of states. However, that intellectual distinction should not be taken to imply that IEAs always, or even in particular cases, operate only through one or the other logic. Indeed, the distinction may be most useful in generating competing predictions about what we should observe that allow the identification of IEAs that work mainly through one logic, those that work mainly through the other, those in which the logics reinforce each other, and those in which the logics undercut each other.

## Explaining compliance and other behavior changes

These models of behavior clarify when we should expect states to comply or violate IEAs and when we should expect evidence of treaty-induced behavioral change. The distinction made above, between treaty-induced and coincidental compliance, sheds light on the factors that can explain, and the conditions that can foster, can behavioral change. Consider first the reasons for coincidental compliance – that is, for why state behavior might conform to the rules of an IEA even though it has no causal influence. How impressed should we be by the claim that 'almost all nations observe almost all principles of international law and almost all of their obligations almost all of the time' (Henkin, 1979: 47)? High compliance levels owe much to the fact that international law reflects negotiation among those actors who will be subject to it. If states often negotiate treaties to promote 'their national interests, and to evade legal obligations that might be harmful to them' (Morgenthau, 1993: 259), then we should begin by assuming that subsequent behavior conforms to agreement rules because of those interests rather than because of some independent influence of international law. Thus, compliance with fishing treaties often reflects the fact that economic and political conflicts lead to agreement on catch limits at or above the levels that the parties could reasonably catch (Peterson, 1993; Miles, 2002a, 2002b). The lack of mining in Antarctica has more to do with the availability of cheap alternatives than with any IEA bans on such mining, which themselves were possible only because the pressures to mine in Antarctica at the time were not particularly strong (Peterson, 1988). Some agreements require little or no change in behavior. Others require behavioral changes that the parties planned to make anyway. Yet others ban states from taking up certain behaviors that no country, as yet, actually engages in. We can expect high compliance levels with all these types of agreements, but we should not interpret such compliance as evidence of agreement influence.

When agreements reflect lowest common denominator negotiations, most states and corporations will find themselves already in compliance. Many states join agreements that regulate behaviors that they do not, or only minimally, engage in, as evidenced in the many countries that are party to, but not significantly engaged in, the behaviors regulated by the ICRW, the International Tropical Timber Agreement (ITTO), or the Montreal Protocol on Substances That Deplete the Ozone Layer (the Montreal Protocol). When leader states convince laggard states to contribute to solving an environmental problem, the former are likely to already have legislation that exceeds the requirements on the books. A 1985 protocol to the Convention on Long-Range Transboundary Air Pollution (LRTAP) required a reduction of sulfur emissions by 30 per cent from 1980 levels by 1993 – a standard that many parties had met before the agreement was signed. Even improvements in laggard state behavior must be examined carefully since leader states might have pressed such laggards to clean up their pollution even if there had been no agreement (for example, because of industry pressure on leader governments to demand that other governments make their competition meet equivalent environmental standards). Reaching agreement may itself be evidence that states' interests have changed; otherwise, that agreement would have been reached earlier. Often such changes in interests could be expected to prompt corresponding changes in behavior even without an agreement. Even agreements that require behaviors that appear costly at the time of negotiation may become cheaper or even economically advantageous if favorable but independent economic or technological changes then occur. In short, a reasonable starting assumption about compliance is that it reflects the short-term and self-interested behavior of the parties, defined narrowly and independent of the actions of other states, and that such behavior would have occurred anyway (Oye, 1986).

## Institutional influence within a logic of consequences

To urge starting with an assumption that compliance is not treaty-induced should not imply ending with it, however. Agreements can and do influence behavior, producing either treaty-induced compliance or good faith non-compliance even within a rationalist logic of consequences. Environmental negotiations can broaden states' definitions of their self-interest by focusing attention on long-term, unclear, ambiguous, or indirect environmental impacts that they might otherwise have chosen to ignore. Joint scientific research may show states how their behaviors harm their own interests, whether or not they harm other states' interests. As a result, some states reduced their emissions of acid precipitants in the 1980s because scientific efforts under LRTAP clarified how their own emissions harmed their own forests, lakes, and fisheries (Levy, 1993: 122). Institutional negotiations and research can make states aware of previously unknown consequences of their behavior and thereby lead them to change their policies and behaviors. Joining an agreement also may raise the expected costs of some behaviors and the expected benefits of others, if other states threaten material or social retaliation in response to agreement-related behaviors. These and other processes can lead states to take actions that are clearly in their interests but that they would not have taken otherwise.

IEAs may also lead states to forego independent decision making in favor of interdependent decision making. States may consider environmental problems as arenas in which the relative gains concerns that dominate security and economic affairs can be ignored safely, allowing each to strive to improve their national well-being in absolute terms through cooperation (Powell, 1991; Snidal, 1991). For various reasons, states can usually assume that other states will not choose their levels of environmentally-harmful behavior as part of a strategic game. Therefore, they need not make worst case assumptions about other states and can more readily use other states' past behaviors to predict their future behavior. For states whose willingness to reduce pollution or protect a species depends on how many and how much other states do, the ability to reliably predict other states' behaviors may provide enough reassurance to take action that might otherwise seem too risky. Over time, reluctant states may gain information and confidence about the behaviors of others and alter their behaviors accordingly.

Habit, institutional inertia, and domestic legal implementation and internalization also can foster institutional effectiveness. These processes are consistent with a logic of consequences but one that recognizes that governments, corporations, and individuals may engage in rational selection among alternatives during treaty adoption but that standard-operating procedures, group think, and bounded rationality may make this choice hard to revisit subsequently (Chayes, 1972). Once agreement-consistent behavior begins, bureaucratic and corporate supporters of such behavior tend to gain power and resources while their opponents lose them. A pollution treaty may help the growth of pollution control companies but harm that of polluting companies. Material capabilities also may atrophy so that violations become more difficult or expensive: the moth-balling of whaling or fur-sealing ships and the retooling of factories that produced chlorofluorocarbons (CFCs) are actions that are more costly to undo than to do. In short, international rules can help actors simplify the number of decisions they must make in a complex decision environment.

## Institutional influence within a logic of appropriateness

Now, consider agreement influence within a logic of appropriateness. When an IEA simply codifies existing environmental norms, any norm-driven behavior cannot be attributed to the IEA's influence. But IEAs sometimes strengthen existing norms or generate new ones. Although it may be difficult to isolate how much an IEA strengthened a norm that would have grown somewhat in influence anyway, this should not lead to discounting norms as potentially powerful paths of IEA influence. Governments often publicly discuss whether to join an agreement or, once they join, whether to take reservations, request extensions, use escape clauses, or withdraw altogether. However, those discussions occur within a changing normative context. When an agreement's norms are weak (as when an IEA has just been signed or has few parties) government officials can legitimately ask 'are these commitments in our country's interest?' As norms strengthen, however, it becomes more difficult to ask that question. For example, the adoption of the Limited

Nuclear Test Ban Treaty in 1960 by the United States and the Soviet Union created a norm that atmospheric testing of nuclear weapons was wrong, which dramatically changed French and Chinese debates over halting atmospheric testing and led to Pakistan and India testing their nuclear weapons underground from the beginning, despite the additional financial costs involved.

Norms may influence all states equally but may operate differentially depending on which of several identities a state seeks to promote. Democratic states tend to value their identities as following the 'rule of law' and may comply more often because they consider doing so a social 'marker' of their identity (Neumayer, 2002a). Some states (for example, the Scandinavian states) may desire self-perceptions and international reputations as environmental leaders – perceptions that failures to meet international environmental commitments undercut. The desire to maintain or promote a particular identity may not determine state behavior if it entails large domestic costs (as is evident in Norway's commitment to commercial whaling), but it may tip the balance in favor of fulfilling IEA commitments in less demanding cases. International law also influences, and is relied on by, judges, bureaucrats, and other actors within states (Alter, 1998). Large numbers of such sub-state actors bringing their behavior, and their expectations of their government, in line with international law can alter domestic legal and political realities in ways that dispose reluctant governments to do so as well.

Norms also are evident when compliant states ask 'should we violate?' and when non-compliant states ask 'should we comply?' A country that has complied with IEA provisions for years may find it difficult to argue that doing so is no longer in its interests. Its previous conformity will have strengthened the normative expectations of conformity held by its own citizens and by other states. Governments can initially use interest-based arguments to reject a norm but need stronger arguments to reject a norm that they have previously supported and urged others to support.

Such forces may influence sub-state actors even more. Businesses promulgate, and train personnel in, corporate procedures that reflect domestic and international laws, even when violations are unlikely to be detected. Corporations cannot flout domestic laws the way governments can flout international law. They cannot publicly discuss whether to comply or violate laws (whether international or not) based on whether doing so is in their interests. Indeed, many multinational corporations adopt international rules even when these rules have yet to be accepted by their home governments simply because doing so aligns with a desire among many corporations to see themselves (and to be seen) as abiding by all legal rules. And the nature of business sometimes means that companies may comply because the companies they do business with will not let them violate. Thus, international oil and cargo transporters depend heavily on companies that build, insure, and classify large tanker and container ships, and the latter have a strong norm that those they do business with must meet international marine pollution standards (Mitchell, 1994a). Companies often do not ask 'is complying with these laws in our interests?' but instead simply ask 'what is the law?'

## Explaining non-compliance, violation, and the failure to change behavior

States may not behave in line with IEA rules for reasons that are simply the converse of those just described. Actors may calculate costs and benefits and find the former exceed the latter. Agreements with normative strength will influence states more than those without it. Yet, beyond interests and norms, three additional factors help explain why IEAs may lack influence. First, consider incapacity. States and sub-state actors may fail to fulfill their IEA commitments because they lack the necessary financial, administrative, or technological resources (Haas et al., 1993; Brown Weiss and Jacobson, 1998). When developing countries fail to meet their environmental commitments, it often reflects a lack of adequate or appropriate resources (and the presence of more pressing concerns) rather than a calculation that non-compliance better fits their interests. Indeed, the shift in environmental agreements over the past two decades from sanctioning violations to facilitating compliance reflects the recognition of how much non-compliance arises from incapacity (Chayes and Chayes, 1995).

Precisely because IEAs often require governments to alter the behavior of numerous sub-state actors, non-compliance is likely among those governments that lack the relevant administrative, informational, or regulatory infrastructures. Incapacities can sometimes affect all countries. International standards intended to prompt technological innovation may fail to do so, leaving companies with no, or only prohibitively expensive, ways to comply. More often, however, incapacities are country-specific. Developing countries may fail to restrict certain types of tree clearing or wetland draining because they cannot identify the peasants who engage in those activities or communicate new rules to them effectively. Governments may lack effective regulatory infrastructures, as with ships that cannot be inspected for compliance with international marine pollution treaties because they rarely enter ports of the state in which they are registered (DeSombre, 2006). Cultural, social, and historical forces make the companies and citizens of some countries less likely than those of others to comply with certain IEAs. The economic trajectories of some states make them harder to alter than those of others, as is evident in the differential treatment provided to post-Soviet 'economies in transition' in many IEAs. And different governments' policy styles may all but preclude the adoption of policy instruments that would be effective with available resources (Boehmer-Christiansen and Skea, 1991; Boehmer-Christiansen, 1992).

Second, states sometimes fall short of intended behavioral changes due to inadvertence. Many policy strategies have inherently uncertain effects, particularly those that give targeted actors flexibility. Thus, a tax established in good faith at a level expected to produce a 7 per cent emission reduction by a certain date may produce only a 3 per cent reduction because of an unexpected economic boom. Programs that perform well in one country may, for various reasons, perform less well when duplicated in others. Innovative policies reflecting sound theoretical predictions may, in the messy world of implementation, face obstacles that reduce or eliminate any significant influence on behavior or environmental quality.

Finally, normative and ideological factors may undercut rather than support an IEA. An IEA that ignores the concerns of particular states may lead those states to reject that IEA completely. Norms regarding equity or the right to develop may trump norms of environmental protection. Developing countries have vigorously objected, for example, to a forestry agreement unless it included temperate and boreal, as well as tropical, forests (Parson et al., 1992). Likewise, many developing countries joined the Montreal Protocol only after their economic situations were properly reflected in that agreement's terms.

## Systems and Strategies for Inducing Behavioral Change

Understanding why states and sub-state actors fulfill, or fail to fulfill, IEA commitments and the general process by which IEAs wield influence leaves unanswered questions about which IEAs perform better, how effective ones promote behavioral change and environmental improvement, and how to improve IEA effectiveness. How do we explain variation in the performance of IEAs? Numerous case studies have demonstrated that some countries are more likely to be influenced by a particular IEA than others (see, for example, Brown Weiss and Jacobson, 1998; Victor et al., 1998a; Young, 1999a). Scholars recently have looked across cases to explain variation across IEAs rather than across countries (Helm and Sprinz, 2000; Miles et al., 2002; Mitchell, 2002).

For over a decade, research has focused on whether IEAs, and international law generally, achieve better results with an 'enforcement' or 'managerial' approach. Proponents of the enforcement view believe states operate according to a logic of consequences but one in which sanctions are more influential than any alternatives. Significant behavioral change requires treaties with 'teeth' in the form of potent sanctions (Downs et al., 1996). In this view, most IEAs are 'shallow' and require the parties to do only what they would have done anyway. If they are 'deep' and require major behavior changes, they only will have influence if they include sanctions that make behavioral change – however costly – the cheapest option. Proponents of the managerial view contend that states use many mechanisms to induce treaty-consistent behavior (Chayes and Chayes, 1995). In this view, state behavior reflects both a logic of consequences and a logic of appropriateness and states' failures to meet their commitments usually reflect incapacity, inadvertence, or normative conflicts. Sanctions are usually, though not always, inappropriate or ineffective and IEA influence is maximized through procedures that encourage and facilitate compliance rather than those that punish non-compliance. The management/enforcement dichotomy captures useful analytic distinctions but also obscures the many other ways that IEAs can influence behavior. IEAs often include components of both models and sometimes have components that do not readily fit into these overly simplified categories.

As noted in the previous chapter, IEAs can be regulatory (delineating proscriptions or prescriptions), procedural (regularizing collective decision making procedures), programmatic (pooling resources for collective projects), or generative (fostering new social practices) (Young, 1999b: 24ff). We might expect each type of IEA to have different behavioral effects. The following discussion focuses on the influence of regulations, whether delineated in a regulatory IEA or promulgated through a procedural IEA's decision-making processes. The non-regulatory strategies of generative and programmatic institutions certainly can influence behavior but are not investigated here, reflecting the fact that these institutions' lack of clear behavioral standards requires more analytic assumptions to evaluate their influence and that limited scholarly attention has left theory regarding their influence far less developed (however, see Keohane and Levy, 1996).

## Systems of regulation

Regulatory and procedural IEAs have three systems that contribute to inducing behavior change (Mitchell, 1996). Effective agreements match all three systems to the problem being addressed. An IEA's primary rule system consists of its overarching goals and specific proscriptions and prescriptions. As noted in the previous chapter, primary rule systems can, inter alia, establish aggressive or limited goals; be specific or vague; proscribe, prescribe, or permit certain actions; ban or only limit behaviors; target relatively few or many actors; or regulate acts of omission or acts of commission. Deciding which activity to regulate determines which actors with what interests and capacities must change their behavior, how large and costly those changes will be, and whether other factors will reinforce or undercut incentives to change.

An IEA's information system seeks to generate indicators of outputs, outcomes, and impacts related to how actors have behaved and what progress has been made toward agreement goals. Regulating highly transparent activities or those involving transactions between actors can reassure actors that they will be aware when others violate an agreement's terms and can respond to protect their interests if needed. Information systems vary widely, from the self-reporting common to most IEAs through systems involving careful implementation review to independent verification systems such as TRAFFIC's database for monitoring the endangered species trade (Brown Weiss and Jacobson, 1998; Victor et al., 1998a). Systems that make reporting both advantageous and easy perform better than others that sanction non-reporting or fail to address practical obstacles to reporting. Many IEAs rely, whether explicitly or implicitly, on NGOs that often have both the incentives and capacity to monitor the agreement-related behaviors of governments and corporations.

Regulatory and procedural IEAs also contain response systems intended to make states and sub-state actors more likely to conform to institutional rules and promote institutional goals. Responses can range from retaliatory non-compliance or retaliation through economic or other mechanisms; the provision of positive incentives or capacity-promoting funding and training; positive and negative diplomatic or public pressures; transparency and market-based systems; and the promotion of norms (even within regulatory IEAs) (Chayes and Chayes, 1995; Wettestad, 1995; Downs et al., 1996; Brown Weiss and Jacobson, 1998; Victor et al., 1998a).

## Strategies of regulation

IEA regulatory systems tend to reflect six ideal types: punitive, remunerative, preclusive, generative, cognitive, or normative (Mitchell, 1997). These categories capture meaningful similarities and differences in how IEAs attempt to influence behavior. IEAs can rely primarily on one approach or combine aspects of several. The available empirical evidence does not support a claim that one strategy is systematically superior to others. Therefore, this section delineates differences in the strategies and conditions under which each is likely to be effective at inducing behavior change.

### Consequence altering strategies

IEAs can influence behaviors by altering the consequences of engaging in them. Both remunerative and punitive strategies – 'carrots' and 'sticks' – assume actors use a logic of consequences. Negative 'punitive' strategies attempt to convince governments that other states, NGOs, or their own citizens will be likely to notice if they do not fulfill their commitments; that those actors will impose economic, political, or social costs when they notice; and that those costs will outweigh the benefits that a violator would otherwise accrue from violating. In short, sanctions must be credible (likely to be imposed) and potent (costly to the target if imposed).

Remunerative strategies involve providing rewards contingent upon states fulfilling their IEA commitments. These benefits are additional to whatever environmental or other benefits accrue directly from fulfilling those commitments. They can involve financial rewards for compliance or positive behavior changes, such as financial aid, improved trade relations, or greater cooperation in other issue areas. Remunerative strategies can be distinguished from generative strategies (see below) in that they address incentive problems rather than incapacity problems.

Strategies of carrots and sticks share several features. Both depend on coupling after-the-fact monitoring with contingent responses. They work by signaling likely responses to behaviors *after* they occur in hopes of influencing choices *before* they occur. They depend on an information system capable of reliably identifying actor behavior and on a response system capable of reliably mobilizing threatened sanctions or promised rewards. Information systems within punitive strategies face particularly demanding requirements. Threats of sanctions drive information underground, creating incentives for targeted actors to find ways to continue their existing behavior in a clandestine manner. By contrast, remunerative strategies can be designed to make rewards contingent on actors performing required behaviors and also on providing convincing evidence of having done so.

Both strategies must overcome the disincentives actors have to imposing sanctions or providing rewards. Although many scholars and practitioners view sanctions as essential to effective international law, states rarely impose them (Chayes and Chayes, 1995; Downs et al., 1996). In some cases, potential sanctioning states lack resources that they are willing to use that would, even potentially, influence the non-compliant actor. In others, the benefits that potential sanctioners expect to receive if sanctions succeed may not outweigh the costs of imposing those sanctions. In yet others, sanctions present a second-order collective action problem in which potential sanctioners value the benefits that collective sanctioning would generate but seek to avoid the costs of contributing to such sanctioning (Axelrod and Keohane, 1986). It also can prove difficult to 'target' sanctions on an offending state without imposing costs on other (innocent) states. And domestic political objections to sanctioning may arise from those sectors that bear the costs of sanctioning and other sectors that demand that all states contribute to the sanctioning effort. This range of obstacles explains both how rarely IEAs incorporate sanctioning provisions, and if incorporated, how rarely they are used (Chayes and Chayes, 1995).

Despite these various obstacles, states are likely to adopt and use sanctions if concern about the environmental problem – and about individual violations of IEA rules – is strong and if retaliatory non-compliance is incentive-compatible, in the sense that sanctioners see it as in their interest to impose sanctions. States are likely to consider sanctions seriously only if they view individual violations of IEA rules as directly and significantly harming their interests. Thus, US domestic outcries about whaling have regularly prompted government officials to impose sanctions on whaling states to fulfill their ICRW commitments. But the effectiveness of such sanctions depends on their being potent, that is, that targeted actors view the sanctions as making it attractive to fulfill their commitments. Retaliatory non-compliance (in which the sanction consists of other countries violating IEA rules) is often not incentive-compatible in cases of environmental degradation: states rarely see sanctioning by polluting their own environment as in their interests or as likely to be effective. However, it is often incentive-compatible in appropriation problems. States do have incentives to increase their own appropriation – of a fish stock, for example – if others are violating established quotas. Sanctions can also become incentive-compatible in a domestic political sense when Baptist-bootlegger coalitions form because enforcing IEAs coincides with the desire of economic sectors for trade protection (DeSombre, 1995, 2000).

Remunerative strategies face similar obstacles to achieving credibility and potency. First, offering rewards must overcome normative resistance to the notion that states capable of meeting their commitments should be rewarded for doing so. IEA membership is voluntary and is usually assumed to include the obligation to fulfill the corresponding commitments without remuneration. Second, such strategies must decide which group of states that could comply should be rewarded for doing so and which should provide those rewards, with most states understandably preferring a 'no rewards' system to one in which they are in the latter category. Third, as with sanctions, states have incentives to shirk in providing rewards in the hope that others will contribute enough to induce a target to respond. Despite such problems, a 1911 agreement provided for Russia and the United States to pay Canada and Japan to stop killing fur seals, and a 1976 agreement provided for the Dutch, Germans, and Swiss to pay France to stop polluting the Rhine (Dorsey, 1991, 1998; Bernauer, 1995b, 1996).

Remunerative strategies are most effective when they are incentive-compatible and are structured to avoid the 'obsolescing bargain' problem. Potential donors must have incentives to contribute to rewards. Those incentives usually consist of the fact that, if not provided, the targeted actor will continue engaging in the environmentally-harmful behavior. Thus, states will offer rewards when they view themselves as sufficiently harmed by another state's activities to offer rewards large enough to convince the targeted actor to discontinue that behavior. To be effective, however, rewards usually must create an ongoing and mutually contingent relationship between compliance and such rewards. Rewards in the fur seal case worked because Russian and American sealers provided a share of their sealskins only after Canadian and Japanese sealers demonstrated they had caught no seals in the prior year, a fact easily verified since London was the only market where sealskins could be sold. Rewards were less effective in the Rhine case both because French behavior was harder to verify and because the rewards involved a one-time contribution to funding a facility to divert chlorides from the

Rhine rather than annual payments contingent upon verified reductions in chloride levels in that river (Bernauer, 1995b, 1996).

Both punitive and remunerative strategies are likely to be effective when victim states are harmed sufficiently in ways that give
them strong incentives to respond and the responses they are willing to undertake are sufficient to alter the calculations of the violating states.

## Opportunity-altering strategies

Though they have received little scholarly attention, IEAs can also
alter the opportunities available to states. Preclusive strategies
remove existing opportunities to engage in proscribed behaviors and
generative strategies create new opportunities to engage in pre-
scribed behaviors. If punitive strategies make it more costly *to have
engaged in* certain behaviors, preclusive strategies make it harder or
more costly *to engage in* those behaviors. The Montreal Protocol bans
parties from exporting specified chemicals to non-parties – to the
extent that parties fulfill this commitment, they prevent non-parties
that cannot produce these chemicals domestically from increasing
their emissions of ozone-depleting substances. The CITES ban
on trade with countries that lack adequate regulatory frameworks
and the Kyoto Protocol's eligibility rules for engaging in emissions
trading illustrate nicely how IEAs can influence state behavior in
ways that a compliance focus misses: such regulations influence
states that, by definition, cannot be evaluated as compliant or not
since they may not be members of the agreement. Similarly, shipbuilders incorporated environmental shipbuilding standards
adopted under the International Convention for the Prevention of
Pollution from Ships (MARPOL) and thereby effectively precluded
any company – whether from a member state or not – from purchasing
a ship that did not meet those standards (Mitchell, 1994a).

Generative strategies, by contrast, create opportunities for, and
enhance the capacities of, actors to meet their IEA commitments. To
be effective, the opportunities created must be seen as preferable by
those who would otherwise ignore or violate their IEA commitments. Rather than rewarding actors for *having engaged in* some
behavior, generative strategies make it easier or cheaper *to engage
in* that behavior. For example, port state control agreements
increase how effective ship inspections are at detecting violations of
marine pollution treaties. They require member maritime authorities to log daily inspections in a central database; such inspection
information helps each maritime authority to target limited inspection resources on ships that have not been inspected recently or that

have been inspected and found to be violating international standards (Kasoulides, 1993). These agreements have created a new
resource, a database that maritime authorities have found it in their
interests to use – and such use does not need to be rewarded but
simply allowed.

Both preclusive and remunerative strategies have the advantage
of not needing well-developed information systems nor of needing
states to have incentives to follow through on their threats and
promises. Neither strategy involves contingent responses, so they
need not monitor behavior to identify non-compliant actors for
sanctions or compliant actors for rewards. Both influence actors
without knowing how those actors would behave with respect to
proscriptions or prescriptions. Just as banks lock their vaults and
place trash cans in their lobbies to make it harder for people to rob
the bank but easier for them not to litter, so too environmental
agreements can be structured to make violating their provisions
more difficult and fulfilling their provisions easier.

Despite these virtues, these strategies are available and effective
only under limited conditions. Preclusive strategies are available
only when a state can violate an agreement through actions entailing cooperation or complicity from other actors. They work only if
the states that support an IEA control resources required by those
states seeking to violate it. Prohibiting the export of banned substances to non-parties has little influence on countries that can produce those substances domestically. Similarly, generative
strategies depend on the availability of processes or technologies
that foster positive behaviors and that, if put in place, would be
viewed as more attractive than existing behaviors. However, such
alternatives may not exist. Generative strategies are most effective
when capacity constraints create a bottleneck that limits the environmental efforts of pro-environment states and when joint capacity creation can remove that bottleneck. Preclusive strategies are
most effective when those engaged in environmentally-harmful
activities require the complicity of actors who support environmental protection or of actors who are sensitive to pressures from pro-
environment actors.

## Perception-altering strategies

IEAs also can influence state behavior by changing perceptions,
providing actors with new information about alternatives or engaging them in normative dialogues about those alternatives. Cognitive
strategies – what might be called 'labels' – involve processes
designed to give states new information about the consequences of

their available choices to alter their calculation of which choices will best promote their interests. This strategy assumes – and is only effective if – targeted actors operate within a logic of consequences and engage in 'undesirable' behaviors only because they lack full and accurate knowledge of the consequences of their choices. IEAs addressing pesticides, hazardous waste, and genetic resources have adopted rules requiring 'prior informed consent' in the belief that providing better information to those at risk from certain activities will make them conduct those activities less often or more safely. States *adopt* these strategies when they seek to balance state sovereignty and environmental protection, when political support for stronger action is lacking, or when faced with strong differences in countries' assessments of and tolerance for environmental risks. Whether these strategies are *effective*, however, depends on whether existing behaviors are caused by actors lacking complete and accurate information about consequences or by deeper forces that would generate the same behaviors even if better information became available.

Normative strategies target deeper change. Rather than target the means by which actors pursue pre-existing ends, such strategies target the ends actors pursue or their beliefs about whether particular means are ever appropriate for pursuing their ends. They seek to get actors to shift from a logic of consequences to a logic of appropriateness. By engaging actors in discussions that frame an environmental problem in particular ways, such strategies can, over time, convince them to adopt new views regarding which goals and means are socially legitimate. Many IEAs include phrases like 'the common heritage of mankind', 'sustainable development', and the 'precautionary principle' in their original texts, regularly refer to them in institutional conversations, and use them to praise or condemn certain behaviors. Embedding these concepts in international law and practice alters the normative and discursive landscape within which governments make choices and are judged – by others and their own polities – with respect to extracting deep sea-bed resources, exploiting their country's natural resources, or releasing genetically modified organisms. Re-framing a debate to delegitimize certain actions does not prevent states from taking such actions but it can create pressures that, at the margin and over time, convince actors who would otherwise have taken such actions that doing so is inappropriate and, therefore, that they should look for alternative options.

Both cognitive and normative strategies, when successful, can produce long-term, internalized shifts in actors that make subsequent monitoring or manipulation of incentives unnecessary to maintain certain behaviors. States that are convinced that certain behaviors harm their own interests – regardless of what other states do – will avoid those behaviors without additional sanctions or rewards being needed. Likewise, actors that become convinced that certain behaviors are truly inappropriate will seek out more socially acceptable alternatives. The fundamental weakness of cognitive strategies is that more accurate information often reinforces, rather than undermines, an actor's view that their behavior is the right course of action, even if it harms the interests of others. Likewise, normative strategies require sustained efforts to shift the terms of debate and the perceptions of targeted actors and may take far longer to induce change than alternative strategies. They are particularly unlikely to work if 'doing the right thing' proves to have significant material costs. Overall, the influence of normative strategies is likely to be long term and marginal rather than immediate and dramatic.

## Explaining Variation in Effectiveness

Researchers have identified numerous variables that explain observed differences in effectiveness. Indeed there is, arguably, an 'embarrassment of riches' of variables, each with a compelling logic and empirical support but which, collectively, lack coherence. Different terms are used to identify conceptually similar variables. Proposed taxonomies identify variables at different levels of resolution and draw boundaries between variables in ways that prevent mapping from one to others. Haas, Keohane, and Levy, identified three broadly-defined factors that explain institutional effectiveness in terms of governmental concern, political and administrative capacity, and the contractual environment (Keohane et al., 1993). Brown Weiss and Jacobson related institutional performance to 12 characteristics of the country, six characteristics of the international environment, eight characteristics of the institution, and four characteristics of the activity involved (Jacobson and Brown Weiss, 1998). Victor and colleagues identified systems of implementation review and other factors as important explanations of the effectiveness of international institutions (Victor et al., 1998a). Young and colleagues highlighted six causal pathways and behavioral mechanisms by which institutions influence behavior (Young, 1999a). Miles and colleagues argued that institutional effectiveness is determined by a problem's structure – in particular, how benign or malign the problem is – and by the institution's problem-solving capacity and the actors concerned about that problem (Miles et al., 2002). Breitmeier and colleagues concluded from data reflecting numerous hypotheses that state behavior is shaped not only by consequences and appropriateness but also by discourse, legitimacy, and habit (Breitmeier et al., 2006: 234–5). Despite these and other differences, some commonalities exist including broad agreement that effectiveness reflects both institutional and non-institutional factors (Young, 1989b; Underdal, 1998a; Breitmeier et al., 2006).

Much of the literature on IEA effects has asked 'how do international environmental institutions influence the behaviors of states?' Yet asking 'what explains variation in the environmental behavior of states?' proves more useful. It broadens our focus beyond institutions to include the many non-institutional forces that can hinder or facilitate IEA efforts. Accounting for economic, technological, political, and other influences on behavior not only makes claims of IEA influence more accurate by refuting alternative explanations but also clarifies whether an IEA's influence depends on (and is 'large' or 'small' relative to) these other influences. Foregoing sections of this chapter have identified how variation in country characteristics and institutional strategies can influence regulated behaviors. But many other factors drive environmental degradation, including the nature of the problem and of the international context (Brown Weiss and Jacobson, 1998). These factors can operate independent of IEAs, requiring that we treat them as alternative explanations, or can facilitate or inhibit IEA influence, requiring that we recognize that IEA influence is contingent on other factors and that we account for that contingency when generalizing to other cases.

The characteristics of environmental problems influence the effects an IEA will have on a given behavior but also generate variation in these behaviors (over time, across actors, and across problems) that are independent of IEA influence. At a broad level, some problems are benign and relatively easy to remedy while others are malign and more challenging to remedy (Underdal, 2002). IEAs that address large, immediate, and visible environmental threats that can be resolved relatively cheaply are likely to produce faster and more dramatic change than those addressing more challenging problems. Problems that require restraint in current behavior may do better than those that require new behaviors or technologies, since the latter face obstacles due to incapacity as well as incentives. IEAs will more readily change those behaviors that are not deeply embedded in social structures and for which relatively cheap and easily-adopted alternatives exist, as evidenced in the greater challenges of regulating greenhouse gases compared to regulating CFCs. Market structures can reinforce or undercut regulatory efforts – the effectiveness of the 1911 fur seal agreement owed much to the fact that a single market for sealskins in London made monitoring easy (Dorsey, 1998). Marine pollution agreements benefit from the incentives that shipbuilders and ship insurers have to monitor and enforce them while, by contrast, endangered species agreements create shortages and price increases that encourage smuggling (Mitchell, 1994a; Jacobson and Brown Weiss, 1998: 521). IEA influence also depends on many factors that negotiators cannot control, including how many states contribute to a problem; scientific uncertainty about a problem and its resolution; the positions of corporate interests; and the level of concentration of the regulated activity (Brown Weiss and Jacobson, 1998: 536 (Figure 15.2)). Scientific research can mobilize action if it uncovers that environmentally-harmful activities impose large, immediate, and tangible costs on those engaged in them or on others who have sufficient sway with those engaged in them. Polluting behaviors often decline if environmentally-friendly technologies become economically attractive, whereas extractive behaviors like fishing are less responsive to technological developments because environmental damage is more inherent to those behaviors. An environmental problem's structure helps us understand such questions as why some IEAs are more effective than others with similar designs and why the effectiveness of IEAs changes over time.

Indeed, the temporal profile of IEA influence deserves separate mention here. Although evaluation of IEA influence over time remains an underdeveloped research area, three points can be offered. First, we should expect IEA influence to reflect a certain lifecycle – starting out relatively weak, gaining strength over time, and then declining after an IEA achieves its major goals. Therefore, assessing whether an IEA is effective or ineffective (whether in an absolute sense or relative to other IEAs) requires having some sense of what point an IEA is at in its lifecycle. Second, differences in temporal profiles may make comparison across IEAs challenging. How should we compare two institutions – one that was quite influential in its first five years but had little influence thereafter, and another that had no influence for its first five years but exercised increasing influence for the next 30 years? Third, what constitutes an 'impressive' temporal profile for an IEA depends on the type of problem being addressed. For pollution and other environmental degradation problems, 'success' most likely consists of inducing a continuing decrease, or a reduction in the rate of increase, of such degradation. By contrast, for fisheries and other appropriation problems such 'success' might consist of a sharp initial decline in catch to allow stocks to recover followed by a modest subsequent increase followed by a leveling off at some sustainable yield. Further theoretical and analytic research is needed to address the issues that temporal aspects of institutional influence raise.

Country-specific economic factors, political forces, policy styles, and demographic and social characteristics can all help explain why countries vary in their environmental degradation as well as in their responsiveness to IEAs. Variation in IEA influence reflects stable forces such as history and social and cultural commitments, geographic size and heterogeneity, and resource endowments; factors that vary more over time such as level of development, type of government, the role of NGOs and environmental parties, and attitudes and values; and immediate drivers such as administrative and financial capacity, leadership changes, and the activities of civil society groups (Jacobson and Brown Weiss, 1998: 535). In some cases, IEAs increase their influence by taking such factors into account. Thus, marine pollution agreements had little influence when flag states were granted sole enforcement rights but became more effective when they extended enforcement rights to the port states that were both more concerned and more able to enforce them (Mitchell, 1994a). IEAs that fail to take country-specific factors into account are less likely to be effective. And certain institutional features may influence actors who lack certain political, financial, and administrative capacities but produce little if any change in the behavior of actors that have those capacities.

The international context also influences IEA effectiveness (Jacobson and Brown Weiss, 1998: 528). Large-scale shifts – globalization, democratization, the development of new technologies, global booms or recessions, the end of the Cold War, and the start of the War on Terror – alter how, how many, and how much countries protect the environment. The ebb and flow of such factors shape global environmental concern which, in turn, shapes the deep and long-term incentives individuals, corporations, and countries have to look for environmental problems, to adopt environmental behaviors, to design clean technologies, and, at the extreme, to alter societal structures to reduce the level and trends in anthropogenic environmental impacts. Global concern can be promoted by international conferences (such as the 1972 UN Conference on the Human Environment, the 1992 UN Conference on Environment and Development, and the 2002 World Summit on Sustainable Development) and by major scientific reports on problems such as climate change, biodiversity, or ozone loss (Clark et al., 2002). NGOs such as the Worldwide Fund for Nature and Greenpeace, and intergovernmental organizations such as the UN Environment Programme and the World Bank, have focused countries' attentions on environmental problems and provided financial and informational resources to address them. These forces overlap and interact with IEAs to promote broad support for environmental protection and corresponding behavioral change. This interplay between individual IEAs and other international institutions increasingly affects IEA influence, as illustrated both by efforts to coordinate the implementation of various species and habitat conventions and by the possibility of incompatibilities between IEA commitments and World Trade Organization (WTO) rules (Ramsar Convention Bureau, 1999; Stokke, 2001; Young, 2002; Oberthür and Gehring, 2006). The dynamics of such interactions among IEAs (and between IEAs and non-environmental institutions) has prompted a lively debate about whether the increasing density of environmental agreements helps or harms the ability of each to achieve its objectives and about whether subsuming IEAs into a global environmental organization would facilitate or impede environmental progress (Biermann, 2001; Biermann and Bauer, 2005).

Research on institutional interplay also has implications for evaluating IEA influence. Interplay may create redundancies and conflict in some cases and healthy competition in others (Stokke, 2001; Young, 2002; Haas, 2004; Oberthür and Gehring, 2006). When institutions are nested, overlap, or otherwise interact, disentangling the influence of individual institutions requires isolating each institution's influence as well as the influence of their interactions (Sprinz et al., 2004; Gehring and Oberthür, 2008). Should reductions of acid precipitants in Europe be attributed to the LRTAP Convention and its protocols, to European Union regulatory efforts, or to synergies between those institutions? Should reductions in whales catches be attributed to the ICRW, the North American Marine Mammal Commission created by whaling states as an alternative to the ICRW, the CITES convention, or agreements protecting cetaceans signed under the Convention On The Conservation Of Migratory Species Of Wild Animals? How do we allocate responsibility for changes in the timber trade given the simultaneous influence of the WTO, the ITTO, and nongovernmental efforts like those of the Forestry Stewardship Council? As institutional interplay increasingly reflects conscious policy coordination rather than the unintended consequence of unilateral institutional action, it may become increasingly difficult to attribute positive – or negative – outcomes to one institution, another, a combination, or the meta-institution constituted by policy coordination efforts.

Institutional interactions also can affect institutional influence through policy diffusion and other, less obvious and direct, mechanisms.

Institutions may observe and adopt the strategies and approaches of other institutions. An institution's influence may include propagating institutional meta-norms or design principles to create emission markets, adopt the precautionary principle, or use a framework-protocol approach to treaty-writing. Indeed, interaction and interplay can occur at and across international, national, and domestic levels. How should we allocate credit for local environmental improvements when they reflect the direct and immediate influence of new local institutions that would not have developed without both the creation of relevant international environmental institutions and deeper, structural shifts in political and economic conditions? These are challenging questions intended to reveal how much remains to be discovered in the realm of institutional effectiveness.

A final caveat is in order regarding the influence of IEAs relative to other international organizations, national governments, and non-state actors. IEAs rarely have persuasive power of their own. Their influence on behavior flows through supportive governments, corporations, NGOs, and individuals taking steps that 'breathe life into' IEA provisions by monitoring behaviors, responding so as to induce behavioral change, identifying the environmental and economic consequences of behaviors, and engaging various actors in normative dialogue. Where a network of supportive actors exists, IEAs may be influential regardless of their precise terms. Where such a network is absent, IEAs will tend to be less influential.

# Beyond the Effectiveness of International Environmental Institutions

Before concluding, a few points are in order on the limitations of focusing on the effectiveness of international environmental institutions. The first involves the importance of also evaluating important but non-environmental aspects of the performance of international environmental institutions. The second involves the importance of evaluating the environmental effects of non-environmental international institutions. And the third involves the importance of recognizing how much non-intergovernmental efforts contribute to resolving international environmental problems.

An exclusive focus on effectiveness as defined above leaves three important aspects of the performance of international environmental institutions unaddressed. First, despite the value placed on behavior and counterfactuals above, we often want to know whether an IEA solved an environmental problem and not just whether it made things better than they would have been otherwise. When looking at institutional performance, analysis often should include actual *vs* aspirational comparisons as well as actual *vs* counterfactual comparisons. Useful institutional analyses must identify how much more work IEAs have to do as well as how much they have already accomplished. Second, although the environmental influences of IEAs are important, publics and policy-makers also rightly care about their non-environmental influence. Stakeholders, policy-makers, and scholars want to know how IEAs have helped or undermined efforts to promote economic development, social equity and justice, indigenous cultures, and other social goals. Third, we also often evaluate the performance of social institutions, including international environmental ones, with respect to procedural standards such as transparency, accountability, and the like. In short, there are both non-behavioral and non-environmental effects of international environmental institutions that deserve our analytic attention but have not been discussed here.

Focusing on the environmental effects of international environmental institutions also draws our attention away from the important environmental impacts of non-environmental international institutions. Institutions like the World Trade Organization, the International Monetary Fund, and the World Bank are larger, more powerful, and better funded than are international environmental institutions. Their actions often have major environmental effects, whether resulting from the promotion of international trade, economic development, or specific infrastructure projects. Institutions that do not have environmental protection as their central mandate still can have major environmental impacts that both attract and deserve attention, particularly since those impacts may be far larger in magnitude than those of the IEAs that have been the focus here.

Finally, focusing on intergovernmental efforts ignores important alternative strategies. Many governments, NGOs, and corporations are now adopting strategies to address international environmental problems outside IEAs. Governments sometimes address international environmental problems unilaterally – funding financial aid, scientific exchanges, environmental projects, or training to help other governments reduce their environmental impacts. NGOs engage in many innovative strategies to influence governments, corporations, and individuals either before intergovernmental efforts begin or in ways that would be unlikely to result from such efforts. Under certain circumstances, corporations find it worthwhile to take actions alone or in concert with other corpora-tions that address international environmental problems. And indi-viduals often take actions that directly help resolve environmental problems and indirectly set examples and persuade others to adopt pro-environmental values and actions. These non-intergovernmental realms often foster greater innovation and allow the use of quite dif-ferent mechanisms of influence. The unilateral and voluntary efforts of such actors are crucial to addressing international environmental problems, since they often start before intergovernmental efforts, demonstrate the availability and effectiveness of untried policies, and contribute additional resources to problems that intergovern-mental efforts are addressing. Fully understanding IEAs requires comparing their effectiveness to that of such non-intergovernmental alternatives. It also requires knowing whether expending a particular amount of resources through an IEA would be more or less effective than through alternatives such as incorporating environmental considerations into non-environmental institutions, convincing corporations to adopt environmental standards, or having NGOs operate alone or in corporate and government part-nerships to improve environmental protection (Brown Weiss, 1997; Andonova and Levy, 2003).

## Conclusion

Accurately assessing IEA influence requires engaging questions of causality in ways that distinguish their influence from the various other factors that influence behavior. The analytic goal should be to identify how much of the policies, behaviors, and environmental quality that we observe after an agreement is signed to attribute to an IEA. Compliance often may not reflect IEA influence but may be due to economic, political, or social circumstances unrelated to that IEA. Nor is non-compliance always evidence of an IEA's lack of influ-ence. IEAs may cause significant progress that falls short of compli-ance for various reasons. Indeed, IEAs sometimes seek to influence non-party states whose behavior cannot even be defined as compli-ant or not. IEA influence on states and sub-state actors operates through two competing logics of consequences and of appropriate-ness. They influence behavior through six strategies that alter the consequences of available alternatives, alter the availability of those alternatives themselves, or alter perceptions of the consequences or norms surrounding those alternatives. How states behave in response to an IEA depends not only on the pre-institutional incentives and norms that determine how likely they are to continue behaviors that they would engage in without an IEA, but also on the particular primary rules, information systems, and response systems that the IEA adopts. Issues related to the underlying problem structure, to the expected temporal profile of an IEA given that problem structure, and to changes in the broader international context all influence whether an IEA is effective and how difficult it is to identify that effectiveness.

# THE FUTURE OF INTERNATIONAL ENVIRONMENTAL POLITICS

Environmental problems will not leave the international scene anytime soon nor will international environmental politics. In the decades – and centuries – ahead, environmental problems will be an increasing part of the international agenda. In part, this will reflect a real increase in environmental degradation due to increases in population, affluence, and the impacts of the technologies humans use. But it will also reflect an increased awareness and attention to such problems. More problems will emerge as scientists or others discover that behaviors previously considered benign damage the environment. They will also emerge as concern grows over known environmental impacts, such as the excessive fixing of nitrogen and other fertilizers in the soil. And they will emerge in response to two dynamics of international environmental politics. The successful management of extant environmental problems will allow governments and intergovernmental institutions – as well as nongovernmental organizations (NGOs), corporations, and individuals – to take up new environmental problems. And those entities may learn new ways to surmount the obstacles that hinder efforts to address and resolve international environmental problems.

This book has provided a framework for understanding the politics that can explain these changes in the problems we face, their emergence on the international stage, the negotiation of intergovernmental agreements to resolve them, and the ability of those agreements to alter behavior. That framework seeks to foster two separate but linked goals. First, it identifies the factors that scholars have hypothesized influence outcomes at each of these four policy stages. More importantly, it provides the reader with methodological skills for evaluating which subset of potential explanations provides the most satisfactory story of a particular outcome. Rather than providing the readers with detailed explanations of outcomes in particular cases, this book has sought to provide them with the tools for undertaking rigorous explanatory analyses themselves and for critically assessing such analyses by others.

This chapter summarizes the major influences on outcomes at each of the four policy stages around which this book has been structured. I then examine the variation in three features that cut across policy stages, exploring how different variables, actors, and processes come to the fore or recede into the background when we attempt to explain outcomes at different policy stages. I then return to the discussion of causality raised in the book's introductory chapter and developed throughout succeeding chapters. To introduce the reader to several major debates – and the corresponding literature – in international environmental politics, I then briefly summarize the discussions surrounding trade and the environment, environmental security, the erosion of sovereignty, and the World Environmental Organization. I outline several questions that remain unanswered, both in this book and in the broader scholarly community. The chapter ends with a discussion of the environmental challenges facing the international community in the decades ahead and the contributions that policy-oriented social science research can make to address those challenges.

## Explaining International Environmental Politics

Building a convincing explanation of any outcome in international environmental politics depends on assembling and evaluating the appropriate subset of variables from a comprehensive list of theoretically likely explanations. Detectives often solve murder cases by systematically examining each of the people on a list of likely suspects. Likewise, researchers can solve the mystery of an international environmental outcome by systematically examining the variables considered as likely explanations of such outcomes. The foregoing chapters have laid out such lists of 'likely suspects' for each of the major outcomes in international environmental politics. Those chapters have encouraged the reader to consider certain factors, processes, and conditions (summarized here) to build convincing explanations of international environmental politics.

To explain why the world is plagued by particular anthropogenic environmental impacts, start by considering the roles that population, affluence, and technology play. Then consider the extent to which the type of environmental degradation, the location and timing of its occurrence, and who is responsible for it corresponds with predictions based on misaligned values, uncertain or inadequate science, lacking or poorly written laws, economic disincentives, a lack of environmentally-friendly alternatives and capacities, or the influence of power and politics.

To explain why some states engage some international environmental impacts more quickly than others, start by comparing the success that governments, scientists, NGOs, and individuals have had at promoting knowledge, concern, and urgency surrounding those impacts. But also consider how a problem's structure (the types of impacts, their magnitude and scope, their behavioral causes, and the availability of solutions) can facilitate or inhibit those efforts to build knowledge, concern, and urgency and the receptiveness of governments and their constituencies to those efforts.

To explain both why states succeed in forming international environmental agreements for some problems but not others and the variation in their content, consider the constellation of relevant actors and the power, interests, science, interdependencies, and existing institutional forums available to them that promote or inhibit international action on an issue. Consider how negotiation processes can strengthen the foundation of knowledge, concern, and urgency and, often through the commitment of particular leaders, can develop and maintain momentum toward mutually agreeable goals and policies. And also consider how all of these variables influence not only whether an agreement is negotiated but also that agreement's fundamental institutional form, its incorporation of science and flexibility, and its systems of primary rules, information, and response mechanisms.

To explain why states, and sub-state actors, alter their behavior in response to some IEAs but not others, it helps to recognize that states respond to factors reflecting both a logic of consequences and a logic of appropriateness (March and Olsen, 1998). IEAs can shift the incentives of engaging in certain behaviors, provide states with improved information regarding their options, and can alter the set of available options – but they can also alter norms related to, and perceptions of, those options. States' and sub-state actors' behavioral choices reflect both instrumental and normative signals, with the influence of institutions dependent on contextual factors and actor characteristics as well as conscious institutional efforts.

Complete and satisfactory explanations of any of these political outcomes rarely depend on either a single one of the variables outlined or on all of them simultaneously. Rather, we develop satisfactory explanations by examining each of numerous *potential* explanations in turn, dismissing those that lack supportive empirical evidence, and by ranking and prioritizing the remainder based on the strength of the supportive evidence, the quality of the correlational evidence, and the persuasiveness of the causal narratives that the analyst can develop.

# Explanatory Variation Across Policy Stages

Looking across the four policy stages used to structure this book, we can observe patterns in how the central explanatory variables, actors, and processes vary depending on what outcomes we seek to explain.

## Variables

Previous chapters have identified extensive lists of potential explanations of outcomes of interest in international environmental politics. Certain factors or variables provide more convincing explanations, however, of the outcomes in certain policy stages while other variables do better for the outcomes in other stages. International environmental problems arise from the interplay among the full array of variables. How much people value environmental protection – in absolute terms and relative to other social, political, and economic values – establishes background conditions the influence of which may be difficult to observe because they are enabling, rather than triggering, forces that exhibit little variation and are common to many environmental problems. But these deep values can help explain why environmental damage appears in so many contexts that otherwise appear to have little in common. It is the other, divergent, aspects that more frequently stand out as explanations against a background 'causal field' of values common to all the cases. If the commonality of human values helps explain the ubiquity of environmental degradation, variation in knowledge, laws, incentives, opportunities and capacities, and power helps to explain why certain types of international environmental problems emerge at certain times and among certain countries but not in other times and places.

If all these factors contribute to our explanations of why humans so frequently damage the environment, knowledge and ideas appear as particularly powerful determinants of which types of such damage end up on the international agenda. The knowledge, concern, and urgency that lead countries to take up an issue for international discussion tend to be more responsive to the persuasion of ideas than to the incentives and coercion of material sources of power. Concerned states engage others in a meaningful discussion of international environmental issues by convincing them that certain impacts on the environment do indeed exist and are a problem. Although powerful states' concerns are more likely to be taken up than those of less powerful states, the persuasion that is central to issue emergence is often more responsive to the ideas and knowledge favored by constructivist perspectives on international relations than to the power and interests favored by realists and institutionalists (Goldstein and Keohane, 1993; Risse, 2000).

Power and interests move back to explanatory 'center stage' in explanations of the negotiation of IEAs. Values, knowledge, and institutional processes can certainly influence international negotiations but the proximate explanations that satisfy our desire to understand why certain negotiations succeed when they do and among the countries they do more often involve reference to the interests of the states involved and the power of each to promote their interests in an intergovernmental setting.

The effectiveness and performance of international environmental institutions once again highlight the numerous influences on what choices people – as individuals and as collective entities – make. Values, knowledge, laws, incentives, opportunities and incapacities, and power all influence whether actors behave differently after an IEA is put in place. Satisfactory explanations of environmentally-related behaviors therefore depend on evaluating the role of all of these factors as deep enabling causes or as proximate triggering ones in explaining whatever differences we observe in behaviors when an IEA is present and when it is not.

In short, although there is a common list of potential explanations for most outcomes in international environmental politics, satisfactory explanations of particular outcomes require us to identify the appropriate subset from that list. And the best subset of variables for explaining outcomes at one stage of the international environmental policy process tends to differ from that which best explains outcomes at some other stage.

## Actors

The people and institutions centrally responsible for outcomes at each policy stage also differ markedly. Although governments, and their attempts at cooperation through intergovernmental institutions, have been central to the arguments in this book, they have not always been the centrally responsible actors. Governments are not the major direct source of most environmental problems. To be sure, governments do cause some environmental problems, such as the habitat destruction and pollution generated by war and military activities, including those related to nuclear weapons (Westing, 1986, 1988). They also generate the legal, regulatory, and economic context that shapes and channels individual and corporate behaviors toward or away from environmental degradation. But it is the behaviors of individuals and the corporations who respond to, stimulate, and shape their economic demands that are directly and primarily responsible for most international environmental problems. Governments also tend to play more reactive roles in international issue emergence. Sometimes governments proactively initiate efforts to address an international environmental problem, but more often they respond reactively to pressures from scientists, NGOs, or individuals – and the countervailing pressures of other actors – to put issues on the agenda.

Governments do take center stage during the negotiation of IEAs, however. Although often operating in response to political pressures for action, governments usually convene the intergovernmental conference to negotiate on a given problem. At times, existing international institutions may initiate such calls but any progress requires that governments respond by coming to the negotiating table. And certainly it is the power, incentives, and strategies of governments that determine whether negotiations succeed and what shape any agreement takes. Governments remain central during the processes that make IEAs effective or ineffective. International institutions (and sometimes NGOs) can play important supporting roles during IEA implementation. However, government policies establish the political, social, and economic context within which corporations and individuals make choices and the effectiveness of IEAs depends on them establishing more environmentally benign laws, policies, markets, and regulations.

Finally, it is noteworthy that IEAs are not the only, nor even the most effective, extant means for addressing international environmental problems. Although they have not been the focus of discussion in this book, the voluntary and unilateral initiatives of governments, multinational corporations, NGOs, and individuals often provide effective alternatives for taking up the range of international environmental problems currently confronting the world. Those initiatives may be intended as synergistic support to IEA efforts, as innovative supplements to those efforts, or as distinct and opposing alternatives to them. But all of them create a context in which governments and the intergovernmental institutions they set up do not exclusively control the landscape of efforts to address international environmental problems.

## Processes

Efforts to explain international environmental politics frequently depend on explanatory variables and the strategies adopted by different actors. Yet foregoing chapters have also demonstrated that the processes of international environmental politics also make a difference. The statics of 'what' and 'who' matter but, at times, so too do the dynamics of 'how'. The influence of process is most pronounced during issue emergence and negotiation. Issue emergence requires that most, if not all, relevant states engage in a discussion of some environmental impact that, at least initially, is the concern of only a subset of people or states. And such emergence depends on scientists, NGOs, and leader states promoting recognition of a problem, diffusing knowledge about it, mobilizing concern, generating a sense of urgency, and framing the issue so that relevant actors become willing to discuss it and, over time, prioritize it for action. It is not the *existence*, in a static sense, of certain ideas, concerns, and framings that explains why issues become internationalized, but the *process* by which ideas, concerns, and framings propagate among different actors and different states that helps to explain their international emergence.

Likewise, satisfactory explanations of why international negotiations succeed when and where they do tend to require reference to the dynamic and often contingent processes by which actors come to believe that accepting the agreement on the table is better than leaving the table or continuing to negotiate (Ikle, 1964). 'Getting to yes' (Fisher and Ury, 1981) in the international arena depends not only on continuing to build on the knowledge, concern, and urgency that placed an issue on the agenda in the first place but also on building a shared understanding of the problem, the need to resolve it, the appropriate ambitiousness for institutional goals, and the best strategies for achieving those goals. Individuals often play crucial roles in maintaining the momentum toward an agreement and in taking advantage of the windows of opportunity created by focusing events to prompt the transition from negotiation to agreement.

We can explain some outcomes in international environmental politics satisfactorily with little attention to process. On the one hand, evidence that a resource is held in common tends to provide a satisfactory explanation of its overappropriation; knowing that one state sits upstream from another tends to provide a satisfactory explanation of why particular types of pollution persist. Particulars about such cases may satisfy our desire to know more about the case in question but do not alter our fundamental understanding of such overappropriation as caused by holding of the resource in common and such pollution as caused by the incentives inherent in upstream/downstream problems. On the other hand, our understanding of many other outcomes in international environmental politics *is* influenced by the processes and causal narratives that the evidence allows us to tell. In many negotiations, the roles of individual leaders and of unexpected and unpredictable focusing events are not simply narrative embellishments but are central to our understanding of why the negotiations succeeded when they did and not at some prior or subsequent point in time. Understanding why certain states take the initiative on a particular environmental problem or begin action to implement a particular IEA after years of indifference often requires that we understand quite particular and contingent processes and histories, without which we cannot fully understand why things happened as they did. In short, although processes are not always crucial to a satisfactory causal explanation, they sometimes are.

## Thinking Causally

Explaining an outcome convincingly in international environmental politics requires not merely knowing the list of potential explanations for that outcome but also being able to gather and evaluate empirical evidence rigorously in light of theoretical insights. This book has highlighted that all international environmental problems are not created equal, that their problem structures vary. Some are Tragedies of the Commons, some are upstream/downstream problems, and some are problems of incapacity. Some involve overappropriation, some involve degradation, and some arise from accidents. And these differences are politically significant and therefore analytically useful because they determine the obstacles to addressing a problem and the best strategies for overcoming them. Problems differ with respect to which and how many countries are relevant to resolving the problem, the rivalry among them, their incentives, power, and capacities, and their domestic political alignments. Problems also differ with respect to the knowledge and uncertainty regarding a problem, the transparency regarding the responsible behaviors, and the values and value conflicts underlying the problem. These categories help us describe international environmental problems accurately but also are central to explaining them. They remind and allow qualitative scholars either to select cases for comparison that are truly comparable in an analytic sense or to take account of how the background conditions, the elements of the 'causal field' and the problem structure, influence the more proximate variables that appear to be doing the causal work. They remind quantitative scholars to keep track of the ways in which problems vary so that the influence of these differences can be controlled for when examining the influence of other variables.

From its first chapter, this book has sought to demonstrate the value of counterfactuals in explanatory accounts. Any causal claim – any claim in which X is said to have caused Y – necessarily involves a counterfactual claim (Fearon, 1991; Biersteker, 1993; Tetlock and Belkin, 1996). Causal claims are made more convincing by an explicit evaluation of both the primary claim and its counterfactual 'mirror image'. General theoretical claims are often phrased as 'X causes Y' or that 'when X occurs, Y becomes more likely to occur'. These claims almost always include, whether implicitly or explicitly, a *ceteris paribus* condition which assumes that the influence of other causal variables have been held in abeyance. Yet a theoretical claim's power depends, at least in part, on how limiting or expansive the *ceteris paribus* clause is. Causal claims that operate over varied conditions tend to be considered more powerful than those that operate only under limited conditions. Yet in most cases, a claim that X causes Y does not imply that if X does not occur Y will not occur. Usually, a particular outcome can be caused by different variables, with Y being capable of being caused by X or by A, B, or C. In these arenas of 'equifinality', the fact that X did not occur need not imply that Y did not occur since A, B, or C might have occurred. Therefore, it appears that a causal claim (X causes Y) does not always imply its counterfactual (if X had not occurred, Y would not have occurred).

Yet, careful causal thinking requires us to distinguish this logic of *theoretical* claims designed to apply across a range of cases from *empirical* claims designed to explain outcomes in a particular case. Empirical claims about a specific case *necessarily* imply counterfactual claims. The claim that 'X caused Y *under the conditions present in a particular case*' necessarily means that 'X occurred and Y occurred under those conditions and if X had not occurred Y would not have occurred under those same conditions'. Causal claims *about* a particular case are constrained by the causal field *of* that case. They are claims that X caused Y under the conditions that prevailed in that case, that X caused Y given that other explanatory variables had the values they actually had. To say that 'Y might have occurred even if X had not occurred' after claiming that 'X caused Y' in that case is either to undercut the original causal claim or to mean that Y might have occurred in that case if explanatory variables other than X had had values other than those they actually had. Empirical explanations involve causal claims about specific cases that necessarily imply counterfactuals. Because of this, such causal claims are strengthened to the extent that empirical evidence, logic, and argument support not only the claim that 'X caused Y under these case-specific conditions' but also the claim that 'under these case-specific conditions, had X not occurred, Y would not have occurred'.

Counterfactual-based arguments can involve thought experiments based on logic alone but become stronger when they are supported by relevant empirical evidence. Such evidence can come from qualitative studies of cases with relatively similar conditions in which, when X did not occur, neither did Y. It can come from quantitative analyses that show, across a wide range of cases, that after controlling for the influence of other variables, the likelihood of Y occurring was greater when X occurred than when it did not. It can come from process tracing in which it is impossible, or at least exceedingly hard, to imagine that the particular types of evidence that appear in the historical record could have appeared had X not occurred. Which of these types of evidence are most compelling may depend on the type of causal claim involved. Thus, the power of certain individuals and their ideas as causes of international environmental outcomes may be less visible in a quantitative analysis than in the fingerprints visible through careful process tracing. The claim that Thomas Lovejoy's idea of linking the interests of debtor countries, financial institutions, and environmental NGOs caused the emergence of debt-for-nature swaps as tools for environmental protection could be supported not merely by the correlational fact that no such swaps occurred before the publication of his 1984 article but also by evidence that the outlines of his strategy had not been publicly delineated prior to that and that the organizations and people involved in the first such swaps described those efforts as prompted by Lovejoy's idea (Lovejoy, 1984; Sheikh, 2007).

Finally, the foregoing chapters have shown the value of thinking of empirical causal claims in probabilistic rather than deterministic terms. Theoretical claims are often made in deterministic rather than probabilistic terms, stating that 'X causes Y' rather than that 'X causes Y to be more likely'. Deterministic causality involves claims that a dependent variable takes on a particular value whenever an explanatory variable takes on a particular value under specified conditions. That is, when X occurs under certain conditions, Y occurs with a 100 per cent probability. But even if such claims were accurate – that X always did cause Y to occur under those conditions – it is more likely that X's relationship with Y will *appear* probabilistic whenever cases thought to meet those conditions do not. In such cases X will occur but Y will not, making X appear as only a probabilistic cause of X. If theoretical claims are treated as deterministic then such evidence would appear to undercut the claim, but if they are treated as probabilistic such evidence allows for a more accurate assessment of the theory's validity.

# Four Debates

This book has focused on the intergovernmental aspects of international environmental politics, concentrating on explaining the causes of why international environmental problems arise and why and when states collectively work to resolve them. The field of international environmental politics, however, has also generated several important debates about the role of environmental politics in international relations. The discussion here seeks to outline major points – and point the reader to important readings – in four of these debates, namely, those related to trade and the environment, environmental security, the erosion of sovereignty, and the value of a World Environment Organization.

## Trade and the environment

One debate central to international environmental politics has been that over the influence of trade and globalization on environmental quality. An early exchange between Bhagwati and Daly has since been developed and extended by numerous other scholars (Bhagwati, 1993; Daly, 1993; Zaelke et al., 1993; Esty, 1994b, 2001; Copeland and Taylor, 2003; Gallagher, 2004; Frankel and Rose, 2005; Prakash and Potoski, 2006). Two separable strands exist in this debate, focused, respectively, on the economic effects and the political effects.

Increased trade, viewed in economic terms, can have both negative and positive environmental impacts. Increased trade generates a 'scale effect' by prompting more production with corresponding increases in the use of natural resources and pollution. Trade openness also generates a countervailing 'competition effect' by encouraging more efficient – and hence less – use of resources as inputs, so long as those resources are priced. Increased trade also has a 'composition effect', with the balance among manufacturing, agriculture, and service sectors shifting as each country develops disproportionately in those sectors in which it has a comparative advantage (Copeland and Taylor, 2003). In addition, increased trade has a 'technique effect' in which price-based choices about where to produce something entrain choices about the environmental effects generated by how something is produced. Finally, to the extent increased trade generates economic growth and corresponding growth in personal income, it may generate a shift toward environmentally-friendly consumer choices, in what is known as an environmental Kuznets curve (Grossman and Krueger, 1995; Harbaugh et al., 2002).

On the political side, the debate has focused on whether international trade causes a race to the bottom, a race to the top, or a race to the middle. Trade liberalization will generate a race to the bottom, even among developed states, if domestic actors succeed in getting their governments to repeal existing – and oppose new – environmental standards because those standards will make the country less economically competitive (Prakash and Potoski, 2006). The related, but distinct, pollution haven hypothesis suggests that economic situations and political preferences may lead developing state governments to establish weaker environmental regulations to attract industrial development (Wheeler, 2002). But international trade may cause a race to the top, with environmental policies converging in an upward, not downward, direction (Holzinger et al., 2008). This upward convergence can reflect powerful leader states making trade expansion contingent on laggard states adopting more stringent environmental standards or a less conscious process of policy diffusion in which governments track and mimic other governments' policies as they learn from successes elsewhere or seek to avoid being labeled as environmental laggards (Holzinger et al., 2008). In powerful developed countries, environmental protection is usually not re-negotiable and their governments cannot readily retreat in their environmental standards. And the desire to access the lucrative markets in such countries – and the necessity of meeting their environmental standards to do so – prompts the corporations and, eventually, the governments in developing countries to match those higher environmental standards. Corporations foster these dynamics by exporting their environmental standards and NGOs influence markets through certification programs and private environmental regimes (Clapp, 1998; Garcia-Johnson, 2000; Espach, 2006). Finally, state behavior may lead to a 'race to the middle' reflecting both self-conscious intergovernmental coordination and less coordinated action by governments and nongovernmental actors, with some states increasing their environmental standards and others reducing, or putting off increasing, theirs (DeSombre, 2006, 2008).

These economic and political theories generate a range of competing predictions, both individually and collectively. Some propositions suggest trade should improve environmental quality and policy, others suggest it should reduce them, and yet others suggest it should leave them relatively unaffected. An accurate judgment of the trade-environment relationship necessarily requires empirically evaluating the net effect of these positive and negative linkages, since theory predicts their individual signs but not their magnitudes or the effect of interactions among them. There is sufficient, and sufficiently ambiguous, empirical evidence that none of these competing views can be completely discounted. The theoretical simplicity desired by many in this debate – that trade either does or does not improve environmental quality – may simply not fit with a complicated economic and political world in which most, if not all, of the alleged influences of trade on environmental quality are operative but their net effects depend on particularities regarding the countries involved, the environmental indicators of concern, and the background context.

## Environmental security

A second important debate explores the relationship of environmental degradation to national security. Beginning in the 1980s, scholars urged an expansion of the concept of national security to acknowledge that environmental degradation increasingly appeared to be threatening the resources and values that traditional efforts to provide national security seek to protect (Galtung, 1982; Ullman, 1983; Myers, 1987, 1989; Mathews, 1989; Fairclough, 1991; Rowlands, 1991). The normative claim that those concerned about national security *should* be concerned about environmental protection was based on an empirical claim that environmental degradation *did*, in fact, increase national security risks. Thomas Homer-Dixon (1991) initiated a major research program focused on evaluating whether environmental degradation increased the likelihood of acute conflict. Declines in the amount and quality of renewable resources produce resource scarcity which can be exacerbated by population growth and unequal access to those resources (Homer-Dixon et al., 1993). Resource scarcity, in turn, can decrease economic productivity and prompt internal conflicts that lead national subgroups to migrate, or be expelled, from their home countries. These dynamics, in turn, weaken the countries in which they occur and can lead to acute conflicts within and across borders (Homer-Dixon et al., 1993). Efforts to evaluate these claims against a set of systematic empirical evidence produced considerable confirmatory evidence and led to the creation of an Environmental Change and Security Program at the Woodrow Wilson International Center for Scholars that continues to foster research on these issues (Homer-Dixon, 1994, 1999; Homer-Dixon and Blitt, 1998; Hauge and Ellingsen, 1998; Tir and Diehl, 1998).

Yet, the empirical claim that environmental scarcity causes violent conflict and the normative claim that environmental protection should be part of the 'portfolio' of those branches of governments providing national security have both been questioned. Deudney argued that the environmental security literature is analytically misleading, empirically inaccurate, and normatively counterproductive (Deudney, 1990, 1991). Linking environment and security is misleading because it focuses attention on the influence of environmental scarcity on war rather than vice versa; because environmental degradation threatens individual security, not national security; because the causes of, harms from, and solutions to environmental damage occur above or below but not at the national level; and because national security entails protection from intentional acts of aggression while environmental degradation is, rather, an unintended by-product of other activities (Deudney, 1990). Empirical studies investigating the environment-security link have been critiqued for problems in defining their main variables, for developing excessively complex and untestable models, for failing to develop appropriate counterfactuals, and for applying theories of interstate conflict to intrastate civil wars (Gleditsch, 1998). The linkage has also been critiqued as 'not primarily descriptive, but polemical [and] a rhetorical device designed to stimulate action' (Deudney, 1990: 465). More damning, Deudney argues that this framing prompts the wrong response, promoting the notion that we can leave environmental protection to government in general and the military establishment in particular and reinforcing an 'us vs them' mentality of nationalism, implications that undermine the argument that environmental protection requires the development of a greater sense of a world community, global citizenship, and individual responsibility (Deudney, 1990; see also Levy, 1995).

Both the empirical and normative aspects of this debate continue to generate scholarly interest (Diehl and Gleditsch, 2001). A particularly valuable aspect of this has been that it has prompted a mature dialogue in which scholars are critically engaging and evaluating each other's claims in ways that foster methodological, theoretical, and empirical progress (see, for example, Gleditsch, 1998; Diehl and Gleditsch, 2001; Schwartz et al., 2001).

## The erosion of sovereignty

A third debate within international environmental politics involves the claim that international environmental politics are eroding sovereignty (Litfin, 1998). If sovereignty is the ability of a government

effectively to control what goes on within its borders, then international environmental politics influence sovereignty in several ways
(Litfin, 1997). First, the growing scope and magnitude of anthropogenic impacts have created international environmental interdependence. Pollution flows cannot be stopped at borders. Migratory
species that one country seeks to preserve can be pushed to extinction by the policy choices or policy failures of other countries.
Continuing fossil fuel use will generate climate change that will
have global impacts, even within the borders of those countries that
have halted their own fossil fuel use. Thus, in a strictly material
sense, governments have less control over what happens within
their borders than they did previously.

Second, the intergovernmental efforts focused on in this book constitute a shift in the locus of policy-making. Intergovernmental agreements involve governments deciding on policies in interdependent
contexts that, at a minimum, ensure that states are aware of other
governments' policies and, at a maximum, encourage them to make
their policies responsive to and contingent on the policies and preferences of other governments. This shift from national toward international governance simultaneously may reduce each government's
sovereign ability to control what goes on within their borders but
increase their ability to influence what goes on in other countries.
Thus, 'by placing states at the centre of institutional responses and
strengthening their capacity to act collectively', international
agreements expand, rather than restrict, 'the menu of choices available to states' (Conca, 1994: 702).

Third, state sovereignty is being eroded by non-state actors taking actions to address international environmental problems in
ways that have been traditionally the sole prerogative of governments. Many multinational corporations can lobby effectively
against costly environmental regulation or avoid its stringent
enforcement but also can 'export environmentalism', promoting
the environmental practices, perceptions, and principles of industrialized countries in developing countries (Garcia-Johnson, 2000).
Other multinationals have negotiated voluntary agreements on
green standards, at times to preempt intergovernmental action and
at other times to motivate it, effectively privatizing global environmental governance (Clapp, 1998). NGOs, often frustrated by the
slow pace of intergovernmental action, frequently take action on
their own, working directly with communities and corporations
and through markets, bypassing governments altogether in their
efforts to address international environmental problems (Cashore
et al., 2004; Espach, 2006). NGOs and global civil society have
sometimes made certain environmentally harmful action – and

environmentally beneficial inaction – so costly that governments, both individually and collectively, have fewer sovereign choices (Wapner, 1996). Such dynamics may not erode sovereignty in the strict sense of dictating what actions governments can and cannot take but they do alter the context within which governments make decisions.

Asking whether these processes erode sovereignty misdirects our attention by oversimplifying the question, however. Even if we could measure 'how much sovereignty' each government has, doing so would fail to answer the question that motivates our interest, namely, how are these processes altering the norms and practice of sovereignty? State policies still are, and are likely to remain, central factors that shape both the causes of international environmental problems and the solutions that people adopt to address them. At the same time, the influences on international environmental problems and their solutions are now shared by other actors in ways that are likely to strengthen government power and sovereignty in some arenas and weaken it in others. What each government is sovereign over and how much influence over outcomes it has is evolving – and will continue to evolve – in response to these pressures. Evaluating what sovereignty means and how the contours of sovereignty are changing frames the question more usefully than whether states have more or less of it.

## A World Environment Organization

The past decade has seen development of a fourth debate over the value of a World Environment Organization (WEO) or Global Environmental Organization. The overarching institutional structure surrounding the international environment differs notably from that surrounding international trade. States have established hundreds of international environmental treaties and corresponding secretariats, commissions, and other institutions (Mitchell, 2003, 2008). Such institutional 'specialization' may appear appropriate if one considers, for example, the differences between the problems of climate change, wetland loss, desertification, fisheries depletion, and river pollution. Indeed, a diversity of specialized institutions has value for various reasons, including allowing for empirical experimentation with different regulatory strategies (Sand, 2001: 297). Yet the value of specialization seems less obvious when one considers that over 30 different international commissions are involved in managing and protecting international fisheries, with responsibilities being divided based on species and ocean region, and sometimes both. The catch of some species are regulated by multiple agreements while the catch of others are not yet regulated. By contrast, a major fraction of all international trade issues is resolved either within the World Trade Organization (WTO) rules or in regional and bilateral trade agreements developed in the shadow of WTO rules and norms.

In light of these considerations, some authors strongly advocate the establishment of a World Environment Organization. The proponents of a WEO have argued that such an institution would improve global environmental governance by eliminating the redundancy and overlap among international environmental institutions; would lead to a more efficient use of the limited financial, administrative, and institutional resources available for international environmental protection; and would provide a more effective voice for environmental protection to counter that of the WTO (Esty, 1994a; Biermann, 2000, 2001; Charnovitz, 2002; Esty and Ivanova, 2002; Biermann and Bauer, 2005). Some have argued that the lack of a WEO demonstrates that 'our planet still lacks effective global environmental governance' (Charnovitz, 2005: 87). Effective global environmental governance, in this view, requires an institutional venue that can facilitate the emergence on the international agenda of 'orphaned' issues, that can foster more rapid agreement on issues that are raised, that can replace existing ad hoc efforts to address global environmental problems with a more systematic review and prioritization of those problems, that can resolve conflicts between different extant environmental agreements, and that can provide an intergovernmental venue in which environmental protection is the primary objective rather than one that must be traded off in pursuit of economic or other goals (Charnovitz, 2005).

An alternative perspective, however, suggests that creating a highly centralized, state-centric WEO is both ill-advised and would undermine existing, positive developments in global environmental governance (Haas, 2004). Actors from governments to corporations to NGOs to individuals no longer see intergovernmental agreements as either the only or the best way to address international environmental problems; 'A new complex decentralized international governance system is emerging [in which] more actors now engage in more governance functions at multiple levels of governance' (Haas, 2004: 13). Although such an organic system may let certain problems 'fall through the cracks' or languish for unnecessarily long periods of time, it also can foster innovation and engage a range of actors with different skills, capabilities, and incentives that may enhance rather than detract from global environmental governance. In this view, what is needed is not a WEO that would compete with or replace the vibrant and growing network of efforts to address international environmental problems but a much more limited and streamlined 'network of networks' that would focus on remedying the functional shortcomings of the existing, organic system of global environmental governance (Haas, 2004). Reform should involve 'multilevel decentralized governance' to improve agenda setting, monitoring and verification, technology and financial transfers, enforcement, and other tasks by coordinating and consolidating them in the United Nations Environment Programme (UNEP) and/or a larger set of existing international institutions (Haas, 2004). Indeed, some international environmental institutions have already taken it upon themselves to address the problems of redundancy and overlap by engaging in self-conscious cross-institutional policy coordination.

The WEO debate is fueled less by disagreement about the inadequacies of existing global environmental governance than about the best strategy for addressing its inadequacies. Existing efforts are certainly not the 'best of all possible worlds': it takes too long for environmental impacts to be recognized and for solutions to be devised and implemented effectively. The question that will likely be debated as long as the world faces international environmental problems is 'how can we best organize local, national, and international efforts – and coordinate those efforts across levels – to maximize the effectiveness of the existing, limited resources devoted to international environmental protection while simultaneously increasing those resources?'

## Unanswered Questions

This book has delineated theoretical and empirical answers to many of the questions of international environmental politics. However, the field abounds with unanswered and inadequately answered questions. We know little about the relative magnitude of the different causes of human environmental impacts. Research into past trends in population, affluence, and technological change, and the tightness of their relationship with different environmental indicators, could clarify whether targeting population growth, consumption patterns and savings rates, or technological innovation is the most likely strategy to bear the most fruit (Pielke et al., 2008). Likewise, scant systematic research has compared the relative efficacy of economic incentives, social norms, or legal coercion at influencing human behavior, although the facile assumption that economic incentives dominate other influences does not appear to be supported by initial research (Schultz et al., 2007; Griskevicius et al., 2008; Nolan et al., 2008). We have little systematic knowledge about how different forms of social organization influence the propensity of a society to generate environmental problems or to resolve them. The influence of national attributes – levels of development, democracy, trade, and personal income – on environmental quality has begun to be investigated, but both the theoretical models as well as the proxies used for explanatory and dependent variables would benefit from fuller development (Grossman and Krueger, 1995; Harbaugh et al., 2002; Neumayer, 2002a, 2002b).

The differential ability of institutions to facilitate issue emergence also remains poorly understood. The strategies that NGOs use in promoting international environmental efforts – from consciousness-raising and lobbying to eco-sabotage – have been common topics of research but rigorous comparative analyses have only recently begun to be undertaken (Betsill and Corell, 2001, 2008; Corell and Betsill, 2001). The involvement of scientists and epistemic communities in promoting international attention to environmental issues is frequently touted at the same time that scientists as well as government and corporate policy-makers lament the lack of rapid communication of scientific knowledge in ways that promote effective and timely decision making (Haas, 1992b; Lubchenco, 1998). Science is insufficiently 'connected to the political agenda for sustainable development' and insufficiently 'focused on the character of nature-society interactions' (Kates et al., 2001: 642). Scholars now recognize that 'usable science' that supports real policy and economic decision making requires re-designing the social institutions involved in knowledge production, knowledge consumption, and the 'boundary work' between them to foster a co-production of knowledge and to address the salience and legitimacy of knowledge as well as its credibility (Guston, 2001; Miller, 2001; Miller and Edwards, 2001; Jasanoff, 2004; Jasanoff and Martello, 2004; Farrell and Jaeger, 2005; Mitchell et al., 2006b; Dilling et al., 2007). Extending these efforts to assess which institutions and which tactics best promote issue emergence remains an important task.

In the realm of negotiations, experience with the Montreal Protocol in addressing stratospheric ozone loss prompted many to argue that 'framework-protocol' approaches to negotiating international environmental agreements were far more effective than the traditional approach of convention followed by subsequent amendment. Yet little rigor has been applied to assessing whether, across environmental problems and with different countries and different numbers of countries, framework-protocol strategies lead to faster intergovernmental agreement on more ambitious regulatory efforts than more traditional strategies. Rigorous comparison requires not only assessing whether different negotiation processes 'get to yes' faster but also whether the 'yes' that states get to is equivalently ambitious and whether the political will of the states involved was equivalent across the cases being compared.

Efforts to evaluate the relative effectiveness of different strategies in resolving international environmental problems have made considerable progress. During the early 1990s, scholars developed theoretical frameworks for thinking about the sources and conditions of regime effectiveness and evaluated the effectiveness of particular IEAs (Haas, 1989, 1990; Chayes and Chayes, 1991, 1993, 1995; Downs et al., 1996, 1998; Mitchell, 1994a, 1994b). Several teams of scholars have compared the effectiveness of different sets of treaties (Haas et al., 1993; Brown Weiss and Jacobson, 1998; Victor et al., 1998a; Miles et al., 2002; Breitmeier et al., 2006). Scholars have developed increasingly rigorous methods to compare the effects of different institutional strategies, developing metrics that allow for systematic comparison while accounting for variation in the difficulty of resolving the problem in question (Sprinz and Helm, 1999; Miles et al., 2002; Hovi et al., 2003a, 2003b; Young, 2003). Progress to date allows for meaningful comparison of variation in IEA effectiveness and compelling explanations of that variation. At the same time, existing analytic methods appear to fall short of being able to provide convincing evidence with sufficient specificity to guide such basic institutional design questions as to whether specific or vague rules are better, whether sanctions or rewards are more effective, or what is the most effective approach to behavioral monitoring.

One area of research that has yet to be engaged is a comparison of the influence of IEAs to that of non-intergovernmental strategies. Given the limited resources that governments will dedicate to international environmental protection in the decades ahead, it is crucial that these resources be deployed as effectively as possible. That requires identifying not only the best design strategies among IEAs but also requires identifying whether unilateral government efforts, nongovernmental programs, and corporate initiatives may be even more effective. These strategies are surely not mutually exclusive and may often be complementary. However, research could identify how IEAs stack up against efforts by governments, NGOs, corporations, or individuals.

Efforts to address international environmental problems could also benefit from a better understanding of how policies to constrain environmentally-damaging behaviors compare with other influences on those behaviors. We need better knowledge of the impact of economic changes relative to policy changes, for example.

Thus, we know that increases in oil prices prompt decreases in fossil fuel consumption and it would be valuable to know how those decreases compare to those attributable to the Kyoto Protocol to the United Nations Framework Convention on Climate Change. Complementarily, knowing how much oil consumption increases in response to a 20 per cent decrease in world prices would provide a benchmark against which to evaluate international efforts to reduce such consumption. Designing institutions to accomplish particular environmental objectives requires knowing how changes in economic, technological, and demographic forces may exacerbate the problem and, perhaps, swamp even the most effective institutional efforts. Being able to compare institutional influence to that of other forces is crucial to knowing whether a solution is adequate to the problem. And being able to estimate our prospects for success, in turn, has implications for our choices among mitigation of, adaptation to, and acceptance of an increasingly wide array of anthropogenic environmental impacts.

Scholars have also identified the importance of interplay, fit, and scale in managing international environmental problems (Young, 2002; Young et al., 2008). As noted above in discussing the WEO, the plethora of international environmental institutions creates a landscape in which institutional efforts are, at times, redundant and overlapping. Interactions among environmental institutions, as well as with non-environmental institutions, can produce synergies that reinforce their effectiveness or conflicts that undermine it (Stokke, 2001; Oberthür and Gehring, 2006). Some of these effects are simply the unintended consequences of simultaneous action by multiple institutions. However, international institutions increasingly have developed inter-institutional processes to manage conflicts and to take advantage of potential synergies. The secretariats of several IEAs regularly coordinate their efforts to reduce redundancy and to foster joint effectiveness. The WTO increasingly seeks to avoid conflicts between trade and environmental treaties. Governments increasingly negotiate whether particular environmental rules will trump or be subordinate to existing trade and economic rules. Trade agreements increasingly have explicit provisions or side agreements that address environmental concerns.

The issue of scale in international environmental politics also is a realm with many open and exciting questions. International institutions influence and are influenced by institutions, actors, and processes at national and sub-national scales (Young, 1994b; Ostrom, 1998; Cash and Moser, 2000; Cash, 2006; Moser, 2006; Gupta, 2008). Effective global environmental governance requires aggregating local knowledge and coordinating local action at higher levels to address global impacts while simultaneously being sensitive to local knowledge, interests, and culture when trying to influence local decision making (Cash, 2006; Patt, 2006). The different scales of international environmental problems – with some local, some national, some regional, and some global – suggests the value of environmental subsidiarity in which governance occurs at the lowest level at which it can be exercised effectively (Wils, 1994; Golub, 1996; Rollo and Winters, 2000). Identifying how to match the scale of solutions to the scale of problems is part of a larger effort to better understand institutional 'fit' (Young, 2002; Galaz et al., 2008). Institutions can fail to remedy a problem due to several types of 'mis-fit': being too small or too large for a problem's spatial dimensions, too slow for its temporal dimensions, ineffective at addressing non-linear 'threshold' effects, or insensitive to positive feedbacks that generate 'cascade effects' across domains (Galaz et al., 2008: see Table 3). More generally, research on institutional fit has highlighted the simple proposition that it is unlikely there is a single institutional design that is best for all problems and all situations. In most areas of human endeavor, solutions are effective when they adapt general principles to the specific conditions presented by the problem at hand. Using this insight requires properly diagnosing the environmental problem and proposing appropriate solutions (Young, 2008). Framework-protocol strategies may facilitate international environmental negotiations on some problems but not others. States will accept, employ, and respond to sanctions in some circumstances but are more likely to accept, employ, and respond to rewards in others (Mitchell and Keilbach, 2001). Monitoring and verification may be unnecessary to address environmental problems that are inherently transparent but crucial to those that are inherently opaque or easily hidden (Mitchell, 1998b). Even claims about international environmental politics that are accurate across a range of cases can be improved by efforts to specify more precisely those conditions where they work best.

All these areas for future research could benefit by continued improvement in the methodological tools used in studying international environmental politics (Sprinz and Wolinsky-Nahmias, 2004; Underdal and Young, 2004). Scholars have proposed various elements of 'good practice' in both qualitative and quantitative methodologies and measurement (Mitchell and Bernauer, 1998; Sprinz and Helm, 1999; Helm and Sprinz, 2000; Hovi et al., 2003a). Methods for evaluating and comparing institutional consequences have attracted significant attention (Haas et al., 1993; Brown Weiss and Jacobson, 1998; Victor et al., 1998a; Miles et al., 2002;

Breitmeier et al., 2006). Self-conscious efforts are also underway to improve analysis of the influence of NGOs and to disentangle the issues raised by the complex causality and institutional interplay common to many aspects of international environmental politics (Homer-Dixon, 1996; Stokke, 2001; Oberthür and Gehring, 2006; Betsill and Corell, 2008). Long-term progress in understanding international environmental politics requires that we continue to develop methodological components of the subfield as well as its theoretical and empirical ones.

# The Importance of Policy-Relevant Research

International environmental politics does present many theoretically, empirically, and methodologically challenging problems. But relatively few people pursue the study of international environmental politics as 'knowledge for knowledge's sake'. Just as those who study war, international trade and finance, and human rights tend to be committed to the goals of peace, economic prosperity, and the protection of human rights, so too do those who study international environmental politics tend to be committed to the goal of environmental protection. That social commitment, in turn, implies – and indeed should imply – that we study international environmental politics in ways that are policy relevant. Intellectual specialization and disciplinarity is a central feature of modern systems of education and facilitates our understanding of the complex phenomena of international environmental politics and the prior theories, methodologies, and empirical analyses developed to explain those phenomena. Yet specialization and disciplinarity often create barriers among scholars from different fields working on a problem and between scholars as a group and policy-makers, decision makers, and the public. Generating policy-relevant research findings (or what is often called 'decision support') requires self-conscious efforts to surmount those barriers (National Oceanic and Atmospheric Administration, 2003). Although the challenges that natural scientists face in communicating research effectively to policy-makers and the public have received considerable attention, social science scholars often face those same challenges (Lubchenco, 1998; Kates et al., 2001).

The desire that one's scholarship contribute to and influence decision making by government officials, corporate executives, or individuals reinforces the traditional demand that scholars 'seek the truth' in as rigorous, unbiased, and self-critical a way as possible. Most institutions of higher learning and most scholars take that commitment seriously on principle. But certainly scholarship that seeks to – or can be expected to – influence policy and behavior in a direct and immediate way incurs the normative burden of ensuring that such influence does not cause harm. Social scientists frequently make recommendations – whether unsolicited or at the request of policy-makers – on how to structure negotiation processes, how to design more effective IEAs, how to ensure that an IEA does not exacerbate existing social inequities, and so on. Scholars, necessarily, cannot have perfect confidence when making such recommendations and they may prove to be in error. But scholars, particularly those who push for adoption of their ideas, assume an obligation to conduct their research in ways that work against their own biases and to have it reviewed critically by skeptical others to avoid all avoidable errors.

For research to be useful to public and private decision makers, it must be salient, credible, and legitimate (Mitchell et al., 2006b). Scholars frequently focus primarily, if not exclusively, on ensuring the 'truth' of their findings. And, certainly, policy-makers generally evaluate research in terms of its credibility, asking whether the scholars responsible have both the expertise to identify the 'truth' and can be trusted to report it honestly. But the likelihood that decision makers will be influenced by scholarship also depends on whether the research is salient and legitimate. Salience exists when research answers questions that are related to real-world decisions (Clark et al., 2006). Research that recommends the imposition of major economic sanctions for violations of environmental treaty provisions can be predicted to have little influence on current policy simply because countries have demonstrated a consistent unwillingness to impose even weak sanctions for treaty violations (Chayes and Chayes, 1993, 1995). Legitimacy exists when those that the research seeks to influence 'believe that the information was produced by a process that took account of the concerns and insights of relevant stakeholders and was deemed procedurally fair' (Clark et al., 2006: 15).

The need for research to be salient, credible, and legitimate if it is to influence policy highlights that the process by which research is generated matters as much as the nature of the findings. To be sure, at times, scientific research has no chance of influencing policy decisions. Governmental, corporate, and individual decisions are susceptible to new information only when the conditions established by existing incentives, capacities, constraints, and values allow. But when new information has the potential for influence, that potential is realized more frequently if research has been generated by a 'process of coproduction of knowledge through participation' (Mitchell et al., 2006a: 324). When scholars conduct 'curiosity driven' research into issues they consider interesting or important and hand decision makers the results, those results tend not to be persuasive. Rather, research tends to be influential when it emerges from long-term interactions that foster communication and mutual understanding between the scholars conducting research and the policy-makers and other potential users of that research (Mitchell et al., 2006a: 325). Ongoing scholar-stakeholder interactions – the 'co-production' of knowledge – foster salience by focusing research on policy-relevant questions; promote credibility by making scholars aware of stakeholder data, evidence, and local knowledge and by helping stakeholders understand research methods and findings and reducing any existing distrust of science; and enhance legitimacy by incorporating stakeholder perspectives and concerns into scientific models and reassuring stakeholders that that has occurred (Mitchell et al., 2006a: 325; see also Dilling et al., 2007).

Managing the many international environmental problems that the Earth currently faces, as well as the many others we will face in the future, requires not only that researchers accurately understand the international environmental policy process but also that their understanding of that process feeds back into and improves that process over time. Such feedback will be fostered by researchers working more closely than they have historically with those whose decisions influence environmental quality – whether they be international negotiators; national or local politicians and government bureaucrats; corporate executives, managers, or employees; those who work with NGOs; or unaffiliated individuals. Scholars often seek to preserve their academic impartiality by maintaining a distance from such actors. The international environmental policy process, however, is likely to be improved more quickly and more completely if scholars can develop ways of collaborating with policy-makers and decision makers without sacrificing this impartiality. Undertaken carefully, the coproduction of knowledge can allow scholars to gain both insights from and influence with whatever audience of decision makers they seek to influence while allowing them to offer those audiences a perspective in which academic rigor, detachment, and incentives encourage a more critical analysis of the policy process and the actors involved than might otherwise be possible.

## Conclusion

The set of international environmental problems currently confronting the world is likely to grow larger, rather than smaller, for the foreseeable future. This book has conceptualized those problems as going through stages that start with the processes that generate human impacts on the environment, through the emergence of those impacts as international problems, through the negotiation of intergovernmental solutions, and through the processes that lead those solutions to be effective or not. The book has introduced the reader to the major factors alleged to explain the outcomes at each stage, as identified by both theoretical and empirical scholarship. By examining international environmental politics through a consistently causal lens, it has sought to give the reader a better understanding of why international environmental problems are so readily generated but their resolution is so difficult to come by. But it has also sought to encourage the reader by identifying the mechanisms by which and the conditions under which international environmental problems can be averted and their resolution facilitated.

The 'transition to a more sustainable world', in which international environmental problems become less rather than more common, is unlikely to be simple or quick. It will require demographic, technological, economic, social, institutional, informational, and ideological transitions that are each challenging in their own rights, let alone when all must occur together (Gell-Mann, 1994). Structural factors that are relatively unsusceptible to rapid change make it unlikely that global society – or any of the national societies of which it is composed – will make those transitions any time soon.

Structural factors create an inertia that dictates that tomorrow's world is likely to look like today's world, with the result that we are likely to face a global environmental predicament for some time to come. Yet structural factors only make that future likely, not necessary. Within the constraints of structural factors there remains considerable room for human agency, for people to make different choices, design different institutions, choose different policies, and adopt different behaviors. Those choices have the potential to reduce, directly and immediately, the environmental problems we face. But they also have the potential over the longer term to loosen the constraints imposed by structural factors and to alter the constellation of structural factors in ways that create a fundamental shift toward a more sustainable future. Those who study international environmental politics have the ability and responsibility to provide better and more complete answers to research questions that can help global society make choices that will foster – and avoid choices that will inhibit – the transitions that global society must make to bring a more sustainable world into being.

# REFERENCES

Abbott, Kenneth W. and Duncan Snidal (2000) 'Hard and soft law in international governance', *International Organization*, 54(3): 421–56.

Alter, Karen J. (1998) 'Who are the "masters of the treaty?" European governments and the European Court of Justice', *International Organization*, 52(1): 121–47.

Anand, Ruchi (2003) *International Environmental Justice: A North-South Dimension*. Aldershot: Ashgate.

Andonova, Liliana B. (2004) *Transnational Politics of the Environment: The European Union and Environmental Policy in Central and Eastern Europe*. Cambridge, MA: MIT Press.

Andonova, Liliana B. and Marc A. Levy (2003) 'Franchising global governance: making sense of the Johannesburg Type II Partnerships', in Olav Schram Stokke and Øystein B. Thommessen (eds), *Yearbook of International Co-operation on Environment and Development 2003/2004*. London: Earthscan. pp. 19–31.

Arvai, Joseph et al. (2006) 'Adaptive management of the global climate problem: bridging the gap between climate research and climate policy', *Climatic Change*, 78(1): 217–25.

Axelrod, Robert (1984) *The Evolution of Cooperation*. New York: Basic Books.

Axelrod, Robert and Robert O. Keohane (1986) 'Achieving cooperation under anarchy: strategies and institutions', in Kenneth Oye (ed.), *Cooperation under Anarchy*. Princeton: Princeton University Press. pp. 226–54.

Barkin, J. Samuel and Elizabeth R. DeSombre (2000) 'Unilateralism and multilateralism in international fisheries management', *Global Governance*, 6(3): 339–60.

Barkin, J. Samuel and Elizabeth R. DeSombre (2002) 'Turbot and tempers in the North Atlantic', in Richard Matthew, Mark Halle and Jason Switzer (eds), *Conserving the Peace: Resources, Livelihoods, and Security*. Winnipeg: International Institute for Sustainable Development. pp. 325–60.

Barrett, Scott (2003) *Environment and Statecraft: The Strategy of Environmental Treaty-Making*. Oxford: Oxford University Press.

Baumol, William J. and Wallace E. Oates (1975) *The Theory of Environmental Policy: Externalities, Public Outlays, and the Quality of Life*. Englewood Cliffs, NJ: Prentice-Hall.

Benedick, Richard E. (1989) 'Ozone diplomacy', *Issues in Science and Technology*, 6(1): 43–50.

Benedick, Richard E. (1998) *Ozone Diplomacy: New Directions in Safeguarding the Planet*. Cambridge, MA: Harvard University Press.

Bernauer, Thomas (1995a) 'The effect of international environmental institutions: how we might learn more', *International Organization*, 49(2): 351–77.

Bernauer, Thomas (1995b) 'The international financing of environmental protection: lessons from efforts to protect the River Rhine against chloride pollution', *Environmental Politics*, 4(3): 369–90.

Bernauer, Thomas (1996) 'Protecting the Rhine River against chloride pollution', in Robert O. Keohane and Marc A. Levy (eds), *Institutions for Environmental Aid: Pitfalls and Promise*. Cambridge, MA: MIT Press. pp. 201–32.

Bernauer, Thomas and Peter Moser (1996) 'Reducing pollution of the Rhine River: the influence of international cooperation', *Journal of Environment and Development*, 5(4): 391–417.

Betsill, Michele M. (2006) 'Transnational actors in international environmental politics', in Michele M. Betsill, Kathryn Hochstetler and Dmitri Stevis (eds), *Palgrave Guide to International Environmental Politics*. New York: Palgrave. pp. 172–202.

Betsill, Michele M. and Elisabeth Corell (2001) 'NGO influence in international environmental negotiations: a framework for analysis', *Global Environmental Politics*, 1(4): 65–85.

Betsill, Michele M. and Elisabeth Corell (2008) *NGO Diplomacy: The Influence of Nongovernmental Organizations in International Environmental Negotiations*. Cambridge, MA: MIT Press.

Betsill, Michele M., Kathryn Hochstetler and Dmitri Stevis (eds) (2006) *Palgrave Guide to International Environmental Politics*. New York: Palgrave.

Bhagwati, Jagdish (1993) 'Does free trade harm the environment: the case for free trade', *Scientific American*, 269(5): 41–57.

Biermann, Frank (2000) 'The case for a World Environment Organization', *Environment*, 42(9): 23–31.

Biermann, Frank (2001) 'The emerging debate on the need for a World Environment Organization', *Global Environmental Politics*, 1(1): 45–55.

Biermann, Frank (2006a) 'Global governance and the environment', in Michele M. Betsill, Kathryn Hochstetler and Dmitri Stevis (eds), *Palgrave Guide to International Environmental Politics*. New York: Palgrave. pp. 237–61.

Biermann, Frank (2006b) 'Whose experts? The role of geographic representation in global environmental assessments', in Ronald B. Mitchell, William C. Clark, David W. Cash and Nancy M. Dickson (eds), *Global Environmental Assessments: Information and Influence*. Cambridge, MA: MIT Press. pp. 87–112.

Biermann, Frank and Steffen Bauer (eds) (2005) *A World Environment Organization: Solution or Threat for Effective International Environmental Governance?* Burlington, VT: Ashgate.

Biersteker, Thomas (1993) 'Constructing historical counterfactuals to assess the consequences of international regimes: the global debt regime and the course of the debt crisis of the 1980s', in Volker Rittberger (ed.), *Regime Theory and International Relations*. New York: Oxford University Press. pp. 315–38.

Birkland, Thomas A. (1998) 'Focusing events, mobilization, and agenda setting', *Journal of Public Policy*, 18(1): 53–74.

Birnie, Patricia W. and Alan E. Boyle (1992) *International Law and the Environment*. Oxford: Oxford University Press.

Boehmer-Christiansen, Sonja A. (1992) 'Anglo-German contrasts in environmental policy-making and their impacts in the case of acid rain abatement', *International Environmental Affairs*, 4(4): 295–322.

Boehmer-Christiansen, Sonja A. and James Skea (1991) *Acid Politics: Environmental and Energy Policies in Britain and Germany*. London: Belhaven.

Boykoff, Maxwell T. and Jules M. Boykoff (2004) 'Balance as bias: global warming and the US prestige press', *Global Environmental Change*, 15(2): 125–36.

Brady, Henry E. and Jason Seawright (2004) 'Framing social inquiry: from models of causation to statistically based causal inference'. Paper presented at the American Political Science Association Annual Meeting, Chicago.

Bratspies, Rebecca M. and Russell A. Miller (2006) *Transboundary Harm in International Law: Lessons from the Trail Smelter Arbitration*. Cambridge: Cambridge University Press.

Breitmeier, Helmut, Oran R. Young and Michael Zürn (2006) *Analyzing International Environmental Regimes: From Case Study to Database*. Cambridge, MA: MIT Press.

Bretherton, Charlotte (2003) 'Movements, networks, hierarchies: a gender perspective on global environmental governance', *Global Environmental Politics*, 3(2): 103–19.

Broadhead, Lee-Anne (2002) *International Environmental Politics: The Limits of Green Diplomacy*. Boulder, Co: Lynne Rienner.

Brown Weiss, Edith (1989) *In Fairness to Future Generations: International Law, Common Patrimony, and Intergenerational Equity*. Dobbs Ferry, NY: Transnational.

Brown Weiss, Edith (ed.) (1997) *International Compliance with Nonbinding Accords*. Washington, DC: American Society of International Law.

Brown Weiss, Edith and Harold K. Jacobson (eds) (1998) *Engaging Countries: Strengthening Compliance with International Environmental Accords*. Cambridge, MA: MIT Press.

Buttel, Frederick H. (1995) 'Rethinking international environmental policy in the late twentieth century', in Bunyan I. Bryant (ed.), *Environmental Justice: Issues, Policies, and Solutions*. Washington, DC: Island Press. pp. 187–207.

Caldwell, Lynton Keith (1972) *In Defense of Earth: International Protection of the Biosphere*. Bloomington: University of Indiana Press.

Caldwell, Lynton Keith (1980) *International Environmental Policy and Law*. Durham, NC: Duke University Press.

Cameron, James, Jacob Werksman and Peter Roderick (eds), (1996) *Improving Compliance with International Environmental Law*. London: Earthscan.

Carpenter, R. Charli (2007) 'Setting the advocacy agenda: theorizing issue emergence and nonemergence in transnational advocacy networks', *International Studies Quarterly*, 51(1): 99–120.

Carr, Edward H. (1964) *The Twenty Years' Crisis: 1919–1939*. New York: Harper and Row.

Carroll, John E. (1983) *Environmental Diplomacy: An Examination and a Prospective of Canadian-U.S. Transboundary Environmental Relations*. Ann Arbor: University of Michigan Press.

Carroll, John E. (ed.) (1988) *International Environmental Diplomacy: The Management and Resolution of Transfrontier Environmental Problems*. Cambridge: Cambridge University Press.

Cash, David W. (2006) 'Mining water, drying wells: multilevel assessment and decision making for water management', in Ronald B. Mitchell, William C. Clark, David W. Cash and Nancy M. Dickson (eds), *Global Environmental Assessments: Information and Influence*. Cambridge, MA: MIT Press. pp. 271–306.

Cash, David W. and Susanne C. Moser (2000) 'Linking global and local scales: designing dynamic assessment and management processes', *Global Environmental Change*, 10(2): 109–20.

Cashore, Benjamin W., Graeme Auld and Deanna Newsom (2004) *Governing through Markets: Forest Certification and the Emergence of Non-State Authority*. New Haven, CT: Yale University Press.

Cass, Loren (2007) 'Measuring the domestic salience of international environmental norms: climate change norms in American, German and British climate policy debates', in Mary E. Pettenger (ed.), *The Social Construction of Climate Change: Power, Knowledge, Norms, Discourses*. Aldershot: Ashgate. pp. 23–50.

Center for Defense Information (1981) 'U.S. nuclear weapons accidents: danger in our midst', *Defense Monitor*, 10(5).

Ceres: Investors and Environmentalists for Sustainable Prosperity (2008) *About Us*. Document last accessed: 10 January 2009. Available at: http://www.ceres.org/NETCOMMUNITY/Page.aspx?pid=415&srcid=705

Charnovitz, Steve (2002) 'A World Environment Organization', *Columbia Journal of Environmental Law*, 27(2): 323–62.

Charnovitz, Steve (2005) 'Toward a World Environment Organization: reflections upon a vital debate', in Frank Biermann and Steffen Bauer (eds), *A World Environment Organization: Solution or Threat for Effective International Environmental Governance?* Burlington, VT: Ashgate. pp. 87–116.

Chatterjee, Pratap and Matthias Finger (1994) *The Earth Brokers: Power, Politics, and World Development*. New York: Routledge.

Chayes, Abram (1972) 'An inquiry into the workings of arms control agreements', *Harvard Law Review*, 85(5): 905–69.

Chayes, Abram and Antonia Chayes (1991) 'Compliance without enforcement: state behavior under regulatory treaties', *Negotiation Journal*, 7(3): 311–30.

Chayes, Abram and Antonia Handler Chayes (1993) 'On compliance', *International Organization*, 47(2): 175–205.

Chayes, Abram and Antonia Handler Chayes (1995) *The New Sovereignty: Compliance with International Regulatory Agreements*. Cambridge, MA: Harvard University Press.

Checkel, Jeffrey T. (2001) 'Why comply? Social learning and European identity change', *International Organization*, 55(3): 553–88.

Checkel, Jeffrey T. (2005) 'International institutions and socialization in Europe: introduction and framework', *International Organization*, 59(4): 801–26.

Chertow, Marian R. (2002) 'The IPAT equation and its variants: changing views of technology and environmental impact', *Journal of Industrial Ecology*, 4(4): 13–29.

Choucri, Nazli (ed.) (1993) *Global Accord: Environmental Challenges and International Responses*. Cambridge, MA: MIT Press.

Clapp, Jennifer (1998) 'The privatization of global environmental governance: ISO 14000 and the developing world', *Global Governance*, 4(3): 295–316.

Clark, William C., Ronald B. Mitchell and David W. Cash (2006) 'Evaluating the influence of global environmental assessments', in Ronald B. Mitchell, William C. Clark, David W. Cash and Nancy M. Dickson (eds), *Global Environmental Assessments: Information and Influence*. Cambridge, MA: MIT Press. pp. 1–28.

Clark, William C., Ronald B. Mitchell, David W. Cash and Frank Alcock (2002) 'Information as influence: how institutions mediate the impact of scientific assessments on global environmental affairs'. Harvard University, Kennedy School of Government, Faculty Research Working Paper RWP02–044.

Clark, William R., Michael J. Gilligan and Matt Golder (2006) 'A simple multivariate test for asymmetric hypotheses', *Political Analysis*, 14(3): 311–31.

Coase, Ronald (1960) 'The problem of social cost', *Journal of Law and Economics*, 3(1): 1–44.

Cobb, Roger and Charles Elder (1972) *Participation in American Politics: The Dynamics of Agenda-Building*. Boston, MA: Allyn and Bacon.

Commoner, Barry (1971) *The Closing Circle: Nature, Man, and Technology*. New York: Knopf.

Conca, Ken (1994) 'Rethinking the ecology-sovereignty debate', *Millennium*, 23(3): 1–11.

Conca, Ken (2006) *Governing Water: Contentious Transnational Politics and Global Institution Building*. Cambridge, MA: MIT Press.

Copeland, Brian R. and Scott M. Taylor (2003) *Trade and the Environment: Theory and Evidence*. Princeton: Princeton University Press.

Corell, Elisabeth and Michele M. Betsill (2001) 'A comparative look at NGO influence in international environmental negotiations: desertification and climate change', *Global Environmental Politics*, 1(4): 86–107.

Cornes, Richard and Todd Sandler (1986) *The Theory of Externalities, Public Goods, and Club Goods*. Cambridge: Cambridge University Press.

Daily, Gretchen C. (ed.) (1997) *Nature's Services: Societal Dependence on Natural Ecosystems*. Washington, DC: Island.

Daly, Herman E. (1993) 'The perils of free trade', *Scientific American*, 269(5): 50–56.

D'Amato, Anthony and Sudhir K. Chopra (1991) 'Whales: their emerging right to life', *American Journal of International Law*, 85(1): 21–62.

Darst, Robert G. (2001) *Smokestack Diplomacy: Cooperation and Conflict in East-West Environmental Politics*. Cambridge, MA: MIT Press.

Dasgupta, Partha (2001) *Human Well-Being and the Natural Environment*. Oxford: Oxford University Press.

Daughton, Christian G. and Thomas A. Ternes (1999) 'Pharmaceuticals and personal care products in the environment: agents of subtle change?' *Environmental Health Perspectives*, 107(Suppl 6): 907–38.

Dauvergne, Peter (1997) *Shadows in the Forest: Japan and the Politics of Timber in Southeast Asia*. Cambridge, MA: MIT Press.

Davies, J. Clarence, III (1974) 'How does the agenda get set?' in Edwin T. Haefele (ed.), *The Governance of Common Property Resources*. Baltimore, MD: Johns Hopkins University Press. pp. 149–77.

Depledge, Joanna (2000) *Tracing the Origins of the Kyoto Protocol: An Article-by-Article Textual History*. Bonn: United Nations Framework Convention on Climate Change.

DeSombre, Elizabeth R. (1995) 'Baptists and bootleggers for the environment: the origins of United States unilateral sanctions', *Journal of Environment and Development*, 4(1): 53–76.

DeSombre, Elizabeth R. (2000) *Domestic Sources of International Environmental Policy: Industry, Environmentalists, and U.S. Power*. Cambridge, MA: MIT Press.

DeSombre, Elizabeth R. (2006) *Flagging Standards: Globalization and Environmental, Safety, and Labor Regulations at Sea*. Cambridge, MA: MIT Press.

DeSombre, Elizabeth R. (2007) *The Global Environment and World Politics*. New York: Continuum.

DeSombre, Elizabeth R. (2008) 'Globalization, competition, and convergence: shipping and the race to the middle', *Global Governance*, 14(2): 179–98.

Dessler, David (1989) 'What's at stake in the agent-structure debate?' *International Organization*, 43(3): 441–73.

Deudney, Daniel (1990) 'The case against linking environmental degradation and national security', *Millennium*, 19(3): 461–76.

Deudney, Daniel (1991) 'Environment and security: muddled thinking', *Bulletin of Atomic Scientists*, 47(3): 22–29.

Devall, Bill and George Sessions (1985) *Deep Ecology*. Salt Lake City, UT: Peregrine Smith.

Diamond, Irene and Gloria Feman Orenstein (eds) (1990) *Reweaving the World: The Emergence of Ecofeminism*. San Francisco, CA: Sierra Club.

Diehl, Paul F. and Nils Petter Gleditsch (2001) *Environmental Conflict*. Boulder, CO: Westview.

Dilling, Lisa, Ronald B. Mitchell, David M. Fairman and Susanne Moser (with Myanna Lahsen, Anthony Patt, Chris Potter, Charles Rice, and Stacy VanDeveer) (2007) 'How can we improve the usefulness of carbon science for decision-making?' in Anthony W. King, Lisa Dilling, Gregory P. Zimmerman, David M. Fairman, R. A. Houghton, G. H. Marland, A. Z. Rose and Thomas J. Wilbanks (eds), *The First State of the Carbon Cycle Report (SOCCR): North American Carbon Budget and Implications for the Global Carbon Cycle (a Report by the U.S. Climate Change Science Program and the Subcommittee on Global Change Research)*. Silver Spring, MD: National Ocean and Atmospheric Administration, Climate Program Office. pp. 5.1–5.16.

Dorsey, Kurkpatrick (1991) 'Putting a ceiling on sealing: conservation and cooperation in the international arena, 1909–1911', *Environmental History Review*, 15(3): 27–45.

Dorsey, Kurkpatrick (1998) *The Dawn of Conservation Diplomacy: U.S.-Canadian Wildlife Protection Treaties in the Progressive Era*. Seattle: University of Washington Press.

Downs, George W., David M. Rocke and Peter N. Barsoom (1996) 'Is the good news about compliance good news about cooperation?' *International Organization*, 50(3): 379–406.

Downs, George W., David M. Rocke and Peter N. Barsoom (1998) 'Managing the evolution of cooperation', *International Organization*, 52(2): 397–419.

Ehrlich, Paul R. and John P. Holdren (1971) 'Impact of population growth', *Science*, 171: 1212–17.

Ehrlich, Paul R. and John P. Holdren (1972a) 'A Bulletin dialogue on 'The closing circle': critique: one dimensional ecology', *Bulletin of Atomic Scientists*, 28(5): 16–27.

Ehrlich, Paul R. and John P. Holdren (1972b) 'Impact of population growth', in R. G. Riker (ed.), *Population, Resources, and the Environment*. Washington, DC: US Government Printing Office. pp. 365–77.

Elvidge, Christopher D., Benjamin T. Tuttle, Paul C. Sutton, Kimberly E. Baugh, Ara T. Howard, Cristina Milesi, Budhendra L. Bhaduri and Ramakrishna

Nemani (2007) 'Global distribution and density of constructed impervious surfaces', *Sensors*, 7: 1962–79.

Espach, Ralph H. (2006) 'When is sustainable forestry sustainable? Comparing the effectiveness of the Forest Stewardship Council in Argentina and Brazil', *Global Environmental Politics*, 6(2): 55–84.

Esty, Daniel C. (1994a) 'The case for a Global Environmental Organization', in Peter B. Kenen (ed.), *Managing the World Economy: Fifty Years after Bretton Woods*. Washington, DC: Institute of International Economics. pp. 287–310.

Esty, Daniel C. (1994b) *Greening the GATT: Trade, Environment, and the Future*. Washington, DC: International Institute for Economics.

Esty, Daniel C. (2001) 'Bridging the trade-environment divide', *Journal of Economic Perspectives*, 15(3): 113–30.

Esty, Daniel C. and Maria H. Ivanova (eds) (2002) *Global Environmental Governance*. New Haven: Yale School of Forestry & Environmental Studies.

Fairclough, A. J. (1991) 'Global environmental and natural resource problems: their economic, political and security implications', *The Washington Quarterly*, 14(1): 81–98.

Falk, Richard (1971) *This Endangered Planet: Prospects and Proposals for Human Survival*. New York: Vintage.

Farrell, Alex and Jill Jaeger (eds) (2005) *Assessments of Regional and Global Environmental Risks: Designing Processes for the Effective Use of Science in Decisionmaking*. Washington, DC: Resources for the Future.

Fearon, James D. (1991) 'Counterfactuals and hypothesis testing in political science', *World Politics*, 43(2): 169–95.

Fearon, James D. and Alexander Wendt (2002) 'Rationalism v. constructivism: a skeptical view', in Walter Carlsnaes, Thomas Risse and Beth Simmons (eds), *Handbook of International Relations*. Thousand Oaks, CA: SAGE. pp. 52–72.

Finnemore, Martha (1993) 'International organizations as teachers of norms: the United Nations Educational, Scientific, and Cultural Organization and science policy', *International Organization*, 47(4): 565–97.

Finnemore, Martha (1996) *National Interests in International Society*. Ithaca, NY: Cornell University Press.

Finnemore, Martha and Kathryn Sikkink (1998) 'International norm dynamics and political change', *International Organization*, 52(4): 887–917.

Fischer-Kowalski, Marina and Christof Amann (2001) 'Beyond IPAT and Kuznets curves: globalization as a vital factor in analysing the environmental impact of socioeconomic metabolism', *Population and Environment*, 23(1): 7–47.

Fisher, Roger and William Ury (1981) *Getting to Yes: Negotiating Agreement without Giving In*. New York: Penguin.

Florini, Ann (1996) 'The evolution of international norms', *International Studies Quarterly*, 40(3): 363–89.

Frankel, Jeffrey and Andrew Rose (2005) 'Is trade good or bad for the environment? Sorting out the causality', *Review of Economics and Statistics*, 87(1): 85–91.

Fudenberg, Drew and Jean Tirole (1991) *Game Theory*. Cambridge, MA: MIT Press.

Gaard, Greta (ed.) (1993) *Ecofeminism: Women, Animals, Nature*. Philadelphia: Temple University Press.

Galaz, Victor, Per Olsson, Thomas Hahn, Carl Folke and Uno Svedin (2008) 'The problem of fit among biophysical systems, environmental and resource regimes, and broader governance systems: insights and emerging challenges', in Oran R. Young, Leslie A. King and Heike Schroeder (eds), *Institutions and Environmental Change: Principal Findings, Applications, and Research Frontiers*. Cambridge, MA: MIT Press. pp. 147–86.

Gallagher, Kevin (2004) *Free Trade and the Environment: Mexico, Nafta, and Beyond*. Stanford: Stanford University Press.

Galtung, Johan (1982) *Environment, Development and Military Activity: Towards Alternative Security Doctrines*. Oslo: Norwegian University Press.

Garcia-Johnson, Ronie (2000) *Exporting Environmentalism: U.S. Multinational Chemical Corporations in Brazil and Mexico*. Cambridge, MA: MIT Press.

Gehring, Thomas and Sebastian Oberthür (2008) 'Interplay: exploring institutional interaction', in Oran R. Young, Leslie A. King and Heike Schroeder (eds), *Institutions and Environmental Change: Principal Findings, Applications, and Research Frontiers*. Cambridge, MA: MIT Press. pp. 187–224.

Gell-Mann, Murray (1994) *The Quark and the Jaguar: Adventures in the Simple and the Complex*. New York: W.H. Freeman.

George, Alexander and Andrew Bennett (2005) *Case Studies and Theory Development in the Social Sciences*. Cambridge, MA: MIT Press.

Gill, Chuck (2007) 'Honey bee die-off alarms beekeepers, crop growers and researchers', *Penn State College of Agricultural Sciences News Releases*.

Giordano, Mark (2002a) 'The internationalization of wildlife and efforts towards its management: a conceptual framework and the historic record', *Georgetown International Environmental Law Review*, 14(4): 607–27.

Giordano, Mark (2002b) 'Wildlife treaties series', *Georgetown International Environmental Law Review*, 14(4): 629–92.

Gleditsch, Nils Petter (1998) 'Armed conflict and the environment: a critique of the literature', *Journal of Peace Research*, 35(3): 381–400.

Gleick, Peter H. (1993) *Water in Crisis: A Guide to the World's Fresh Water Resources*. New York: Oxford University Press.

Goertz, Gary, Tony Hak and Jan Dul (2008) 'Ceilings and floors: theoretical and statistical considerations when the goal is to draw boundaries of data, not lines through the middle'. Paper presented at the American Political Science Association Annual Meeting, Boston.

Goldstein, Judith and Robert O. Keohane (eds) (1993) *Ideas and Foreign Policy: Beliefs, Institutions, and Political Change*. Ithaca, NY: Cornell University Press.

Golub, Jonathan (1996) 'Sovereignty and subsidiarity in EU environmental policy', *Political Studies*, 44(4): 686–703.

Griskevicius, Vladas, Robert B. Cialdini and Noah J. Goldstein (2008) 'Social norms: an underestimated and underemployed lever for managing climate change', *International Journal of Sustainability Communication*, 3: 5–13.

Grossman, Gene M. and Allen B. Krueger (1995) 'Economic growth and the environment', *Quarterly Journal of Economics*, 110(2): 353–75.

Gruber, Lloyd (2000) *Ruling the World*. Princeton: Princeton University Press.

Gupta, Joyeeta (2008) 'Global change: analyzing scale and scaling in environmental governance', in Oran R. Young, Leslie A. King and Heike Schroeder (eds), *Institutions and Environmental Change: Principal Findings, Applications, and Research Frontiers*. Cambridge, MA: MIT Press. pp. 225–58.

Guston, David H. (2001) 'Boundary organizations in environmental policy and science: an introduction', *Science, Technology & Human Values*, 26(4): 399–408.

Gutner, Tamar L. (2002) *Banking on the Environment: Multilateral Development Banks and Their Environmental Performance in Central and Eastern Europe*. Cambridge, MA: MIT Press.

Haas, Peter M. (1989) 'Do regimes matter? Epistemic communities and Mediterranean pollution control', *International Organization*, 43(3): 377–403.

Haas, Peter M. (1990) *Saving the Mediterranean: The Politics of International Environmental Cooperation*. New York: Columbia University Press.

Haas, Peter M. (1992a) 'Banning chlorofluorocarbons', *International Organization*, 46(1): 187–224.

Haas, Peter M. (1992b) 'Epistemic communities and international policy coordination', *International Organization*, 46(1): 1–35.

Haas, Peter M. (ed.) (1992c) *Knowledge, Power, and International Policy Coordination*. Columbia: University of South Carolina Press.

Haas, Peter M. (2004) 'Addressing the global governance deficit', *Global Environmental Politics*, 4(4): 1–15.

Haas, Peter M., Robert O. Keohane and Marc A. Levy (eds) (1993) *Institutions for the Earth: Sources of Effective International Environmental Protection*. Cambridge, MA: MIT Press.

Harbaugh, William, Arik Levinson and David Wilson (2002) 'Re-examining the empirical evidence for an environmental Kuznets curve', *Review of Economics and Statistics*, 84(3): 541–51.

Hardin, Garrett (1968) 'The tragedy of the commons', *Science*, 162(3859): 1243–48.

Hart, Jeffrey A. (1976) 'The Anglo-Icelandic Cod War of 1972–1973: a case study of a fishery dispute'. PhD Thesis, University of California, Berkeley.

Hasenclever, Andreas, Peter Mayer and Volker Rittberger (1997) *Theories of International Regimes*. Cambridge: Cambridge University Press.

Hauge, Wenche and Tanja Ellingsen (1998) 'Beyond environmental security: causal pathways to conflict', *Journal of Peace Research*, 35(3): 299–317.

Helm, Carsten and Detlef F. Sprinz (2000) 'Measuring the effectiveness of international environmental regimes', *Journal of Conflict Resolution*, 44(5): 630–52.

Hempel, Lamont C. (1996) *Environmental Governance: The Global Challenge*. Washington, DC: Island.

Henkin, Louis (1979) *How Nations Behave: Law and Foreign Policy*. New York: Columbia University Press.

Holzinger, Katharina, Christoph Knill and Bas Arts (2008) *Environmental Policy Convergence in Europe: The Impact of International Institutions and Trade*. Cambridge: Cambridge University Press.

Homer-Dixon, Thomas F. (1990) *Environmental Change and Violent Conflict*. Cambridge: American Academy of Arts and Sciences.

Homer-Dixon, Thomas F. (1991) 'On the threshold: environmental changes as causes of acute conflict', *International Security*, 16(2): 76–116.

Homer-Dixon, Thomas F. (1994) 'Environmental scarcities and violent conflict: evidence from cases', *International Security*, 19(1): 5–40.

Homer-Dixon, Thomas F. (1996) 'Strategies for studying causation in complex ecological political systems', *Journal of Environment and Development*, 5(2): 132–48.

Homer-Dixon, Thomas F. (1999) *Environment, Scarcity, and Violence*. Princeton: Princeton University Press.

Homer-Dixon, Thomas F. and Jessica Blitt (1998) *Ecoviolence: Links among Environment, Population and Security*. Lanham, MD: Rowman & Littlefield.

Homer-Dixon, Thomas F., Jeffrey H. Boutwell and George W. Rathjens (1993) 'Environmental change and violent conflict: growing scarcities of renewable resources can contribute to social instability and civil strife', *Scientific American*, 268(2): 38–45.

Hovi, Jon and Detlef F. Sprinz (2006) 'The limits of the law of the least ambitious program', *Global Environmental Politics*, 6(3): 28–42.

Hovi, Jon, Detlef F. Sprinz and Arild Underdal (2003a) 'The Oslo-Potsdam solution to measuring regime effectiveness: critique, response, and the road ahead', *Global Environmental Politics*, 3(3): 74–96.

Hovi, Jon, Detlef F. Sprinz and Arild Underdal (2003b) 'Regime effectiveness and the Oslo-Potsdam solution: a rejoinder to Oran Young', *Global Environmental Politics*, 3(3): 105–7.

Humphreys, David (2001) 'Forest negotiations at the United Nations: explaining cooperation and discord', *Forest Policy and Economics*, 3(3–4): 125–35.

Ikle, Fred (1964) *How Nations Negotiate*. New York: Harper and Row.

Inglehart, Ronald M. (1990) *Culture Shift in Advanced Industrial Society*. Princeton: Princeton University Press.

Inglehart, Ronald M. (1995) 'Public support for environmental protection: the impact of objective problems and subjective values in 43 societies', *Political Science and Politics*, 27(1): 57–71.

Inglehart, Ronald, Miguel Basanez, Jaime Diez-Medrano, Loek Halman and Ruud Luijkx (2002) *World Values Surveys and European Values Surveys, 1981–1984, 1990–1993, and 1995–1997*. Ann Arbor, MI: Institute for Social Research, Inter-University Consortium for Political and Social Research (computer file).

Jacobson, Harold K. and Edith Brown Weiss (1998) 'Assessing the record and designing strategies to engage countries', in Edith Brown Weiss and Harold K. Jacobson (eds), *Engaging Countries: Strengthening Compliance with International Environmental Accords*. Cambridge, MA: MIT Press. pp. 511–54.

Jäger, Jill with, Nancy M. Dickson, Adam Fenech, Peter M. Haas, Edward A. Parson, Vassily Sokolov, Ferenc L. Tóth, Jeroen van der Sluijs and Claire Waterton (2001) 'Monitoring in the management of global environmental risks', in Social Learning Group (ed.), *Learning to Manage Global Environmental Risks, Volume 2: A Functional Analysis of Social Responses to Climate Change, Ozone Depletion and Acid Rain*. Cambridge, MA: MIT Press. pp. 31–48.

Jasanoff, Sheila (1990) *The Fifth Branch: Science Advisers as Policymakers*. Cambridge, MA: Harvard University Press.

Jasanoff, Sheila (1995) *Science at the Bar: Law, Science, and Technology in America*. Cambridge, MA: Harvard University Press.

Jasanoff, Sheila (2004) *States of Knowledge: The Co-Production of Science and Social Order*. New York: Routledge.

Jasanoff, Sheila and Marybeth Long Martello (eds) (2004) *Earthly Politics: Local and Global in Environmental Governance*. Cambridge, MA: MIT Press.

Kammen, Daniel M. and Michael R. Dove (1997) 'The virtues of mundane science', *Environment*, 39(6): 10–19.

Kasoulides, George C. (1993) *Port State Control and Jurisdiction: Evolution of the Port State Regime*. Dordrecht and Boston: M. Nijhoff.

Kates, Robert W., William C. Clark, Robert Corell, J. Michael Hall, Carlo C. Jaeger, Ian Lowe, James J. McCarthy, Hans Joachim Schellnhuber, Bert Bolin, Nancy M. Dickson, Sylvie Faucheux, Gilberto C. Gallopin, Arnulf Grübler, Brian Huntley, Jill Jäger, Narpat S. Jodha, Roger E. Kasperson, Akin Mabogunje, Pamela Matson, Harold Mooney, Berrien Moore III, Timothy O'Riordan and Uno Svedin (2001) 'Sustainability science', *Science*, 292(5517): 641–42.

Kay, David A. and Eugene B. Skolnikoff (1972) *World Eco-Crisis: International Organizations in Response*. Madison, WI: University of Wisconsin Press.

Kay, David A. and Harold K. Jacobson (eds) (1983) *Environmental Protection: The International Dimension*. Totowa, NJ: Allanheld, Osmun & Co.

Keck, Margaret E. and Kathryn Sikkink (1998) *Activists Beyond Borders: Advocacy Networks in International Politics*. Ithaca, NY: Cornell University Press.

Kennan, George F. (1970) 'To prevent a world wasteland: a proposal', *Foreign Affairs,* 48(2): 401–13.

Keohane, Robert O. (1984) *After Hegemony: Cooperation and Discord in the World Political Economy*. Princeton: Princeton University Press.

Keohane, Robert O. (1988) 'International institutions: two approaches', *International Studies Quarterly*, 32(4): 379–96.

Keohane, Robert O. (1989) 'Neoliberal institutionalism: a perspective on world politics', in Robert O. Keohane (ed.), *International Institutions and State Power: Essays in International Relations*. Boulder, CO: Westview. pp. 1–20.

Keohane, Robert O. (1993) 'The Analysis of international regimes: towards a European-American research programme', in Volker Rittberger (ed.), *Regime Theory and International Relations*. New York: Oxford University Press. pp. 23–45.

Keohane, Robert O. (1996) 'Analyzing the effectiveness of international environmental institutions', in Robert O. Keohane and Marc A. Levy (eds), *Institutions for Environmental Aid: Pitfalls and Promise*. Cambridge, MA: MIT Press. pp. 3–27.

Keohane, Robert O. and Marc A. Levy (eds) (1996) *Institutions for Environmental Aid: Pitfalls and Promise*. Cambridge, MA: MIT Press.

Keohane, Robert O. and Lisa L. Martin (1995) 'The promise of institutionalist theory', *International Security*, 20(1): 39.

Keohane, Robert O. and Joseph S. Nye (1989) *Power and Interdependence: World Politics in Transition (2nd edition)*. Boston, MA: Little, Brown.

Keohane, Robert O., Peter M. Haas and Marc A. Levy (1993) 'The effectiveness of international environmental institutions', in Peter Haas, Robert O. Keohane and Marc Levy (eds), *Institutions for the Earth: Sources of Effective International Environmental Protection*. Cambridge, MA: MIT Press. pp. 3–26.

Kindleberger, Charles P. (1981) 'Dominance and leadership in the international economy: exploitation, public goods, and free rides', *International Studies Quarterly*, 25(2): 242–54.

King, Gary, Robert O. Keohane and Sidney Verba (1994) *Designing Social Inquiry: Scientific Inference in Qualitative Research*. Princeton: Princeton University Press.

Kingdon, John W. (1995) *Agendas, Alternatives, and Public Policies*. Boston, MA: Little, Brown and Co.

Koh, Harold (1997) 'Why do nations obey international law?' *Yale Law Journal*, 106(8): 2598–659.

Kolstad, Charles D. (2000) *Environmental Economics*. New York: Oxford University Press.

Koremenos, Barbara, Charles Lipson and Duncan Snidal (2001) 'The rational design of international institutions', *International Organization*, 55(4): 761–99.

Koremenos, Barbara, Charles Lipson and Duncan Snidal (eds) (2004) *The Rational Design of International Institutions*. New York: Cambridge University Press.

Krasner, Stephen D. (ed.) (1983) *International Regimes*. Ithaca, NY: Cornell University Press.

Krasner, Stephen D. (1991) 'Global communications and national power: life on the Pareto frontier', *World Politics*, 43(3): 336–66.

Krasner, Stephen D. (1999) *Sovereignty: Organized Hypocrisy*. Princeton: Princeton University Press.

Kuran, Timur and Cass R. Sunstein (1999) 'Availability cascades and risk regulation', *Stanford Law Review*, 51(4): 683–768.

Leiserowitz, Anthony A., Robert W. Kates and Thomas M. Parris (2006) 'Sustainability values, attitudes, and behaviors: a review of multinational and global trends', *Annual Review of Environment and Resources*, 31: 413–44.

LeMarquand, David G. (1977) *International Rivers: The Politics of Cooperation*. Vancouver, BC: Westwater Research Centre, University of British Colombia.

Leon H. Sullivan Foundation (2008) *Global Sullivan Principles of Social Responsibility*. Document last accessed: 25 September 2008. Available at: http://www.globalsullivanprinciples.org/principles.htm

Levy, Marc A. (1993) 'European acid rain: the power of tote-board diplomacy', in Peter Haas, Robert O. Keohane and Marc Levy (eds), *Institutions for the Earth: Sources of Effective International Environmental Protection*. Cambridge, MA: MIT Press. pp. 75–132.

Levy, Marc A. (1995) 'Is the environment a national security issue?' *International Security*, 20(2): 35–62.

Lipschutz, Ronnie D. and Ken Conca (eds) (1993) *The State and Social Power in Global Environmental Politics*. New York: Columbia University Press.

Lipschutz, Ronnie D. and Judith Mayer (1996) *Global Civil Society and Global Environmental Governance: The Politics of Nature from Place to Planet*. Albany: State University of New York.

Lipson, Charles (1991) 'Why are some international agreements informal?' *International Organization*, 45(4): 495–538.

List, Martin and Volker Rittberger (1998) 'The role of intergovernmental organizations in the formation and evolution of international environmental regimes', in Arild Underdal (ed.), *The Politics of International Environmental Management*. Dordrecht: Kluwer. pp. 67–81.

Litfin, Karen T. (1994) *Ozone Discourses: Science and Politics in Global Environmental Cooperation*. New York: Columbia University Press.

Litfin, Karen T. (1997) 'Sovereignty in world ecopolitics', *Mershon International Studies Review*, 41(4): 167–204.

Litfin, Karen T. (ed.) (1998) *The Greening of Sovereignty in World Politics*. Cambridge, MA: MIT Press.

Litfin, Karen T. (2005) 'Gaia theory: intimations for global environmental politics', in Peter Dauvergne (ed.), *Handbook of Global Environmental Politics*. Northampton, MA: Edward Elgar. pp. 502–17.

Livingston, Steven G. (1992) 'The politics of international agenda-setting: Reagan and North-South relations', *International Studies Quarterly*, 36: 313–30.

Lovejoy, Thomas E. (1984) 'Aid debtor nations' ecology', *The New York Times* (4 October): p. A–31.

Lovelock, James (1979) *Gaia: A New Look at Life on Earth*. Oxford: Oxford University Press.

Lovelock, James (1990) *The Ages of Gaia: A Biography of the Living Earth*. New York: Bantam.

Lowi, Miriam R. (1995) *Water and Power: The Politics of a Scarce Resource in the Jordan River Basin*. Cambridge: Cambridge University Press.

Lubchenco, Jane (1998) 'Entering the century of the environment: a new social contract for science', *Science* 279: 491–97.

Maine Department of Marine Resources (2004) *Maine's Sea Urchin Fishery*. Document dated: 26 July 2004. Document last accessed: 16 October 2008. Available at: http://maine.gov/dmr/rm/seaurchin/Urchin%20report%207-04.pdf

Maine Department of Marine Resources (2008) *Historical Maine Sea Urchin Landings*. Document dated: 2 July 2008. Document last accessed: 16 October 2008. Available at: http://www.maine.gov/dmr/commercialfishing/documents/Urchin.pdf

March, James and Johan Olsen (1998) 'The institutional dynamics of international political orders', *International Organization*, 52(4): 943–70.

Marini, Margaret M. and Burton Singer (1988) 'Causality in the social sciences', *Sociological Methodology*, 18: 347–409.

Martin, Lisa L. (1992a) *Coercive Cooperation: Explaining Multilateral Economic Sanctions*. Princeton: Princeton University Press.

Martin, Lisa L. (1992b) 'Interests, power, and multilateralism', *International Organization*, 46(4): 765–92.

Mathews, Jessica Tuchman (1989) 'Redefining security', *Foreign Affairs*, 68(2): 162–77.

Mathews, Jessica Tuchman (ed.) (1991) *Preserving the Global Environment: The Challenge of Shared Leadership*. New York: Norton.

Matthews, Geoffrey V. T. (1993) *The Ramsar Convention on Wetlands: Its History and Development*. Gland, Switzerland: Ramsar Convention Bureau.

May, Peter (1990) 'Reconsidering policy design: policies and publics', *Journal of Public Policy*, 11(2): 187–206.

McCubbins, Mathew and Thomas Schwartz (1984) 'Congressional oversight overlooked: police patrols versus fire alarms', *American Journal of Political Science*, 28(1): 165–79.

Mearsheimer, John (1995) 'The false promise of international institutions', *International Security* 19(3): 5–49.

Media Research Center (1998) *MRC Releases Primer for Reporters Covering Climate Change: Special Report Exposes Common Myths, Provides Media with Credible Sources Who Have a Free Market Perspective*. Document last accessed: 10 December 2007. Available at: http://www.mediaresearch.org/press/1998/press19981029.asp

Merchant, Carolyn (1990) 'Ecofeminism and feminist theory', in Irene Diamond and Gloria Feman Orenstein (eds), *Reweaving the World: The Emergence of Ecofeminism*. San Francisco, CA: Sierra Club. pp. 100–5.

Merchant, Carolyn (1996) *Earthcare: Women and the Environment*. New York: Routledge.

Meyer, John W., David John Frank, Ann Hironaka, Evan Schofer and Nancy Brandon Tuma (1997) 'The structuring of a world environmental regime, 1870–1990', *International Organization*, 51(4): 623–51.

M'Gonigle, R. Michael and Mark W. Zacher (1979) *Pollution, Politics, and International Law: Tankers at Sea*. Berkeley: University of California Press.

Miles, Edward L. (2002a) 'The management of high seas salmon in the North Pacific, 1952–1992', in Edward L. Miles, Arild Underdal, Steinar Andresen, Jørgen Wettestad, Jon Birger Skjærseth and Elaine M. Carlin (eds), *Environmental Regime Effectiveness: Confronting Theory with Evidence*. Cambridge, MA: MIT Press. pp. 249–68.

Miles, Edward L. (2002b) 'The management of tuna fisheries in the west central and southwest Pacific', in Edward L. Miles, Arild Underdal, Steinar Andresen, Jørgen Wettestad, Jon Birger Skjærseth and Elaine M. Carlin (eds), *Environmental Regime Effectiveness: Confronting Theory with Evidence*. Cambridge, MA: MIT Press. pp. 117–48.

Miles, Edward L., Arild Underdal, Steinar Andresen, Jørgen Wettestad, Jon Birger Skjærseth and Elaine M. Carlin (eds) (2002) *Environmental Regime Effectiveness: Confronting Theory with Evidence*. Cambridge, MA: MIT Press.

Mill, John Stuart (1950) *Philosophy of Scientific Method*. New York: Hafner.

Mill, John Stuart (1988) *A System of Logic, Ratiocinative and Inductive*. New York: Harper.

Miller, Alan S. (1991) *Gaia Connections: An Introduction to Ecology, Ecoethics, and Economics*. Lanham, MD: Rowman & Littlefield.

Miller, Clark A. (2001) 'Hybrid management: boundary organizations, science policy, and environmental governance in the climate regime', *Science, Technology & Human Values*, 26(4): 478–500.

Miller, Clark A. and Paul N. Edwards (eds) (2001) *Changing the Atmosphere: Expert Knowledge and Environmental Governance*. Cambridge, MA: MIT Press.

Miller, Marian A. L. (1995) *The Third World in Global Environmental Politics*. Boulder, CO: Lynne Rienner.

Milner, Helen V. (1997) *Interests, Institutions, and Information: Domestic Politics and International Relations*. Princeton: Princeton University Press.

Minkel, J. R. (2007) *Scientific American: Mysterious Honeybee Disappearance Linked to Rare Virus*. Document last accessed: 7 September 2007. Available at: http://www.sciam.com/article.cfm?id=bees-ccd-virus

Mitchell, David (2005) *Making Foreign Policy: Presidential Management of the Decision-Making Process*. Aldershot: Ashgate.

Mitchell, Ronald B. (1994a) *Intentional Oil Pollution at Sea: Environmental Policy and Treaty Compliance*. Cambridge, MA: MIT Press.

Mitchell, Ronald B. (1994b) 'Regime design matters: intentional oil pollution and treaty compliance', *International Organization*, 48(3): 425–58.

Mitchell, Ronald B. (1996) 'Compliance theory: an overview', in James Cameron, Jacob Werksman and Peter Roderick (eds), *Improving Compliance with International Environmental Law*. London: Earthscan. pp. 3–28.

Mitchell, Ronald B. (1997) 'International control of nuclear proliferation: beyond carrots and sticks', *The Nonproliferation Review*, 5(1): 40–52.

Mitchell, Ronald B. (1998a) 'Discourse and sovereignty: interests, science, and morality in the regulation of whaling', *Global Governance*, 4(3): 275–93.

Mitchell, Ronald B. (1998b) 'Sources of transparency: information systems in international regimes', *International Studies Quarterly*, 42(1): 109–30.

Mitchell, Ronald B. (2002) 'A quantitative approach to evaluating international environmental regimes', *Global Environmental Politics*, 2(4): 58–83.

Mitchell, Ronald B. (2003) 'International environmental agreements: a survey of their features, formation, and effects', *Annual Review of Environment and Resources*, 28: 429–61.

Mitchell, Ronald B. (2006) 'Problem structure, institutional design, and the relative effectiveness of international environmental agreements', *Global Environmental Politics*, 6(3): 72–89.

Mitchell, Ronald B. (2008) *International Environmental Agreements Database Project*. Document last accessed: 20 January 2008. Available at: http://iea.uoregon.edu/

Mitchell, Ronald B. (2009) 'The influence of international institutions: institutional design, compliance, effectiveness, and endogeneity', in Helen V. Milner (ed.), *Power, Interdependence and Non-State Actors in World Politics: Research Frontiers*. Princeton: Princeton University Press. pp. 66–83.

Mitchell, Ronald B. and Thomas Bernauer (1998) 'Empirical research on international environmental policy: designing qualitative case studies', *Journal of Environment and Development*, 7(1): 4–31.

Mitchell, Ronald B. and Patricia Keilbach (2001) 'Reciprocity, coercion, or exchange: symmetry, asymmetry and power in institutional design', *International Organization*, 55(4): 891–917.

Mitchell, Ronald B., William C. Clark and David W. Cash (2006a) 'Information and influence', in Ronald B. Mitchell, William C. Clark, David W. Cash and Nancy M. Dickson (eds), *Global Environmental Assessments: Information and Influence*. Cambridge, MA: MIT Press. pp. 307–38.

Mitchell, Ronald B., William C. Clark, David W. Cash and Nancy M. Dickson (eds) (2006b) *Global Environmental Assessments: Information and Influence*. Cambridge, MA: MIT Press.

Molina, Mario J. and Frank S. Rowland (1974) 'Stratospheric sink for chlorofluoromethanes: chlorine atom-catalysed destruction of ozone', *Nature*, 249(5460): 810–12.

Morgenthau, Hans Joachim (1993) *Politics among Nations: The Struggle for Power and Peace*. New York: McGraw-Hill.

Moser, Susanne C. (2006) 'Climate change and sea-level rise in Maine and Hawai'i: the changing tides of an issue domain', in Ronald B. Mitchell, William C. Clark, David W. Cash and Nancy M. Dickson (eds), *Global Environmental Assessments: Information and Influence*. Cambridge, MA: MIT Press. pp. 201–40.

Myers, Norman (1987) 'Linking environment and security', *Bulletin of the Atomic Scientists*, 43(5): 46–7.

Myers, Norman (1989) 'Environmental security: the case of South Asia', *International Environmental Affairs*, 1(2): 138–54.

Naess, Arne (1973) 'The shallow and the deep, long-range ecology movement: a summary', *Inquiry*, 16(1): 95–100.

National Oceanic and Atmospheric Administration (2003) *Decision Support Research: Bridging Science and Service*. Document dated: 21 April 2003. Document last accessed: 19 June 2008. Available at: http://www.oar.noaa.gov/spotlite/archive/spot_risa.html

Neumayer, Eric (2002a) 'Do democracies exhibit stronger international environmental commitment?' *Journal of Peace Research*, 39(2): 139–64.

Neumayer, Eric (2002b) 'Does trade openness promote multilateral environ-
    mental cooperation?' *The World Economy*, 25(6): 815–32.
New York State Department of Environmental Conservation (2008) 'Bat die-off
    prompts investigation', *New York State Department of Environmental
    Conservation News Release*.
Newell, Peter (2000) *Climate for Change: Non-State Actors and the Global
    Politics of Greenhouse*. Cambridge: Cambridge University Press.
Nolan, Jessica M., P. Wesley Schultz, Robert B. Cialdini, Noah J. Goldstein and
    Vladas Griskevicius (2008) 'Normative social influence is underdetected',
    *Personality and Social Psychology Bulletin*, 34(7): 913–23.
Nordhaus, William D. and Edward Charles Kokkelenberg (1999) *Nature's
    Numbers: Expanding the National Economic Accounts to Include the
    Environment*. Washington, DC: National Academy Press.
Nye, Joseph S. (2000) *Understanding International Conflicts: An Introduction to
    Theory and History*. New York: Addison Wesley Longman.
Oberthür, Sebastian and Thomas Gehring (eds) (2006) *Institutional Interaction
    in Global Environmental Governance: Synergy and Conflict among
    International and EU Policies*. Cambridge, MA: MIT Press.
Olson, Mancur (1965) *The Logic of Collective Action: Public Goods and the
    Theory of Groups*. Cambridge: Harvard University Press.
O'Neill, Kate (2000) *Waste Trading among Rich Nations*. Cambridge, MA: MIT
    Press.
Ophuls, William (1977) *Ecology and the Politics of Scarcity: Prologue to a
    Political Theory of the Steady State*. San Francisco, CA: W. H. Freeman.
Orr, David W. and Marvin S. Soroos (eds) (1979) *The Global Predicament:
    Ecological Perspectives on World Order*. Chapel Hill: The University of North
    Carolina Press.
Ostrom, Elinor (1998) 'Scales, polycentricity, and incentives: designing com-
    plexity to govern complexity', in Laksham D. Guruswamy and Jeffrey A.
    McNeely (eds), *Protection of Biodiversity: Converging Strategies*. Durham:
    Duke University Press. pp. 149–67.
Oye, Kenneth A. (1986) 'Explaining cooperation under anarchy: hypotheses
    and strategies', in Kenneth Oye (ed.), *Cooperation under Anarchy*. Princeton:
    Princeton University Press. pp. 1–24.
Oye, Kenneth A. and James M. Maxwell (1994) 'Self-interest and environmen-
    tal management', *Journal of Theoretical Politics*, 6(4): 191–221.
Parker, Richard W. (1997) 'Choosing norms to promote compliance and effec-
    tiveness: the case for international environmental benchmark standards', in
    Edith Brown Weiss (ed.), *International Compliance with Nonbinding Accords*.
    Washington, DC: American Society of International Law. pp. 145–203.
Parson, Edward A. (2003) *Protecting the Ozone Layer: Science and Strategy*.
    Oxford: Oxford University Press.
Parson, Edward A., Peter M. Haas and Marc A. Levy (1992) 'A summary of
    major documents signed at the earth summit and the global forum',
    *Environment*, 34(4): 12–15, 34–36.
Patt, Anthony G. (1999) 'Separating analysis from politics: acid rain in Europe',
    *Review of Policy Research*, 16(3–4): 104–37.
Patt, Anthony G. (2006) 'Trust, respect, patience, and sea-surface temperatures:
    useful climate forecasting in Zimbabwe', in Ronald B. Mitchell, William C. Clark,
    David W. Cash and Nancy M. Dickson (eds), *Global Environmental Assessments:
    Information and Influence*. Cambridge, MA: MIT Press. pp. 241–70.

Peterson, M.J. (1988) *Managing the Frozen South: The Creation and Evolution of the Antarctic Treaty System*. Berkeley: University of California Press.

Peterson, M.J. (1993) 'International fisheries management', in Peter Haas, Robert O. Keohane and Marc Levy (eds), *Institutions for the Earth: Sources of Effective International Environmental Protection*. Cambridge, MA: MIT Press. pp. 249–308.

Pettenger, Mary E. (ed.) (2007) *The Social Construction of Climate Change: Power, Knowledge, Norms, Discourses*. Aldershot: Ashgate.

Pielke, Jr., Robert, Tom Wigley and Christopher Green (2008) 'Dangerous assumptions', *Nature*, 452(7187): 531–32.

Plaza, Fernando (1997) 'Port state control: an update', *IMO News*, 1997(4): 30–34.

Pollack, Mark A. (1997) 'Delegation, agency, and agenda setting in the European Community', *International Organization*, 51(1): 99–134.

Postel, Sandra (1999) *Pillar of Sand: Can the Irrigation Miracle Last?* New York: Norton.

Powell, Robert (1991) 'Absolute and relative gains in international relations theory', *American Political Science Review*, 85(4): 1303–20.

Prakash, Aseem and Matthew Potoski (2006) 'Racing to the bottom? Trade, environmental governance, and ISO 14001', *American Journal of Political Science*, 50(2): 350–64.

Princen, Thomas and Matthias Finger (1994) *Environmental NGOs in World Politics: Linking the Local and the Global*. New York: Routledge.

Princen, Thomas, Matthias Finger and Jack Manno (1995) 'Nongovernmental organizations in world environmental politics', *International Environmental Affairs*, 7(1): 42–58.

Princen, Thomas, Michael Maniates and Ken Conca (2002) *Confronting Consumption*. Cambridge, MA: MIT Press.

Putnam, Robert D. (1988) 'Diplomacy and domestic politics: the logic of two-level games', *International Organization*, 42(3): 427–60.

Raiffa, Howard (1982) *The Art and Science of Negotiation*. Cambridge, MA: Harvard University Press.

Ramsar Convention Bureau (1999) *Memoranda of Understanding and Cooperation with Other Conventions and International Organizations*. Document last dated: 26 June 1999. Document last accessed: 29 September 2008. Available at: http://www.ramsar.org/index_mou.htm

Raustiala, Kal (1997a) 'Domestic institutions and international regulatory cooperation: comparative responses to the Convention on Biological Diversity', *World Politics*, 49(4): 482–509.

Raustiala, Kal (1997b) 'States, NGOs, and international environmental institutions', *International Studies Quarterly*, 41(4): 719–40.

Raustiala, Kal (2004) 'Police patrols & fire alarms in the NAAEC', *Loyola of Los Angeles International and Comparative Law Review*, 26(3): 389–413.

Raustiala, Kal and Anne-Marie Slaughter (2002) 'International law, international relations and compliance', in Walter Carlsnaes, Thomas Risse and Beth Simmons (eds), *Handbook of International Relations*. Thousand Oaks, CA: SAGE. pp. 538–58.

Reeve, Rosalind (2002) *Policing International Trade in Endangered Species: The Cites Treaty and Compliance*. London: Royal Institute of International Affairs and Earthscan.

Risse, Thomas (2000) '"Let's argue": communicative action in world politics', *International Organization*, 54(1): 1–39.

Rittberger, Volker (1993) 'Research on international regimes in Germany: the adaptive internalization of an American social science concept', in Volker Rittberger (ed.), *Regime Theory and International Relations*. New York: Oxford University Press. pp. 3–22.

Rittberger, Volker and Michael Zürn (1991) 'Regime theory: findings from the study of East-West regimes', *Cooperation and Conflict*, 26(4): 165–83.

Rollo, Jim and L. Alan Winters (2000) 'Subsidiarity and governance challenges for the WTO: environmental and labour standards', *The World Economy*, 23(4): 561–76.

Rosenau, James N. (1993) 'Environmental challenges in a global context', in Sheldon Kamieniecki (ed.), *Environmental Politics in the International Arena*. Albany: State University of New York Press. pp. 257–74.

Rosendorff, B. Peter and Helen V. Milner (2001) 'The optimal design of international trade institutions: uncertainty and escape', *International Organization*, 55(4): 829–57.

Rowlands, Ian H. (1991) 'The security challenges of global environmental change', *The Washington Quarterly*, 14(1): 99–114.

Ruggie, John Gerard (1998) 'What makes the world hang together? Neo-utilitarianism and the social constructivist challenge', *International Organization*, 52(4): 855–85.

Sabatier, Paul A. (ed.) (2007) *Theories of the Policy Process (2nd edition)*. Boulder, CO: Westview.

Sand, Peter H. (2001) 'Environment: nature cooperation', in P. J. Simmons and Chantal de Jonge Oudraat (eds), *Managing Global Issues: Lessons Learned*. Washington, DC: Carnegie Endowment for International Peace. pp. 281–309.

Sand, Peter H. (2008) 'Japan's 'research whaling' in the Antarctic Southern Ocean and the North Pacific Ocean in the face of the endangered species convention (CITES)', *RECIEL*, 17(1): 56–71.

Sands, Philippe (ed.) (1994) *Greening International Law*. New York: The New Press.

Schattschneider, Elmer E. (1975 [1960]) *The Semisovereign People: A Realist's View of Democracy in America*. Hinsdale, IL: Dryden.

Schreurs, Miranda A. (1997) 'Domestic institutions and international environmental agendas in Japan and Germany', in Miranda A. Schreurs and Elizabeth Economy (eds), *The Internationalization of Environmental Protection*. Oxford: Oxford University Press. pp. 134–61.

Schultz, P. Wesley, Jessica M. Nolan, Robert B. Cialdini, Noah J. Goldstein and Vladas Griskevicius (2007) 'The constructive, destructive, and reconstructive power of social norms', *Psychological Science*, 18(5): 429–34.

Schwartz, Daniel M., Tom Deligiannis and Thomas Homer-Dixon (2001) 'The environment and violent conflict', in Paul F. Diehl and Nils Petter Gleditsch (eds), *Environmental Conflict*. Boulder, CO: Westview. pp. 273–94.

Sebenius, James K. (1983) 'Negotiation arithmetic: adding and subtracting issues and parties', *International Organization*, 37(2): 281–316.

Sessions, George (1991) 'Ecocentrism and the anthropocentric detour', *ReVISION*, 13(3): 109–15.

Sharma, Shalendra D. (1996) 'Building effective international environmental regimes: the case of the global environment facility', *Journal of Environment and Development*, 5(1): 73.

Sheikh, Pervaze A. (2007) *Debt-for-Nature Initiatives and the Tropical Forest Conservation Act: Status and Implementation*. Washington, DC: Congressional Research Service.

Simmons, Beth A. and Daniel J. Hopkins (2005) 'The constraining power of international treaties', *American Political Science Review*, 99(4): 623–31.

Simmons, P.J. (1998) 'Learning to live with NGOs', *Foreign Policy*, (112): 82–96.

Sjostedt, Gunnar (ed.) (1993) *International Environmental Negotiation*. Newbury Park, CA: SAGE.

Smith, J. Eric (1972) 'The role of special purpose and non-governmental organizations in the environmental crisis', *International Organization*, 26(2): 302.

Snidal, Duncan (1985) 'Coordination versus prisoner's dilemma: implications for international cooperation and regimes', *American Political Science Review*, 79(4): 723–42.

Snidal, Duncan (1991) 'Relative gains and the pattern of international cooperation', *American Political Science Review*, 85(3): 701–26.

Social Learning Group (ed.) (2001a) *Learning to Manage Global Environmental Risks, Volume 1: A Comparative History of Social Responses to Climate Change, Ozone Depletion and Acid Rain*. Cambridge, MA: MIT Press.

Social Learning Group (ed.) (2001b) *Learning to Manage Global Environmental Risks, Volume 2: A Functional Analysis of Social Responses to Climate Change, Ozone Depletion and Acid Rain*. Cambridge, MA: MIT Press.

Spretnak, Charlene (1990) 'Ecofeminism: our roots and flowering', in Irene Diamond and Gloria Feman Orenstein (eds), *Reweaving the World: The Emergence of Ecofeminism*. San Francisco, CA: Sierra Club. pp. 3–14.

Sprinz, Detlef F. and Carsten Helm (1999) 'The effect of global environmental regimes: a measurement concept', *International Political Science Review*, 20(4): 359–69.

Sprinz, Detlef F. and Tapani Vaahtoranta (1994) 'The interest-based explanation of international environmental policy', *International Organization*, 48(1): 77–105.

Sprinz, Detlef F. and Yael Wolinsky-Nahmias (eds) (2004) *Models, Numbers, and Cases: Methods for Studying International Relations*. Ann Arbor: University of Michigan Press.

Sprinz, Detlef F., Jon Hovi, Ronald B. Mitchell and Arild Underdal (2004) 'Separating and aggregating regime effects'. Paper presented at the International Studies Association Conference, Montreal, Canada.

Sprout, Harold H. and Margaret T. Sprout (1971) *Toward a Politics of the Planet Earth*. New York: Van Nostrand Reinhold.

Stein, Janice Gross (ed.) (1989) *Getting to the Table: The Processes of International Prenegotiation*. Baltimore, MD: Johns Hopkins University Press.

Stoett, Peter J. (1997) *The International Politics of Whaling*. Vancouver: University of British Columbia Press.

Stokke, Olav Schram (1997) 'Regimes as governance systems', in Oran R. Young (ed.), *Global Governance: Drawing Insights from the Environmental Experience*. Cambridge, MA: MIT Press. pp. 27–63.

Stokke, Olav Schram (1998) 'Understanding the formation of international environmental regimes: the discursive challenge', in Arild Underdal (ed.), *The Politics of International Environmental Management*. Dordrecht: Kluwer. pp. 129–48.

Stokke, Olav Schram (ed.) (2001) *Governing High Seas Fisheries: The Interplay of Global and Regional Regimes*. Oxford: Oxford University Press.

Stone, Christopher D. (1974) *Should Trees Have Standing? Toward Legal Rights for Natural Objects*. Los Altos: Kaufmann.

Stone, Deborah A. (1989) 'Causal stories and the formation of policy agendas', *Political Science Quarterly*, 104(2): 281–300.

Strange, Susan (1983) '*Cave! hic dragones*: a critique of regime analysis', in Stephen D. Krasner (ed.) *International Regimes*. Ithaca, NY: Cornell University Press. pp. 337–54.

Sunstein, Cass R. (2006) 'The availability heuristic, intuitive cost-benefit analysis, and climate change', *Climatic Change*, 77(1–2): 195–210.

Swanson, Timothy M. and Sam Johnston (1999) *Global Environmental Problems and International Environmental Agreements: The Economics of International Institution Building*. Cheltenham: Edward Elgar.

Taylor, Paul Graham and A. J. R Groom (eds.) (1988) *International Institutions at Work*. New York: St. Martin's Press.

Tesh, Sylvia N. and Bruce A. Williams (1996) 'Identity politics, disinterested politics, and environmental justice', *Polity*, 28(3): 285–305.

Tetlock, Philip and Aaron Belkin (eds) (1996) *Counterfactual Thought Experiments in World Politics: Logical, Methodological, and Psychological Perspectives*. Princeton: Princeton University Press.

Thucydides (1982) *The Peloponnesian War*. New York: Modern Library.

Tietenberg, Thomas H. (1988) *Environmental and Natural Resource Economics*. Glenview, IL: Scott, Foresman.

Tir, Jaroslav and Paul F. Diehl (1998) 'Demographic pressure and interstate conflict: linking population growth and density to military disputes and war, 1930–1989', *Journal of Peace Research*, 35(3): 319–39.

Torrance, Wendy E. F. (2006) 'Science or salience: building an agenda for climate change', in Ronald B. Mitchell, William C. Clark, David W. Cash and Nancy M. Dickson (eds), *Global Environmental Assessments: Information and Influence*. Cambridge, MA: MIT Press. pp. 29–56.

Tufte, Edward R. (2006) *The Cognitive Style of Powerpoint: Pitching out Corrupts Within*. Cheshire, CT: Graphics.

Turner, B. L., II, William C. Clark, Robert W. Kates, John F. Richards, Jessica T. Mathews and William B. Meyer (1990) *The Earth as Transformed by Human Action: Global and Regional Changes in the Biosphere over the Past 300 Years*. Cambridge: Cambridge University Press with Clark University.

Ullman, Richard (1983) 'Redefining security', *International Security*, 8(1): 129–53.

Underdal, Arild (1980) *The Politics of International Fisheries Management: The Case of the Northeast Atlantic*. Oslo: Universitetsforlaget.

Underdal, Arild (1992) 'The concept of regime 'effectiveness'', *Cooperation and Conflict*, 27(3): 227–40.

Underdal, Arild (1998a) 'Explaining compliance and defection: three models', *European Journal of International Relations*, 4(1): 5–30.

Underdal, Arild (ed.) (1998b) *The Politics of International Environmental Management*. Dordrecht: Kluwer.

Underdal, Arild (2002) 'One question, two answers', in Edward L. Miles, Arild Underdal, Steinar Andresen, Jørgen Wettestad, Jon Birger Skjærseth and Elaine M. Carlin (eds), *Environmental Regime Effectiveness: Confronting Theory with Evidence*. Cambridge, MA: MIT Press. pp. 3–45.

Underdal, Arild and Kenneth Hanf (eds) (2000) *International Environmental Agreements and Domestic Politics: The Case of Acid Rain*. Aldershot: Ashgate.

Underdal, Arild and Oran R. Young (eds) (2004) *Regime Consequences: Methodological Challenges and Research Strategies*. Dordrecht: Kluwer.

UNEP GEMS/Water Programme (2007) *Water Quality Outlook*. Ontario, Canada: UN GEMS/Water Programme Office.

United Nations System-Wide Earthwatch (2007) *Emerging Environmental Issues*. Document dated: 12 September 2007. Document last accessed: 17 April 2008. Available at: http://earthwatch.unep.net/emergingissues/index.php

United States Geological Survey (2001) 'Amphibian malformations', *USGS National Wildlife Health Center Information Sheet*.

Utton, Albert E. and Daniel H. Henning (eds) (1973) *Environmental Policy: Concepts and International Implications*. New York: Praeger.

Victor, David G., Kal Raustiala and Eugene B. Skolnikoff (eds) (1998a) *The Implementation and Effectiveness of International Environmental Commitments: Theory and Practice*. Cambridge, MA: MIT Press.

Victor, David G., Kal Raustiala and Eugene B. Skolnikoff (1998b) 'Introduction and overview', in David G. Victor, Kal Raustiala and Eugene B. Skolnikoff (eds), *The Implementation and Effectiveness of International Environmental Commitments: Theory and Practice*. Cambridge, MA: MIT Press. pp. 1–46.

Vitousek, Peter M., John Aber, Robert W. Howarth, Gene E. Likens, Pamela A. Matson, David W. Schindler, William H. Schlesinger and G. David Tilman (1997) 'Human alteration of the global nitrogen cycle: causes and consequences', *Issues in Ecology*, (1): 1–16.

von Stein, Jana (2005) 'Do treaties constrain or screen? Selection bias and treaty compliance', *American Political Science Review*, 99(4): 611–22.

Waggoner, Paul E. and Jesse H. Ausubel (2002) 'A framework for sustainability science: a renovated IPAT identity', *Proceedings of the National Academy of Sciences*, 99(12): 7860–65.

Walsh, Virginia M. (2004) *Global Institutions and Social Knowledge: Generating Research at the Scripps Institution and the Inter-American Tropical Tuna Commission 1900s–1990s*. Cambridge, MA: MIT Press.

Waltz, Kenneth (1979) *Theory of International Politics*. Reading, MA: Addison-Wesley.

Wapner, Paul (1996) *Environmental Activism and World Civic Politics*. Albany: State University of New York Press.

Wapner, Paul (1997) 'Environmental ethics and global governance: engaging the international liberal tradition', *Global Governance*, 3(2): 213–31.

Warren, Karen (2000) *Ecofeminist Philosophy: A Western Perspective on What It Is and Why It Matters*. Lanham, MD: Rowman & Littlefield.

Warren, Karen and Barbara Wells-Howe (1994) *Ecological Feminism*. New York: Routledge.

Weber, Max (1957 [1922]) *The Theory of Social and Economic Organization*. Glencoe, IL: Free Press.

Wendt, Alexander (1987) 'The agent structure problem in international relations theory', *International Organization*, 41(3): 335–70.

Wendt, Alexander (1999) *Social Theory of International Politics*. New York: Cambridge University Press.

Werksman, James, Jacob Cameron and Peter Roderick (eds) (1996) *Improving Compliance with International Environmental Law*. London: Earthscan.

Westing, Arthur H. (1986) *Global Resources and International Conflict: Environmental Factors in Strategic Policy and Action*. Oxford: Oxford University Press.

Westing, Arthur H. (1988) *Cultural Norms, War and the Environment*. Oxford: Oxford University Press.

Wettestad, Jørgen (1995) 'Science, politics and institutional design: some initial notes on the Long-Range Transboundary Air Pollution Regime', *Journal of Environment and Development*, 4(2): 165–83.

Wettestad, Jørgen (1999) *Designing Effective Environmental Regimes: The Key Conditions.* Cheltenham: Edward Elgar.

Wheeler, David (2002) 'Beyond pollution havens', *Global Environmental Politics* 2(2): 1–10.

Wilen, James E. (1976) *Common Property Resources and the Dynamics of Overexploitation: The Case of the North Pacific Fur Seal.* Vancouver, Canada: Department of Economics, University of British Columbia.

Wilkening, Kenneth E. (2004) *Acid Rain Science and Politics in Japan: A History of Knowledge and Action toward Sustainability.* Cambridge, MA: MIT Press.

Wils, Wouter P. J. (1994) 'Subsidiarity and EC environmental policy: taking people's concerns seriously', *Journal of Environmental Law*, 6(1): 85–91.

Wood, Dan and Jeffrey S. Peake (1998) 'The dynamics of foreign policy agenda setting', *American Political Science Review*, 92(1): 173–84.

World Commission on Environment and Development (1987) *Our Common Future.* New York: Oxford University Press.

Young, H. Peyton and Amanda Wolf (1992) 'Global warming negotiations: does fairness matter?' *Brookings Review*, 10(2): 46–51.

Young, Oran R. (1981) *Natural Resources and the State: The Political Economy of Resource Management.* Berkeley: University of California Press.

Young, Oran R. (1989a) 'The power of institutions: why international regimes matter', in Oran R. Young (ed.), *International Cooperation: Building Regimes for Natural Resources and the Environment.* Ithaca, NY: Cornell University Press. pp. 58–80.

Young, Oran R. (1989b) 'The politics of international regime formation: managing natural resources and the environment', *International Organization*, 43(3): 349–76.

Young, Oran R. (1991) 'Political leadership and regime formation: on the development of institutions in international society', *International Organization*, 45(3): 281–308.

Young, Oran R. (1994a) *International Governance: Protecting the Environment in a Stateless Society.* Ithaca, NY: Cornell University Press.

Young, Oran R. (1994b) 'The problem of scale in human/environment relationships', *Journal of Theoretical Politics*, 6(4): 429–47.

Young, Oran R. (1998) *Creating Regimes: Arctic Accords and International Governance.* Ithaca, NY: Cornell University Press.

Young, Oran R. (ed.) (1999a) *The Effectiveness of International Environmental Regimes: Causal Connections and Behavioral Mechanisms.* Cambridge, MA: MIT Press.

Young, Oran R. (1999b) *Governance in World Affairs.* Ithaca, NY: Cornell University Press.

Young, Oran R. (1999c) 'Regime effectiveness: taking stock', in Oran R. Young (ed.), *Effectiveness of International Environmental Regimes: Causal Connections and Behavioral Mechanisms.* Cambridge, MA: MIT Press. pp. 249–79.

Young, Oran R. (2002) *The Institutional Dimensions of Environmental Change: Fit, Interplay, and Scale.* Cambridge, MA: MIT Press.

Young, Oran R. (2003) 'Determining regime effectiveness: a commentary on the Oslo-Potsdam solution', *Global Environmental Politics*, 3(3): 97–104.

Young, Oran R. (2008) 'Building regimes for socioecological systems: institutional diagnostics', in Oran R. Young, Leslie A. King and Heike Schroeder (eds), *Institutions and Environmental Change: Principal Findings, Applications, and Research Frontiers*. Cambridge, MA: MIT Press. pp. 115–43.

Young, Oran R. and Gail Osherenko (1993a) 'International regime formation: findings, research priorities, and applications', in Oran R. Young and Gail Osherenko (eds), *Polar Politics: Creating International Environmental Regimes*. Ithaca, NY: Cornell University Press. pp. 223–61.

Young, Oran R. and Gail Osherenko (eds) (1993b) *Polar Politics: Creating International Environmental Regimes*. Ithaca, NY: Cornell University Press.

Young, Oran R. and Gail Osherenko (1993c) 'Preface', in Oran R. Young and Gail Osherenko (eds), *Polar Politics: Creating International Environmental Regimes*. Ithaca, NY: Cornell University Press. pp. vii–xi.

Young, Oran R. and Marc A. Levy (1999) 'The effectiveness of international environmental regimes', in Oran R. Young (ed.), *The Effectiveness of International Environmental Regimes: Causal Connections and Behavioral Mechanisms*. Cambridge, MA: MIT Press. pp. 1–32.

Young, Oran R., Leslie A. King and Heike Schroeder (eds) (2008) *Institutions and Environmental Change: Principal Findings, Applications, and Research Frontiers*. Cambridge, MA: MIT Press.

Young, Zoe (1999) 'NGOs and the Global Environmental Facility: friendly foes?' *Environmental Politics*, 8(1): 243–67.

Zaelke, Durwood, Paul Orbuch and Robert F. Housman (eds) (1993) *Trade and the Environment: Law, Economics, and Policy*. Washington, DC: Island.

Zald, Mayer N. (1996) 'Culture, ideology, and strategic framing', in Doug McAdam, John D. McCarthy and Mayer N. Zald (eds), *Comparative Perspectives on Social Movements: Political Opportunities. Mobilizing Structures, and Cultural Framings*. Cambridge: Cambridge University Press. pp. 261–74.

Zartman, I. William (1985) *Ripe for Resolution: Conflict and Intervention in Africa*. New York: Oxford University Press.

Zürn, Michael (1998) 'The rise of international environmental politics: a review of current research', *World Politics*, 50(4): 617–49.

Zürn, Michael and Jeffrey T. Checkel (2005) 'Getting socialized to build bridges: constructivism and rationalism, Europe and the nation-state', *International Organization*, 59(4): 1045–79.

# INDEX